Financial Inclusion in Emerging Markets

Ananda S. · Dharmendra Singh
Editors

Financial Inclusion in Emerging Markets

A Road Map for Sustainable Growth

palgrave
macmillan

Editors
Ananda S.
Department of Postgraduate Studies & Research
College of Banking & Financial Studies
Muscat, Oman

Dharmendra Singh
Department of Finance, Accounting & Economics
Faculty of Business and Economics, Modern College of Business and Science
Muscat, Oman

ISBN 978-981-16-3822-0 ISBN 978-981-16-2652-4 (eBook)
https://doi.org/10.1007/978-981-16-2652-4

This Palgrave Macmillan imprint is published by the registered company Springer Nature Singapore Pte Ltd.
The registered company address is: 152 Beach Road, #21-01/04 Gateway East, Singapore 189721, Singapore

Foreword

Strong financial system is the backbone of every economy as it facilitates financing of productive sectors by channeling resources from less efficient to more efficient sectors of the economy. Financial inclusion has been recognized as an important condition for strong financial system and sustainable economic development by individual nations as well as global financial institutions. It is gaining increasing attention from the policymakers as it supports inclusive growth and wider participation of public. It has also been positioned as an enabler of development goals by the UN in its 2030 agenda. All governments, especially those of the emerging markets, are striving hard to increase financial inclusion in their country through innovative methods of promoting financial access, such as mobile banking, micro-finance, and micro-insurance. Other factors that affect the growth of financial inclusions include the usage of the banking products and channels provided by the government. The critical hurdles in the success of the government efforts can be low income, lack of sufficient financial literacy, and the quality of the banking products and services.

This book provides a comprehensive analysis and discussion of issues pertinent to financial inclusion in different parts of the world. All sixteen chapters, under seven sub-themes, are highly relevant and address contemporary issues. I hope that the new body of knowledge introduced and developed by the authors in this book will enrich the readers' knowledge and ideas about financial inclusion. I also expect the book to serve as a convincing source of information to regulators, policymakers, students, and researchers on various aspects of financial inclusion and the challenges faced by in its development. The initiative of publishing this book is a significant milestone toward raising awareness on the importance of financial inclusion practices around the world.

I would like to extend my acknowledgment and appreciation to the editors of the book for taking up this knowledge transfer initiative for the benefit of the community and commend the authors of the chapters for their considerable efforts in sharing their scholarly thoughts and insights on these important issues.

I wish the Editors the very best for their endeavors and look forward to reading many more contributions and scholarly publications from them in the future.

Krishna Paudyal
Vice Dean (Research)
Strathclyde Business School
University of Strathclyde
Glasgow, UK

Preface

The level of economic activities determines the growth and sustainability of an economy, and the level of economic activities depends upon the basic infrastructure and the resources. Financial resources are one of the important resources required for the development of the economic activities. The economy can have sustainable growth only if all the individuals participate in the economic activities. One of the requirements for the economic participation is the proper circulation of money which is only possible if there is easy access to finance and it is used by all. With this background the critical role of the financial inclusion for the overall sustainable development of the economy is evident. Financial inclusion leads more individuals to get access to funding for business and personal requirement. This would create more investment, employment, and demand and thus generates more employment and disposable income in society. Financial inclusion also helps savings mobilization and encourage to use various forms of financial products and services, so that hidden money will be in circulation in the economy. Overall, financial inclusion ensures ease of access, availability, and usage of the formal financial system, product, and services for all members, especially of an emerging economy. Hence, there is a strong need of useful literature to the stakeholders on financial inclusion in framing policies, guidelines, strategic planning, and designing initiatives and activities and to set future directions. This book seeks to bring global experiences and findings of the researchers in the form of chapters for providing useful insights to boost up the financial inclusion by minimizing the hurdles in the path of development.

The book aims to explore the various strategic issues and ideas about financial inclusion through the lens of theoretical, practical, and empirical research. This book focuses on key developments in financial inclusion, as well as its contributions to the sustainable economic development of emerging economies. The book consists of sixteen informative scientific papers and essays under seven sub-themes. These papers were selected after a double-blind peer review process. The chapters are authored by thirty-two researchers and practitioners across the globe. In this book we have tried to capture a comprehensive picture on the financial inclusion practices, products, issues, and challenges in the emerging markets. The book is representing the financial inclusion scenario from the various parts of the world, like chapters have covered financial inclusion practices in the group of western Balkan countries, and Organization of Islamic Cooperation (OIC) countries, Egypt, Saudi Arabia, and India. The key areas captured in the book are the determinants of financial inclusion; different financial inclusion products like micro-insurance, micro-financing, and cooperative societies; role of financial literacy and self-help groups in development of financial inclusion; important issues in sustainable development of financial inclusion like digital finance and minimizing economic inequality. We hope the book fills the gap in the academic and policy literature on financial inclusions topics by sharing the original ideas covering the theoretical and empirical issues related to the financial inclusion in emerging economies.

We recognize the sincere efforts and time devoted by the authors in sharing their invaluable thoughts by way of chapters in this edited book. We express our deepest sense of gratitude to all the authors for their efforts in transferring their knowledge through this book. We are thankful to all the reviewers for their constructive feedback in bringing improvement of overall quality of this book. We also thank Ms. Sandeep Kaur, Associate Editor of Palgrave Macmillan for her continuous support and guidance in publishing this book. We certainly hope that the insightful ideas of this book will receive widespread acceptance in the community.

Muscat, Oman

Ananda S.
Dharmendra Singh

Contents

Editors and Contributors

About the Editors

Ananda S. is the Director of the Postgraduate Studies and Research Department at the College of Banking and Financial Studies, Muscat, Sultanate of Oman. He has a Ph.D. in Finance, with over thirty years of expertise in management education, consulting, and the financial services industry. He has also been a visiting professor at leading B-schools in Dubai, Germany, and India. He has published around 50 articles in peer-reviewed journals indexed by Scopus, Web of Sciences and ABDC ranking list, and presented 40 research papers in national and international conferences. He has written books on Mutual Funds, Mergers & Acquisitions and Financial Systems & Commercial Banking and edited books on Banking Sector of Oman, Financial Sector of Oman, and Diversification of Oman Economy. He is a Guest Editor, member of the Editorial Board, and Reviewer for refereed International Research Journals. He has been a member of the subject expert committee to review the master and undergraduate curriculum in universities in India and Oman. He has also conducted training courses for leading corporates in India and Oman.

Dharmendra Singh is an Assistant Professor at Modern College of Business and Science, Muscat. He has over 20 years of professional experience in the field of finance. He has a Ph.D. (Finance), and professional certifications: Chartered Financial Analyst (ICFAI), Certified Financial

Planner (CFP), and Associate Diploma (Life Insurance). He has published a number of articles and research papers in international and refereed journals, some of them listed in ABDC and Scopus. His research areas include banking, corporate finance, and financial markets. He also serves as a reviewer for select journals. He is a member of the Financial Planning Standard Board (FPSB), Indian Econometric Society, and Insurance Institute of India.

Contributors

Dr. Pankaj K. Agarwal is currently working as Associate Professor of Finance at Indian Institute of Management, Jammu, India. He possesses a rich professional experience of over 22 years in the field of finance and banking. He holds two Ph.Ds (Asset Pricing/Banking), an M.B.A. (Finance) and professional certifications like CFA (ICFAI) & CAIIB.

Dr. Shailja Agarwal is currently working as Associate Professor and Chairperson (PGDM-Part Time) at Institute of Management Technology, Ghaziabad, India. She possesses a rich professional experience of over two decades in the field of business education. She holds Ph.D. (English Literature), and certifications from Universities like Harvard and Columbia.

Dr. Amal Khairy Amin is currently working as Economic Researcher and Lecturer at the National Center for Statistical Training (NCST) in the Central Agency for Public Mobilization and Statistics (CAPMAS), Cairo, Egypt. She possesses a rich professional experience of over 25 years in the field of economics. She holds Ph.D. (economics) from Cairo University, Egypt.

Prof. Lidija Barjaktarović has a Ph.D. in Economic Sciences in sectors banking and finance. At the University Singidunum in Belgrade she teaches Banking, Risk Management and Corporate Finances (from 2008). Prior to joining academia, Professor Barjaktarovic had rich professional career in banking sector, with different high-level managerial roles. She has been Head of Master study programs Business Economics since 2014. She used to be Vice-Dean at the Faculty of Business in Belgrade (University Singidunum) in the period of 2012 to 2015. Professor Barjaktarovic is also a lecturer on different business schools in Republic of Serbia.

Dr. Savitha Basri is currently working as Associate Professor at Manipal Institute of Management, Manipal Academy of Higher Education (an Institution of Eminence), Manipal, India. She is the coordinator, Centre for Advanced research in Financial Inclusion established at Manipal Institute of Management. She has evaluated the impact of micro health insurance schemes in Karnataka for her Ph.D. study at National Institute of Technology Karnataka. She possesses a rich professional experience of over 15 years. She has published several research articles in national and international journals. Her main areas of research interests include micro health insurance, banking and insurance and capital markets.

Dr. Amitabha Bhattacharyya is presently working as an Assistant Professor in Commerce at Balurghat College, West Bengal, India. The author has a teaching experience of twenty-two years and research experience of more than fifteen years during which he published numerous book chapters and articles.

Dr. Elizabeth Chacko is an Associate Professor at Center for Management Studies, Jain University (deemed to be). She is having 12 years of work experience teaching in management. She has completed her doctorate in Economics from Banasthali Vidhyapeeth, Jaipur. She has published a number of papers and presented papers in conferences.

Dr. Srimoyee Datta is presently working as Assistant Professor in Bengal Institute of Science & Technology, West Bengal, India. She has over 14 years of academic experience in various institutes. She is an M.B.A. from Maulana Abul Kalam Azad University of Technology. She has published various research articles in different journals in the area of financial inclusion, microfinance, women empowerment.

Noreha Halid is a research and teaching faculty member at the Department of Economics—College of Business and administration—Princess Nourah bint Abdulrahman University (PNU) in Riyadh, Saudi Arabia. She holds a Ph.D. in Economics from the National University of Malaysia. Her thesis developed a model of the monetary policy impact on the current account, first of a kind in the College of Economics and Business Administration. She currently holds a position as the Program Director for the Economics Program at the Department of Economics.

Dr. Uvesh Husain has more than 15 years of teaching and research experience. He is presently working as Head of Economics and Business

Studies Department, Mazoon College, Muscat, Sultanate of Oman. He has published research and articles in various national and international journals and sound research publications.

Dr. Pooja Jain is presently working as Associate Professor in Department of Commerce, CHRIST (Deemed to be University), Bengaluru. She has 16 years of teaching experience and holds a Ph.D. from CHRIST University. Her area of specialization is Marketing.

Dr. Sarfaraz Javed is an Assistant Professor and has completed his education at Aligarh Muslim University (AMU), Aligarh, India. He is a laurel award winner from AMU. He is an active researcher and published papers in peer-reviewed journals, edited books, and presented papers in seminar and conferences. He is managing editor of the International Journal of Economics Business and Human Behaviour (USA). His research area mainly focuses on Corporate Finance, Intellectual Capital, CSR, Environmental, Financial and Management Accounting.

Dr. M. Krishna Murthy is currently working as Faculty at University of Technology and Applied Sciences in the Department of Business Studies, Muscat, Sultanate of Oman. He holds Ph.D. in Commerce and M.B.A. in finance and has teaching and research experience over twenty years in academics. He has presented and published articles in international conferences.

Dr. Jyothi Kumar is currently Professor and Dean at CHRIST (Deemed to be University), Bangalore, India. He possesses a rich professional experience of 22 years in teaching and other academic engagements. He holds a Ph.D. in the area of Strategic Management and her research was on Organizational Sustainability.

Fatma Mabrouk is a researcher and teaching faculty member at the Department of Economics, College of Business and Administration, Princess Nourah bint Abdulrahman University (PNU) in Riyadh, Saudi Arabia. She holds a Ph.D. in Economics from both the University of Bordeaux (France) and the University of Tunis El Manar (Tunisia) with a highest honor and a Master's degree in Economics from the University Paris Dauphine (France). She is an affiliate researcher at the Center for Economic and Social Studies and Research (CERES-Tunisia), the CBA research Centre (Saudi Arabia) and at the Research Group in Theoretical and Applied Economics (GREThA—University of Bordeaux-France).

CMA Sudarshan Maity is presently Deputy Director in the Directorate of Examination, The Institute of Cost Accountants of India, Kolkata, West Bengal, India. He has over 18 years of administrative experience in various industries. He is a postgraduate from Calcutta University and all India rank holder in the Final Examination of The Institute of Cost Accountants of India. He has published more than thirty five research articles in different journals published by different reputed publishers.

Dr. Priya Makhija is an Associate Professor at Centre of Management Studies, Jain University, Bangalore, India. She has completed her M.Com, M.B.A, PGDHRM, M.Phil and Ph.D. She has 15 years of academic work experience. She has published over 28 research papers in journals and presented her research work at various national and international conferences.

Dr. Prabhakar Nandru currently serves as a Guest Faculty at School of Management, Pondicherry University, Karaikal Campus (India). He was awarded Ph.D. in Management from Pondicherry University. He is a recipient of Rajiv Gandhi National Fellowship during his doctoral research. His areas of research interest are financial inclusion, microfinance, and development studies.

Dr. Geetanjali Purswani is currently working as Assistant Professor in Department of Commerce, CHRIST (Deemed to be University), Bangalore, India. She possesses an experience of 13 years in the field of teaching. She holds Ph.D. in Commerce from Bharathiar University, Coimbatore. She specializes in the area of Accountancy and Finance.

Dr. P. V. Raveendra is currently working as Professor and Head of the Department at Department of Management Studies, Ramaiah Institute of Technology, Bangalore, India. He has professional experience of 25 years in the field of Finance. He holds Ph.D. in Finance and works on various Research and consultancy projects from the Indian Government and Private sector firms.

Dr. Satyanarayana Rentala is an Assistant Professor in Marketing at Bharathidasan Institute of Management, Tiruchirappalli (India). He holds a Ph.D. in Management from Pondicherry University. He completed B.Pharmacy BITS, Pilani and completed his Post Graduation in Management from Goa Institute of Management, Panaji.

Dr. M. Rizwana is currently working as Associate Professor and Academic coordinator at Department of Management Studies, Ramaiah Institute of Technology, Bangalore, India. She has professional experience of 15 years in the field of Marketing and Entrepreneurship Development. She holds Ph.D. in Management and works on various research and consultancy projects from the Indian Government and Private sector firms.

Dr. Tarak Nath Sahu is currently working as an Assistant Professor in the Department of Commerce, Vidyasagar University, Midnapore, West Bengal, India. He has over 13 years of postgraduate teaching and research experience. Dr. Sahu, a gold medalist at both graduate and postgraduate level, has authored three books, and co-edited five books. Dr. Sahu has published more than eighty research articles in different refereed and indexed journals published by different reputed publishers.

Dr. H. N. Shivaprasad is currently working as Director and Professor, DVHIMSR, Dharwar, Karnataka, India. He possesses rich professional experience of over 23 years in the field of strategy and finance. He holds Ph.D. (Finance) and has guided around 8 students toward their doctoral research successfully. His research areas include banking, behavioral finance, and financial inclusion.

Dr. H. N. Shylaja is currently working as Associate Professor, School of Management Studies, Dayananda Sagar University, Bengaluru. She has completed her Ph.D. from Visvesvaraya Technological University, Belgavi, Karnataka. She has over 13 years of academic experience with specialization in Finance, Banking, Communications, Strategy. She has to her credit various certifications from Coursera learning platform and a PG Diploma in HRM. Her research areas include banking, stock market, behavioral finance, and financial inclusion.

Dr. Padmalini Singh is currently working as Assistant Professor and Coordinator of Teaching Learning Centre (TLC) and Member of IQAC (Internal Quality Assurance Cell) at RV Institute of Management, Bangalore, India. She has professional experience of 12 years in the field of Marketing. She holds Ph.D. in Management and works on research and consultancy project from the Indian Government and Private sector firms.

Dr. Abhijit Sinha is an Associate Professor in Commerce at Vidyasagar University in West Bengal, India. He has a teaching and research experience of more than fifteen years during which he published numerous articles in national and international journals apart from authoring and editing few books.

Dr. Mudita Sinha is currently associated with Christ University as Faculty of Marketing. She has completed her Ph.D., Masters in Marketing Management, and M.B.A. Dr. Sinha is an experienced researcher, faculty, and salesperson with proven abilities. She is a competent professional with over 12 years of combined experience in Industry, Business Education, Institutional Affairs & administrative functions. Dr. Sinha has published several articles in various national and international journals of repute in Marketing and General Management. To keep her knowledge updated and deliver best quality, she participates and presents research articles in different national and international level conferences.

Dr. Nikola Stakić is the Assistant Professor at the Faculty of Business at Singidunum University, Belgrade, Serbia. He possesses a rich academic experience of 15 years in the field of financial markets, securities valuation, financial institutions, and corporate finance with various managerial roles in HEI sector. He holds Ph.D. in Economics and Certified Financial Analyst, USA.

Dr. Vidya Suresh is currently working as an Assistant Professor at College of Banking and Financial Studies, Muscat, Sultanate of Oman. She possesses a rich professional experience of over 23 years in the field of Economics. She holds Ph.D. (Economics), from Bharathiar University in India.

Dr. Jesu Raju Thomas is currently working as Senior Area Manager (South India) at Maanaveeya Development & Finance Private Ltd (wholly owned subsidiary of Oikocredit), Bengaluru, India. He possesses a rich professional experience of eighteen years in the field of Social Performance Management, Microfinance, Social and Financial sustainability, and Women Empowerment. He holds Ph.D. (Management) from CHRIST (Deemed to be University), Bengaluru, Karnataka, India.

Dr. Deepika Upadhyay is currently working as Assistant Professor in Department of Commerce, CHRIST (Deemed to be University), Bengaluru. She has 12 years of experience in teaching and holds a Ph.D.

in Commerce from Faculty of Commerce, Banaras Hindu University. Her area of specialization is Finance and Accountancy.

Dr. S. Varalakshmi has thirteen years of academic experience in teaching and research which includes seven and half years as Assistant Professor at Muscat College, Department of Business and Accounting, Muscat, Sultanate of Oman. She holds Ph.D. in commerce and has presented and published articles in International Conferences.

List of Figures

Financial Inclusion in Organization of Islamic Cooperation Countries: Challenges and Opportunities

Impact of Microcredit on Livelihood Status of Women in Rural India

Determinants of Trust, Security, Privacy and Risk Factors in Embracing Online Banking

Microfinance Sector and the Supportive Role of Regulator in its Transformation: A Case Study from India

Impact of Financial Factors on Social and Financial Sustainability in Banking Sector: A Mediating Role of Financial Literacy

Digital Financial Inclusion: Strategic Issues and Imperatives

List of Tables

Key Determinants of Financial Inclusion: An Empirical Evidence from Western Balkan Countries

Business Correspondents' Perspective on Financial Inclusion Initiatives: An Empirical Analysis

Assessing the Performance of District Cooperative Banks: An Efficiency-Based Approach

Role of Non-governmental Organizations in Micro Health Insurance Schemes: A Case Study from India

Assessing the Performance of Primary Agricultural Credit Societies: A Non-traditional Multi-Dimensional Index Approach

Are Indian Microfinance Institutions Efficient? A Two-Stage Double Bootstrapped DEA Based Analysis

Impact of Microcredit on Livelihood Status of Women in Rural India

Determinants of Trust, Security, Privacy and Risk Factors in Embracing Online Banking

Microfinance Sector and the Supportive Role of Regulator in its Transformation: A Case Study from India

Impact of Financial Factors on Social and Financial Sustainability in Banking Sector: A Mediating Role of Financial Literacy

Promoting Financial Inclusion Through Digital Wallets: An Empirical Study with Street Vendors

Inclusive Finance and Income Inequality: An Evidence from Saudi Arabia

Financial Inclusion Practices

Demographic Discriminators in the Adoption of Banking Services: Evidence from the Primitive Tribal Households

Prabhakar Nandru, Satyanarayana Rentala, and Vidya Suresh

1 Introduction

The concept of financial inclusion has become a prominent agenda for the governments and financial institutions both at national and global levels. It has caught significant attention of researchers, policymakers, financial service providers, and economists (Srinivasan, 2007; Allen et al., 2012; Gupte et al., 2012; Amidzic et al., 2014; Camara et al., 2014). A well-structured financial system serves as a basic tool for providing the wide range of banking services like savings, payments, credit, and insurance products to vast segments of population (Demirguc-Kunt & Klapper, 2013). The banking services are intended for public good and

P. Nandru (✉)
Department of Commerce, School of Management, Pondicherry University, Karaikal, India

S. Rentala
Bharathidasan Institute of Management, Tiruchirappalli, India

V. Suresh
Professional Studies and Undergraduate Department, College of Banking and Financial Studies, Muscat, Sultanate of Oman

Ananda S. and D. Singh (eds.), *Financial Inclusion in Emerging Markets*,
https://doi.org/10.1007/978-981-16-2652-4_1

hence it is essential that the government and financial institutions take effective measures for providing basic banking services to the unbanked population—particularly the low-income and underprivileged sections of the society (Leeladhar, 2005). In India, the central government, Reserve Bank of India (RBI), and banking sector are making great efforts to bring many segments of unbanked population into mainstream of formal banking system. There is evidence that after nationalization of 14 banks in 1969, the banking sector has shown significant improvement in terms of financially accessibility, availability, profitability and increase competitiveness among service providers. Globally, various attempts have been made to examine the triggers of financial exclusion and develop strategies to enhance access to various financial services for the poor and disadvantaged sections. The World Bank had also declared an goal of accomplishing universal access by 2020 which signifies that financial inclusion has been accepted as a fundamental strategy for economic growth (Leeladhar, 2005; Camara et al., 2014). In India, the main agenda of government and policymakers is to ensure access to at least one bank account for every household. This is the reason the Government of India started a national level financial inclusion initiative named as "Pradhan Mantri Jan Dhan-Yojana (PMDJY)" with an intention that every Indian household should maintain an account in a formal financial institution.

Efforts are being made at the global level to study the causes of financial exclusion that need to be viewed in a much wider perspective. But having a bank account (current/saving) may not be an exact sign of financial inclusion. It majorly depends on the effective use of banking services like savings, availing bank credit, payments, and remittances (Leeladhar, 2005; Ranjani & Bapat, 2015). Hence, the financial institutions and RBI are trying to ensure that a wide assortment of appropriate financial products are offered to every individual and facilitate them to use those services (Rangarajan, 2008). World Bank Global Findex Survey (2014) shows that the account penetration in India is almost 52.8% among all the adults, up from 35.2%, in 2011. The survey results reveal that 11.6% adults saved money in financial institutions in 2011 while it has increased up to 14.4% in 2014. The borrower percentage from financial institutions had decreased from 7.7 in 2011 to 6.4% of adults in 2014. It was also observed that more than 50% of Indian population had bank account but only 6.4% of adults have borrowed money from formal banking system. It can thus be posited that the policymakers and government should make more efforts and design appropriate strategies for increasing the usage of the bank accounts.

Many empirical research studies and publicly available data have researched the financial inclusion outreach at national and international levels. The present literature review of this research is broadly categorized into two categories:

i. Role of banks in promoting financial inclusion;
ii. Demographic characteristics influencing financial inclusion.

1.1 Role of Banks in Promoting Financial Inclusion

With an objective of expanding banking services to all sections of the society, the government decided to nationalize 14 commercial banks on 19th July 1969. There is evidence that the Indian banking sector has achieved considerable growth rate in terms of branch and ATMs penetration during the last few decades. A keynote address by Dr. K.C Chakrabarty (2011)—Deputy Governor of the Reserve Bank of India (RBI)—highlighted the issues concerning the status of financial inclusion and banks. Currently, inclusive growth is a focus area for enhancing financial inclusion at national and international levels. Empirical evidence demonstrates that nations with large sections of their population excluded from financial systems lead to higher poverty levels and discrimination. Therefore, the concept of financial inclusion is a priority policy choice and it is considered that banking system is a key driver for inclusive growth in all developing and developed nations.

Bansal (2014) stated that efficient financial system enables the underprivileged people to use financial services more effectively without any social and economic discrimination. The financial institutions like banks and microfinance organizations are providing affordable financial services like savings, credit, payments, and insurance services to the low income and weaker section population and make part of the formal financial system. Kendall et al. (2010) measured the status of financial access around the world and found that in countries like India, institutions that include commercial banks, rural banks, various types of urban and rural cooperatives, and microfinance institutions typically play a more active role in promoting financial inclusion. Another study (Han & Melecky, 2013) found that there is a close relation between financial inclusion and financial stability. The study notes that greater access to bank deposits (financial inclusion) can enhance the banking sector funding and will be able to provide loans to industries for productive purposes. This leads to disappearing financial crises and enables maintenance of financial stability in the country.

1.2 Demographic Characteristics Influencing on Financial Inclusion

Many studies have empirically explored the influence of demographic characteristics on financial inclusion in national and global contexts. In the Indian context, Bhanot et al. (2012) explored the factors that determine the extent of financial inclusion in the states of Assam and Meghalaya. The study concluded that income level, financial literacy, awareness of self-help groups (SHGs) are influential key factors leading to financial inclusion. Nandru et al. (2015) observed that the demographic factors which extend the usage of banking services as determinants of the financial inclusion outreach in Pondicherry region. It was found that factors like higher education, better education, gender, and occupation levels have a significant influence on usage of banking services. It was also found that macro-level dimensions like ease of accessing bank products, physical distance of bank branches, and usage of banking services have a potential to determine the financial inclusion outreach. Bapat (2010) observed that there is a relationship between bank account ownership and several demographic factors. It was found that factors like income, occupation, and asset holding pattern show significant relation with the status of ownership of bank accounts.

Research done at global level (Demirguc-Kunt & Klapper, 2012, 2013; Efobi et al., 2014; Fungacova & Weill, 2015; Saunders et al., 2007; Sinclair, 2013) has used World Bank findex database to study the relation of demographic characteristics with financial inclusion. Saunders et al. (2007) stated that owning a bank account is the most significant indicator of financial inclusion and that it has a relationship with other demographic variables. It was stated that the demographic factors such as income level, employment status, and level of education have significant association with ownership of an account at a bank. Other study by Demirguc-Kunt and Klapper (2012) reviewed the connection between ownership of bank accounts and usage of formal accounts among 123 countries. The results of the research indicated that higher financial inclusion levels are correlated with lesser banking expenses, more proximity to the branches, and a smaller number documentation necessities to open an account. It was concluded that there are substantial disparities across regions and individual characteristics. Demirguc-Kunt and Klapper (2013) investigated gender differences in the use of financial services among 98 developing countries. It was found that the individual characteristics including income, education, employment status, age, and gender show significant impact on usage of financial services. Sinclair (2013) explored several aspects of financial exclusion in the context of Britain. It was found that factors such as low income of customers, lack of appropriate financial means, and affordable credit provision influence access to mainstream banking services. Research by Efobi et al. (2014) asserted that individual attributes—income, ICT (information, communication, and technology) inclination of individuals and age—have great influence on the access to and usage of bank services in Nigeria. Fungacova and Weill (2015) explored the status of financial inclusion in China using Global Findex database during 2011. The study compared the status of financial inclusion of China with other nations comprising Brazil, Russia, India, and South Africa (BRICS). The results revealed that China has achieved higher levels of financial inclusion owing to greater usage of formal accounts and savings in comparison with the other nations. Moreover, other factors like higher educational qualifications, better incomes, and gender influences also have a significant positive impact on better use of formal accounts and availability of formal credit.

The literature review clearly provides the evidence that most of the global studies have used publicly available data to determine the demographic characteristics to establish the relation with financial inclusion. Even in Indian context, a few studies (Bapat, 2010; Bhanot et al., 2012; Nandru & Rentala, 2019) have used primary data. Bapat (2010) and Bhanot et al. (2012) studied the influence of demographics on the access to bank account. It was found that financial inclusion has multiple dimensions such as accessibility, availability, and usage of banking services. Based on evidence from literature, in this research an attempt was made to find out the demographic discriminators in relation with dimensions of financial inclusion. The present study, for the first time, focuses the status of financial inclusion among underprivileged population. The study was confined to primary data which have been collected from Scheduled Tribes (ST's) who are socially and economically discriminated in the society in the state of Telangana, India.

2 Research Methodology

2.1 *Objectives of the Study*

To study the financial inclusion among the Scheduled Tribes (ST's) , the following three objectives have been formed.

i. To study the level of financial inclusion for the Scheduled Tribal households.
ii. To explore the dimensions of financial inclusion.
iii. To find the significant difference among various demographic characteristics on different dimensions of financial inclusion.

2.2 *Hypothesis of the Study*

The following hypothesis have been formed and tested.

H_{01}: *There is no significant difference among various demographic factors and with awareness* of banking services.
H_{02}: *There is no significant difference among various demographic factors and with accessibility* of banking services.
H_{03}: *There is no significant difference among various demographic factors and with affordability* of banking services.
H_{04}: *There is no significant difference among various demographic factors and with usage of banking services.*

2.3 *Data Source*

The data employed in this research was collected through a household level survey using a structured questionnaire which covered dimension of access to and usage of banking services with a sample of 300 respondents based on convenience sampling methodology in Khammam district in state of Telangana. Out of this sample of 300 respondents, 25 were rejected because of missing data and this research was finally confined to a sample size of 275. The analysis indicates a gender distribution of the selected respondents as 69.1% males and 30.9% females. The socio-demographic profile of the respondents is shown in Table 1.

Table 1 Demographic characteristics of the respondents

Demographic variable	*Frequency*	*%*
Gender		
Male	190	69.1
Female	85	30.9
Total	275	100.0
Age		
25 yrs or less	6	2.2
26–35 yrs	120	43.6
36–45 yrs	91	33.1
46–55 yrs	50	18.2
55 yrs and above	8	2.9
Total	275	100.0
Education		
Illiterate	89	32.4
Primary level	67	24.4
High school level	63	22.9
Intermediate/diploma	37	13.5
UG Degree	12	4.4
PG Degree	7	2.5
Total	275	100.0
Occupation		
Govt. employed	11	4.0
Pvt. employed	53	19.3
Daily labor	78	28.4
Farmer	35	12.7
Self-employed	25	9.1
Agricultural labor	73	26.5
Total	275	100.0

Source Primary data results

It can be noted from Table 2 that most of the respondents had a bank account in formal financial institutions, i.e., 81.8% of respondents had bank account and only 18.2% respondents do not have a bank account.

Table 2 Number of respondents having bank account

Particular	*Category*	*Frequency*	*%*
Have a bank account	Yes	225	81.8
	No	50	18.2
Total		275	100.0

Source Primary data results

In the procedure of assessing financial inclusion, a formal bank account functions as an entry step into formal financial segment. This ensure easy transfer of—money, wages, remittances and government payments and receipts. It also encourages saving of money and access to bank credit (Demirguc-Kunt & Klapper, 2012). In this study, most of the respondents have a bank account but having a bank account is only one aspect to measure the financial inclusion outreach whereas the other aspect is about how the account holder uses various banking services like savings, withdrawals, credit, and remittances.

Table 3 shows clearly that most of the respondents who have a bank account have not been interested to approach bank for availing credit services. Interestingly, most of the respondents have membership in SHGs. There is evidence that the SHGs provide supplementary credit requirement for clients and reduce the influence of informal financial sector role in rural areas.

Table 4 shows that who has approached bank for a loan and who had got the loan and who did not get the loan.

Table 5 shows there are several reasons for rejection of loans by the banks. The primary reason for rejection of bank loans was that there was no security offered by the customers. The other reasons were lack of documentation, poor maintenance of account, insufficient income, and lack of a loan guarantor.

Table 3 Respondents who approached a bank credit

Particular	*Category*	*Frequency*	*%*
Approached bank credit	Yes	72	0.32
	No	163	0.68
Total		225	100.0

Source Primary data results

Table 4 Respondents who got a loan from bank

Particular	*Category*	*Frequency*	*%*
Got bank loan	Yes	18	0.25
	No	54	0.75
Total		72	100.0

Source Primary data results

Table 5 Reasons for loans reject by banks

Reasons for bank loan rejection	*Frequency*	*%*
No security	16	29.63
Lack of documentation	14	25.93
Poor maintain account	11	20.37
No loan guarantor	5	9.26
Insufficient income	8	14.81
Total	54	100.0

Source Primary data results

2.4 *Variable Measurement*

A structured feedback form was created to gather data and measure the status of financial inclusion by taking micro-level indicators into account with the help of multiple item measures using a 5-point Likert scale. In this scale, strongly disagree represented (1) and strongly agree represented (5). Overall, 11 items had been developed to obtain four factors. Each item was measured by the five-point Likert scale. 1 = strongly disagree, 2 = disagree, 3 = neutral, 4 = agree and 5 = strongly agree. Finally, four factors have been constructed to measure the perception of tribal households regarding various dimensions of financial inclusion.

2.5 *Results of Factor Analysis and Scale Reliability*

The foremost objective of factor analysis is the methodical simplification of a high number of intercorrelated characteristics to a few representative constructs or factors (Ho, 2006). In this research, factor analysis characterizes a set of detected variables—23 items of a number of "common" factors plus a factor which is unique to each variable. These core dimensions are known as factors. Data set is reduced to a smallest set of factors of interrelated variables. This helps in achieving parsimony by being able to explain maximum variance with a minimum number of constructs. All items loaded with a value of >0.5 (Hair et al., 2006) factor loading can be considered significant. In this research, all those items with a loading value of >0.5 have been accepted for further analysis.

Two important measures are considered to check appropriateness of factor analysis. The first measure, known as Kaiser–Meyer–Olkin (KMO) measure, gives an overall sampling adequacy (Kaiser, 1974). The KMO value can vary between 0 and 1. In this research, the scales are within the

Table 6 Results of KMO and Bartlett's test for overall sampling adequacy

Kaiser–Meyer–Olkin measure of sampling adequacy 0.827		
Bartlett's test of sphericity	Approx. χ^2	596.510
	Df	55
	Sig.	0.000

Source Primary data results

acceptable range, i.e., 0.827 and it is also seen that the composite reliability of all the latent constructs is more than 0.5. This suggests that the measurement is good. Bartlett's test of sphericity is the second measurement considered and its value was found to be 596.510 at 1% level of significance as $p < 0.001$. This measure signifies that there is a high significant correlation among the items of the constructs in the survey. Table 6 shows the results of the KMO-Bartlett's test. KMO measure indicates that the sample size is adequate.

2.6 *Reliability*

Reliability of any measurement items is evaluated by calculating Cronbach's alpha value that confirms internal consistency and checking reliability. Kline (2013) asserted that the generally acceptable value of 0.80 is appropriate to ascertain reliability. It was also noted that the value between 0.60 and 0.70 is also acceptable. Hence, a minimum cut off value of 0.60 for Cronbach's alpha reliability was employed in the present research to determine the reliability of each measure to ascertain the overall reliability. All Cronbach's alpha values in the present study were found to be greater than 0.80 and only the factor value of accessibility was 0.65 and this may also be considered as reliable. Values of Cronbach's alpha are shown in below Table 7.

3 Results of Exploratory Factor Analysis

23 items were used for identification of factors that have been used in this research. All the extraction values in the communities ranged between 0.853 and 0.645 which are higher than the minimum accepted value of 0.5. After Varamix rotation, all the 23 items were grouped into 4 factors which put together accounted for 69.825 of total variance loading. These

Table 7 Results of factors analysis (factor loading) and reliability test (Cronbach's alpha)

Factors constructed	*Items measurement*	*Item loading*	*Cronbach's α value*
Awareness	I aware use of ATMs	0.704	0.830
	I aware filling bank challan	0.757	
	I aware Kisan Credit Card (KCC)	0.742	
	I aware No-frills (Zero Balance) accounts	0.645	
	Aware of saving account	0.718	
	Aware of life insurance products	0.675	
Accessibility	Location of bank branches are highly accessible	0.702	0.649
	Opening bank account is very easy	0.665	
	Availability of ATMs are convenient places	0.659	
Affordability	I find there are no hidden charges in the services	0.653	0.819
	Bank charges normal fee for lockers	0.735	
	Bank charges reasonable fee of services	0.853	
	I find bank loan are very affordable than credit avail from moneylenders	0.848	
	I find bank charge less fee for Internet banking	0.852	
	I find flexibility to repay bank loans	0.714	
	The time required to processing the bank loan is very less than informal sources	0.800	
Usage	I save money into bank very frequently	0.788	0.901
	I withdrawal money very frequently	0.756	
	I opened bank account for getting bank loan	0.688	

(continued)

Table 7 (continued)

Factors constructed	*Items measurement*	*Item loading*	*Cronbach's α value*
	I use ATMs for withdrawal money	0.805	
	I feel use of ATMs is very comfortable	0.802	
	I use bank account for receiving government benefits	0.689	
	Have very interest to use bank account	0.801	

Source Primary data results

factors were identified as awareness, accessibility, affordability, and usage of banking services. Each of these factors were observed to have initial eigenvalues of 46.24, 9.38, 8.50, and 5.70%, respectively. The results of the total variance explained by different factors have been shown in Table 8.

The following factors have been formed with factor analysis.

3.1 Awareness

Awareness of banking services among the public influences the usage of various banking services. In India, RBI has taken initiatives regarding promoting "Project Literacy" program at national level to provide awareness regarding use of basic banking services. Through factor analysis, the first dimension that was constructed was named "awareness," which explained 46.241% of the total variance. There were 6 items extracted to construct this factor, (a) I am aware of use of ATMs (Item loaded = 0.704), (b) I am aware of filling bank challan (Item loaded = 0.757), (c) I am aware of Kisan Credit Card (KCC) (Item loaded = 0.742), (d) I am aware of No-frills (Zero Balance) accounts (Item loaded = 0.645), (e) I am aware of saving account (Item loaded = 0.718), and (f) I am aware of life insurance products (Item loaded = 0.675).

Table 8 Total variance explained by different items

No	*Initial eigenvalues*			*Extraction of squared loading*			*Rotation sums of squared loadings*		
	Total	*% Variance*	*Cumulative %*	*Total*	*% Variance*	*Cumulative %*	*Total*	*% Variance*	*Cumulative %*
1	10.64	46.24	46.24	10.64	46.24	46.24	9.09	39.52	39.53
2	2.16	9.38	55.62	2.16	9.38	55.62	2.88	12.53	52.06
3	1.96	8.50	64.12	1.96	8.50	64.12	2.60	11.30	63.36
4	1.31	5.70	69.82	1.31	5.70	69.83	1.4	6.47	69.83
5	1.01	4.371	74.196						
6	0.82	3.551	77.748						
7	0.77	3.336	81.084						
8	0.64	2.774	83.858						
9	0.61	2.646	86.504						
10	0.58	2.505	89.009						
11	0.51	2.225	91.235						
12	0.38	1.661	92.896						
13	0.32	1.391	94.287						
14	0.29	1.255	95.543						
15	0.19	0.816	96.358						
16	0.18	0.772	97.130						
17	0.17	0.719	97.849						
18	0.13	0.544	98.393						
19	0.12	0.507	98.900						
20	0.09	0.376	99.276						
21	0.07	0.318	99.593						
22	0.05	0.224	99.817						

(continued)

Table 8 (continued)

No	*Initial eigenvalues*			*Extraction of squared loading*			*Rotation sums of squared loadings*		
	Total	*% Variance*	*Cumulative %*	*Total*	*% Variance*	*Cumulative %*	*Total*	*% Variance*	*Cumulative %*
23	0.04	0.183	100.000						

Note Extraction method: Principal component analysis
Source Primary data results

3.2 *Accessibility*

Reaching the unreached segment of people is the main agenda of financial institutions and financial service providers. Making bank branches and ATMs accessible for people are both good practices that can be followed not only for business development, but also for making sound commercial decisions. Accessibility means improved convenience resulting from more use of banking and ATMs services. It provides the opportunity to the public to open a savings account and make possible use of banking services like savings, deposits, and credit. The government of India and RBI have been taking so many initiatives regarding expanding bank branches and ATMs to the people at the bottom of the pyramid.

It is considered that improving accessibility enhances access to banking services for all users and makes it possible for them to use more of banking services. On the other hand, there are a few issues regarding accessibility of banking services—a few environmental and demographic factors which determine the bank and ATMs penetration. A study by Evanoff (1988) stated that certain issues like population and per capita income are expected to have a positive impact on accessibility and they have a direct influence on the demand for banking services. Beck et al. (2007) found that geographic access to banking services is positively correlated with population density and access to and use of banking services. It was also found that country characteristics as well as policy variables also have a significant relation with higher outreach. Through factor analysis, "accessibility" dimension has been constructed, which explained 9.382% of the total variance. It could be constructed with extraction of 3 items which are (a) Location of bank branches highly accessible (Item loaded = 0.702), (b) Opening bank account is very easy (Item loaded = 0.665), (c) Availability of ATMs is at convenient places (Item loaded = 0.659).

3.3 *Affordability*

Financial inclusion is defined as providing the banking and financial services at affordable cost to the disadvantaged and underprivileged section of population. It involves the costs in terms of minimum balance requirement and fees that clients need to pay to avail services from banks. Availability of formal and affordable financial services for the unbanked segment of population largely contributes to bringing them into formal banking system. Additionally, it could have positive consequences on the lives of these people. For the result of factor analysis, "affordability" dimensions have been captured and the factor explained 9.382% of the total variance. It could be constructed from extraction of 7 items (a) I find there are no hidden charges in the services (Item loaded = 0.653), (b) Bank charges normal fee for lockers (Item loaded = 0.735), (c) Bank charges reasonable fee for services (Item loaded = 0.853), (d) I find bank loan are very affordable than credit availed from moneylenders (Item loaded = 0.848), (e) I find bank charges less fee for Internet banking (Item loaded = 0.852), (f) I find flexibility to repay bank loans (Item loaded = 0.714), (g) The time required to processing the bank loan is very less than informal sources (Item loaded = 0.800).

3.4 *Usage of Banking Services*

Currently in India, the focus of financial inclusion is restricted to ensure a minimum level of access to a savings bank account. Ownership of a bank account alone is not regarded as an accurate indicator of financial inclusion and there could be multiple modes of determining financial inclusion. It can be measured based on level of use of banking services for deposits, credit, and withdrawal. The fourth factor has been confined to usage of banking services with extraction of 7 items namely (a) I save money into bank very frequently (Item loaded = 0.788), (b) I withdraw money very frequently (Item loaded = 0.756), (c) I opened bank account for getting bank loan (Item loaded = 0.688), (d) I use ATMs for withdrawal money (Item loaded = 0.805), (e) I feel use of ATMs is very comfortable (Item loaded = 0.802), (f) I use bank account for receiving government benefits (Item loaded = 0.689), (g) Have high interest to use bank account (Item loaded = 0.801).

3.5 *One-Way ANOVA*

The one-way analysis of variance (ANOVA) is a statistical technique that is used to compare the means of (>2) groups. Lahari et al. (2010) asserted that ANOVA can be prescribed to estimate the statistically significant mean difference between customers of banks and SERVQUAL dimensions. Ranjani and Bapat (2015) employed ANOVA test to measure the significant differences between perceptions of respondents who had a bank account. In this research, one-way ANOVA test had been applied to weigh the significant mean differences among various financial inclusion dimensions such as awareness, accessibility, affordability, and usage of banking services. Different demographic factors of the respondents such as gender, age, level of education, level of occupation, and household income status were considered in the research. The results of analysis of variance (ANOVA) and independent samples *t*-test are shown Table 9.

Table 10 gives an account of results of independent samples *t*-test with various dimensions of financial inclusion.

4 Conclusion

This study widely documented the demographic characteristics of household in relation to the various dimensions of financial inclusion such as awareness, accessibility, affordability, and use of various banking services. This research captures various dimensions of financial inclusion. Firstly, financial inclusion, which is measured by the proportion of individuals who have a bank account. The results indicate that about 82% of the respondents have bank accounts. The second issue is that ownership of a bank account alone is not the only indicator of financial inclusion since there could be usage of banking services also that show significant impact on the status of financial inclusion. The study finds that only 25% of respondents have borrowed money from the banks. The security and lack of documentation are main cause for limited approach to banks for credit. Studies by Bapat (2010) and others (Ranjani & Bapat, 2015) found that there is a significant disparity between the respondents who hold bank accounts and those availing loans from the bank because the account holders are not comfortable in approaching bank for their credit needs. The present study identified that the demographic characteristics including age, gender, income, level of education, and occupation status remain significantly related to the various dimensions of financial inclusion among the ST's. The results of one-way ANOVA and independent sample t-test confirm that there is a demographic discrimination with the awareness, accessibility, affordability, and usage of banking services. Therefore, the results of this study reject the null hypothesis H_{01}, H_{02}, H_{03}, and H_{04} and confirm that there is a significant relationship between demographic characteristics and dimensions of financial inclusion. Finally the results are also similar to other studies conducted by researchers like Saunders et al. (2007), Bapat (2010), Bhanot et al. (2012), Demirguc-Kunt and Klapper (2012), Demirguc-Kunt and Klapper (2013), Sinclair (2013), Efobi et al.

Table 9 Results of analysis of variance (ANOVA) and independent sample *t*-test

Factors	*Statement of hypothesis*	*F-value*	*p-value*	*Decision*
Awareness (H_{01})	$\mathbf{H_{01a}}$: there is no significant difference between different gender-based groups and on their awareness level of banking services	14.07	0.000***	Rejected H_{01a}
	$\mathbf{H_{01b}}$: there is no significant difference among different age level groups and on their awareness level of banking services	12.96	0.000***	Rejected H_{01b}
	$\mathbf{H_{01c}}$: there is no significant difference among different level of households income and on their awareness of banking services	45.75	0.000***	Rejected H_{01c}
	$\mathbf{H_{01d}}$: there is no significant difference among different level of occupation groups and on their awareness level of banking services	48.78	0.000***	Rejected H_{01d}
	$\mathbf{H_{01e}}$: there is no significant difference among different level of education and on their awareness level of banking services	44.36	0.000***	Rejected H_{01e}
Accessibility (H_{02})	$\mathbf{H_{02a}}$: there is no significant difference between different gender-based groups and on accessibility of banking services	49.70	0.000***	Rejected H_{02a}

(continued)

(2014), Fungacova and Weill (2015), and Nandru et al. (2015). Prior research studies concluded that there is a significant association between the various demographic characteristics and financial inclusion dimensions that include awareness, accessibility, affordability, and usage of various banking services.

Table 9 (continued)

Factors	*Statement of hypothesis*	*F-value*	*p-value*	*Decision*
	H_{02b}: there is no significant difference among different age level groups and on accessibility of banking services	13.36	0.000***	Rejected H_{02b}
	H_{02c}: there is no significant difference among different level of households income and on accessibility of banking services	23.46	0.000***	Rejected H_{02c}
	H_{02d}: there is no significant difference among level of occupation and on accessibility of banking services	13.77	0.000***	Rejected H_{02d}
	H_{02e}: there is no significant difference among different level of education and on accessibility of banking services	9.93	0.000***	Rejected H_{02e}
Affordability (H_{03})	**H_{03a}**: there is no significant difference between different gender-based groups and on affordability of banking services	4.38	0.000***	Rejected H_{03a}
	H_{03b}: there is no significant difference among different age level groups and on affordability of banking services	9.92	0.000***	Rejected H_{03b}

(continued)

The present research highlights a few directions that can be considered for further future research in the same field. First, the present study was restricted to assess the financial inclusion among Scheduled Tribes (ST's) only. Future research could be extended to other underprivileged sections of the society and even extended to rural areas. Second, the present study

Table 9 (continued)

Factors	*Statement of hypothesis*	*F-value*	*p-value*	*Decision*
	$\mathbf{H_{03c}}$: there is no significant difference among different level of households income and on affordability of banking services	38.20	0.000***	Rejected H_{03c}
	$\mathbf{H_{03d}}$: there is no significant difference among different level of occupation groups and on affordability of banking services	73.63	0.000***	Rejected H_{03d}
	$\mathbf{H_{03e}}$: there is no significant difference among different level of education and on affordability of banking services	44.63	0.000***	Rejected H_{03e}
Usage (H_{04})	$\mathbf{H_{04a}}$: there is no significant difference between different gender-based groups and on usage of banking services	23.71	0.000***	Rejected H_{04a}
	$\mathbf{H_{04b}}$: there is no significant difference among different age level groups and on usage of banking of banking services	14.31	0.000***	Rejected H_{04b}
	$\mathbf{H_{04c}}$: there is no significant difference among different level of households income and on usage of banking of banking services	45.19	0.000***	Rejected H_{04c}
	$\mathbf{H_{04d}}$: there is no significant difference among different level of occupation groups and on usage of banking of banking services	74.12	0.000***	Rejected H_{04d}

(continued)

Table 9 (continued)

Factors	*Statement of hypothesis*	*F-value*	*p-value*	*Decision*
	$\mathbf{H_{04e}}$: there is no significant difference among different level of education and on usage of banking of banking services	32.70	0.000***	Rejected H_{04e}

Note ***Denotes significant at 1% level
Source Primary data results

Table 10 Results of independent samples *t*-test with dimensions of financial inclusion

Factors	*Segmentation*	*Leven's test for equality of variances*		*t-value*	*Sig (2-tailed)*
		F-value	*P-value*		
Awareness	Equal variance assumed	14.07	0.000	6.72***	0.000
Accessibility	Equal variance assumed	49.70	0.000	4.86***	0.000
Affordability	Equal variance assumed	4.38	0.000	4.09***	0.000
Usage	Equal variance assumed	23.71	0.000	3.72***	0.000

Note ***Denotes significance at 1% level
Source Primary data results

found demographic characteristics in relation to only four financial inclusion dimensions such as awareness, accessibility, affordability, and usage of banking services. Further research can be extended by including a higher number of explanatory dimensions like availability, payment measures, cost of usage dimension, and quality dimension.

References

Allen. F., Demirguc-Kunt, A., Klapper, L., & Peria Martinez, S. M. (2012). *The foundations of financial inclusion understanding ownership and use of formal Accounts* (Policy Research Working Paper 6290). World Bank, Washington, DC.

Amidzic, G., Massara, A., & Mialou, A. (2014). *Assessing countries' financial inclusion standing—A new composite index* (IMF working paper WP/14/36)

Bansal, S. (2014). Perspective of technology in achieving financial inclusion in rural India. *Procedia Economics and Finance, 11*, 472–480.

Bapat, D. (2010). Perceptions on banking service in rural India: An empirical study. *International Journal of Rural Management, 6*(2), 303–321.

Beck, T., Demirguc-Kunt, A., & Peria Martinez, S. M. (2007). Reaching out: Access to and use of banking services across countries. *Journal of Financial Economics, 85*, 234–266.

Bhanot, D., Bapat, V., & Bera, S. (2012). Studying financial inclusion in north-east India. *International Journal of Bank Marketing, 30*(6), 465–484.

Camara, N., Pena, X., & Tuesta, D. (2014). *Factors that matter for financial inclusion: Evidence from Peru* (No. 1409).

Chakrabarty, K. C. (2011, November). Financial inclusion and banks: Issues and perspectives. *RBI Bulletin*.

Demirguc-Kunt, A., & Klapper, L. (2012). *Measuring financial inclusion: The Global Findex database* (Policy Research Working Paper 6025). World Bank, Washington, DC.

Demirguc-Kunt, A., & Klapper, L. (2013, Spring). Measuring financial inclusion: Explaining variation in use of financial services across and within countries. *Paper Economic Activity.*

Efobi, U., Beecroft, I., & Osabuohien, E. (2014). Access to and use of bank services in Nigeria: Micro-econometric evidence. *Review of Development Finance, 4*(2), 104–114.

Evanoff, D. D. (1988). Branch banking and service accessibility. *Journal of Money, Credit and Banking, 20*(2), 191–202.

Fungacova, Z., & Weill, L. (2015). Understanding financial inclusion in China. *BOFIT Discussion Papers, 2014*(10), 1.

Gupte, R., Venkataramani, B., & Gupata, D. (2012). Computation of financial inclusion index for India. *International Journal of Procedia - Social and Behavioral Sciences, 37*(133), 149.

Hair, J. F., Black, W. C., Babin, B. J., Anderson, R. E., & Tatham, R. L. (2006). *Multivariate data analysis* (Vol. 6). Pearson Prentice Hall.

Han, R., & Melecky, M. (2013). *Financial inclusion for financial stability: access to bank deposits and the growth of deposits in the global financial crisis* (World Bank policy research working paper (6577)).

Ho, R. (2006). *Handbook of univariate and multivariate data analysis and interpretation with SPSS*. CRC Press. Google Scholar.

Kaiser, H. F. (1974). An index of factorial simplicity. *Psychometrika, 39*(1), 31–36.

Kendall, J., Ponce, A., & Mylenko, N. (2010). *Measuring financial access around the world*. The World Bank.

Kline, P. (2013). *Handbook of psychological testing*. Routledge.

Leeladhar, V. (2005). *Taking banking services to the common man—Financial inclusion*. Commemorative Lecture at the Fedbank Hormis Memorial Foundation at Ernakulum. Retrieved from https://www.rbi.org.in/scripts/BS_SpeechesView.aspx?Id=218

Nandru P., Anand, B., & Rentala., S. (2015). Financial inclusion in Pondicherry region: Evidence from accessibility and usage of banking services. *TSM Business Review, 3*(2), 2348–3784.

Nandru, P., & Rentala, S. (2019). Demand-side analysis of measuring financial inclusion: Impact on socio-economic status of primitive tribal groups (PTGs) in India. *International Journal of Development Issues, 19*(1), 1–24.

Ranjani, K. S., & Bapat, V. (2015). Deepening financial inclusion beyond account opening: Road ahead for banks. *Business Perspectives and Research, 3*(1), 52–65.

Rangarajan, C. (2008). *Report of the committee on financial inclusion, Government of India*. New Delhi. Retrieved from https://www.sksindia.com/downloads/Report_Committee_Financial_Inclusion.pdf

Saunders, S. G., Bendixen, M., & Abratt, R. (2007). Banking patronage motives of the urban informal poor. *Journal of Services Marketing, 21*(1), 52–63.

Sinclair, S. (2013). Financial inclusion and social financialisation: Britain in a European context. *International Journal of Sociology and Social Policy, 33*(11/12), 658–676.

Srinivasan, N. (2007). Policy issues and Role of banking system in financial inclusion. *Economic and Political Weekly*, 3091–3095.

Financial Inclusion in Organization of Islamic Cooperation Countries: Challenges and Opportunities

Amal Khairy Amin

1 Introduction

After the global financial crisis in 2008, Financial Inclusion has attracted global attention with the realization that many people around the globe are denied access to financial services. Therefore, issues of financial exclusion and the importance of expanding Financial Inclusion were included in the international political agenda. In the countries of the Organization of Islamic Cooperation (OIC), which includes in its membership 57 countries with a Muslim majority, and a population of 1.8 billion people, 17.05% of the total population still lives below the global poverty line, and the average of the OIC countries in the Human Development Index (HDI), which is developed by the United Nations and indicates the level of welfare of people in the world, is 0.63, that is less than the global average of 0.73 for 2018 (OICStat).

At the same time, the Financial Development Index, which is published annually by the World Economic Forum to measure and analyze the factors that enable the development of financial systems between different

A. K. Amin (✉)
Economic Researcher, Central Agency for Public Mobilization and Statistics, Cairo, Egypt

Ananda S. and D. Singh (eds.), *Financial Inclusion in Emerging Markets*,
https://doi.org/10.1007/978-981-16-2652-4_2

economies, is valued at 0.2. This value is lower than the global average of 0.3, which indicates the weakness of financial systems in these countries (OICStat). Financial Inclusion is seen as one of the economic growth engines, so this study seeks to explore the state of Financial Inclusion in the OIC countries. It will provide a brief introduction to Financial Inclusion, its importance and its most important indicator, as well as monitor the state of Financial Inclusion in OIC countries according to the Financial Inclusion index, then clarify the most important challenges facing promoting Financial Inclusion in these countries besides the most important opportunities that can contribute to promoting Financial Inclusion in OIC countries.

2 Financial Inclusion—A Brief Overview

2.1 *Financial Inclusion Meaning*

As the World Bank stated, Financial Inclusion means that "individuals and businesses have access to useful and affordable financial products and services that meet their needs – transactions, payments, savings, credit, and insurance – delivered in a responsible and sustainable way" (World Bank, 2018a, para. 1).

Financial Inclusion refers to ensuring that all groups of society (individuals, families, and institutions) have the mandatory financial services which could enhance their conditions and lives regardless of income level, by generalizing financial and banking products and services at reasonable costs.

On the contrary, financial exclusion "refers to a process whereby people encounter difficulties accessing and/or using financial services and products in the mainstream market that are appropriate to their needs and enable them to lead a normal social life in the society in which they belong" (Financial Services, 2008, p. 9).

2.2 *The Significance of Financial Inclusion*

The eighth goal of the SDGs (decent work and economic growth) included "strengthen the capacity of domestic financial institutions to encourage and expand access to banking, insurance, and financial services for all, by raising the percentage of adults (15+) who have accounts with banks, financial institutions, or mobile financial service providers" (United Nations, 2016, para. 10).

Numerous studies have shown the positive role of Financial Inclusion in boosting economic, financial, social, and political stability. Including people in the formal financial system helps to facilitate daily transactions including transferring and receiving funds, protecting savings, and managing costs of unexpected crises as medical emergencies or death or natural disasters, as well as improving overall living standards and helping individuals out of the poverty cycle.

Thus, Financial Inclusion has become a priority for policymakers and international institutions. The G20 has recognized the importance of Financial Inclusion as an essential pillar of global development, and pledged to promote Financial Inclusion worldwide, which prompted the World Bank to adopt a vision to mainstream financial services by 2020 (World Bank, UFA2020 Overview: Universal Financial Access by 2020, 2018b). Since 2011 more than 60 countries have started implementing reform programs aimed at improving Financial Inclusion (World Bank, Financial Inclusion, 2018a, Para. 12).

2.3 Financial Inclusion Index

The Global Financial Inclusion Database (Findex), which is developed by the World Bank, is an important tool for measuring the level achieved by countries in Financial Inclusion in more than 140 countries and is based on more than 150,000 interviews conducted in different countries of the world. This database has been published every three years since 2011 (Demirgüç-Kunt et al., 2018, p. xv).

The 2017 index results showed that about 69% of adults in the world (3.8 billion people) currently own accounts in banks or other financial institutions. This percentage varies between countries according to income level, where 94% of adults in high-income countries have an account, compared to 64% in developing countries. A variation in this percentage between countries according to income level, where 94% of adults in high-income countries get an account, compared to only 63% in developing countries.

3 Financial Inclusion in OIC

According to the OIC Statistics (OICStat) Database, there are 8.96 commercial bank branches per 100,000 people aged 15 years and above, and there are 81,301 ATMs (OICStat, 2019). We can identify Financial Inclusion status in the OIC countries by monitoring the data of Findex for the year 2017, related to adults who have an account and those who are unbanked, inactive accounts, patterns of use of the account, patterns of payments, as well as patterns of savings, borrowing and access to funds in emergency situations.

3.1 Account Ownership

The percentage of adults who own accounts in a bank or any other kind of financial institution or mobile money service in OIC is 45%. This percentage is less than the global average and the Middle East and North Africa average, while it exceeds its counterpart in the Arab region and in sub-Saharan Africa (Fig. 1).

The Republic of Iran came first in the Findex with 94%, followed by the Emirates with 88%, Malaysia with 85%, and Bahrain with 83%, and in the fifth place, Kuwait was 80%. In contrast, the least Financial Inclusion country was Afghanistan at 15% (Fig. 2).

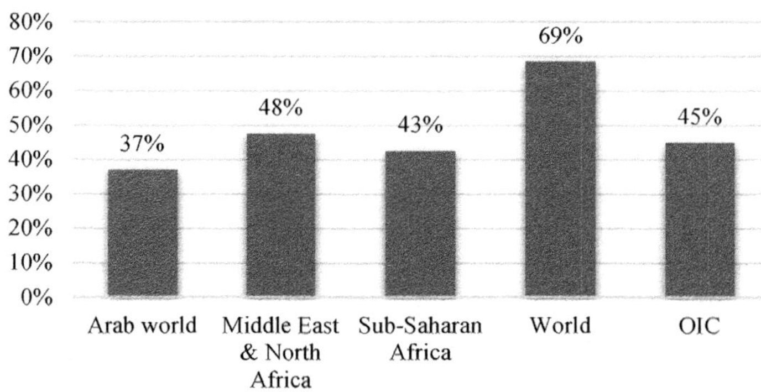

Fig. 1 Financial Account ownership 2017 (%, Age 15+) (*Source* Prepared by the author based on The World Bank Global Findex database [2017])

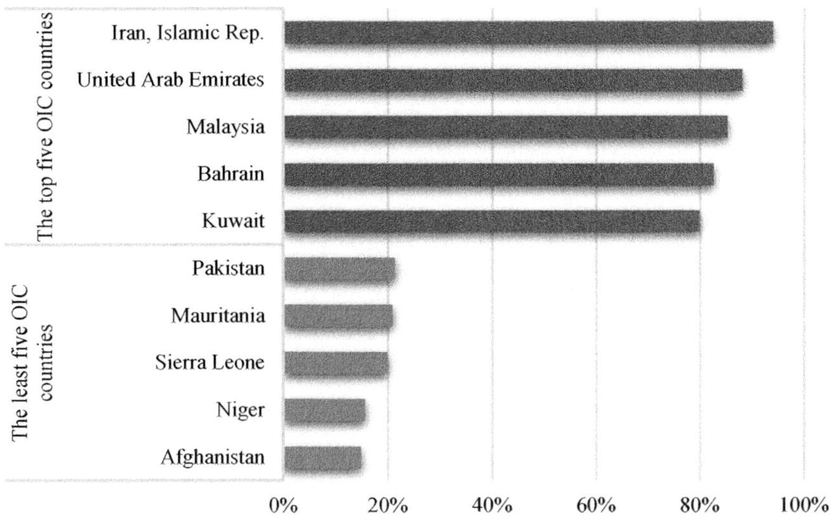

Fig. 2 Top and Least OIC countries in Financial Inclusion 2017 (%, Age 15+) (*Source* Prepared by the author based on The World Bank Global Findex database [2017])

The results indicate a gender gap related to account ownership, besides a disparity by age group, by education, by income, and by workforce (Fig. 3).

The percentage of males who own an account is 51% compared to only 38% for females. 56% of those who have completed secondary education or higher have an account, while those with a low educational level have only 34%.

There is a gap between the richest and poorest groups in owning an account in the OIC countries. Among those belonging to the richest 60% of households there are 51% own an account, while only 36% of "the poorest 40% of households" have an account.

Account ownership decreases among youth in the OIC (15–24 years), as only 36% of this age group has an account compared to 48% of those over the age of 24. 53% of those in the active workforce have an account, while 33% of adults outside the workforce have one.

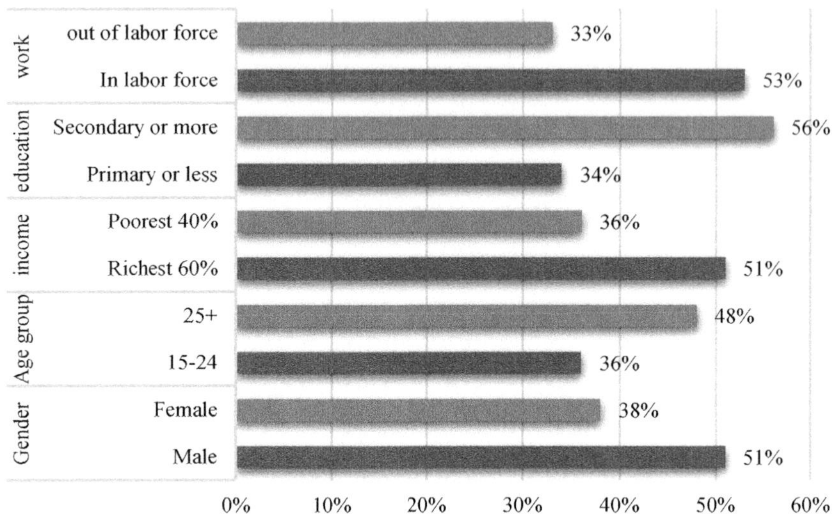

Fig. 3 Financial Account ownership in OIC by individual characteristics 2017 (%, Age 15+) (*Source* Prepared by the author based on The World Bank Global Findex database [2017])

Regarding mobile money accounts, 15% of adults in the OIC countries own a mobile money account. They can be classified according to personal characteristics as in (Fig. 4).

By gender, 18% of adult males have a mobile account, compared to 12% of females. In terms of age group, there is a rapprochement between youth and adults, as 16% of young people (15–24 years) have a mobile money account, compared to 15% among adults (25+).

Education plays a major role in attitudes toward mobile money account, 11% of those with primary education or less have a mobile money account, compared to 23% among those with secondary education or more.

The same applies to the standard of living, 18% of "the richest 60% of households" own a mobile account, compared to 11% for "the poorest 40% of households." As for work, those inside the labor force have 18% of them with a mobile account, while those outside the workforce only 10% have one. Also, 13% of the rural population owns a mobile account.

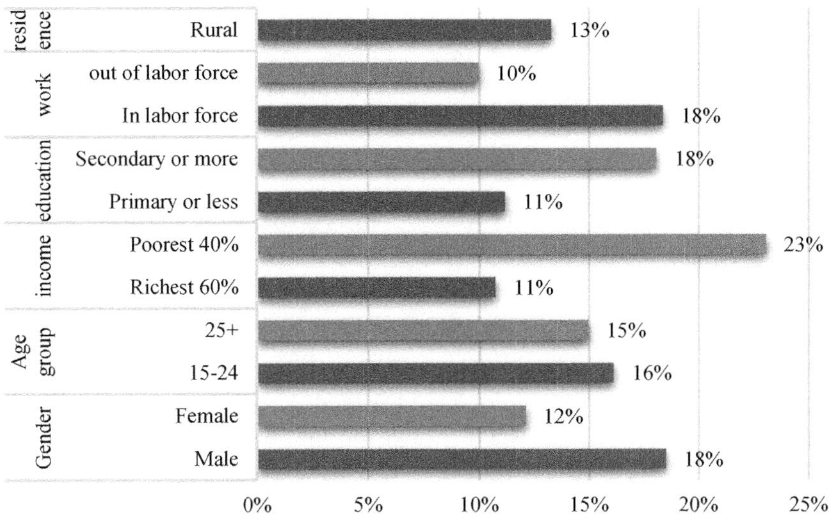

Fig. 4 Mobile money account in OIC by individual characteristics 2017 (%, Age 15+) (*Source* Prepared by the author based on The World Bank Global Findex database [2017])

3.2 *Patterns of Using Accounts*

The first step in achieving Financial Inclusion is having an account, whereas just having an account is not enough, it must be used in convenient and secure ways. Findex data show that 64% of the OIC adults reported that they made deposits past year with a financial institution's account, while 21% did not make any banking operations, whether by deposits or withdrawals in the last year.

10% of adults in OIC paid bills using the Internet last year, and 8% made their purchases using the Internet, and 43% of online buyers pay online, while 54% made pay by cash when delivering goods.

Findex data also show that 8% of the OIC adults have a "credit card", and 22% used a "credit card" during the past year. About 16% of adults accessed an account via a mobile phone or the Internet and 12% checked their account balance through a mobile phone or the Internet to in the last year.

Also, 28% of adults used an account to pay their bills, while 21% pay these bills via a financial institution account, and 63% preferred to use cash only, compared to 14% prefer to use a mobile phone.

3.3 Payments Patterns in OIC

Most people receive payments either from the government, from wages, pensions, self-employment, selling agricultural products, or domestic money transfers.

3.3.1 Payments from the Government

About 19% of the OIC adults stated that they received government payments last year, 16% received them into a financial institution account, and only 2% received them via a mobile phone, while 5% received these payments in cash only. And 7% opened the first account to receive government payments. 37% of adults used digital payment services last year, either by payment or receiving.

3.3.2 Work Payments

Findex data for work payments include wage payments, whether from the public or private sector, as well as payments from self-employment and the sale of agricultural products.

26% of the OIC adults received wages last year, and the rate of receiving wages from the private sector exceeds the public sector, as 19% received wages from the private sector during the past year, compared to 7% who received wages from the public sector.

The percentage of wages received in an account whether a financial institution or other account reached 48% of the total wage recipients, and the proportion of private sector wages received in an account reached 40% of the wage recipients, and 90% of them received wages from the public sector in an account.

Regarding receiving wages through a mobile phone, there are 11% of the wage recipients, and 9% received wages from the private sector, while 15% received wages from the public sector through a mobile phone.

On the other hand, 45% of the wage recipients received their wages in cash only, and 53% received the wages of the private sector in cash, compared to 9% of the wages of the public sector.

42% of the wage recipients opened the first account to receive wages, the percentage reached 38% for private sector wages, and 54% for public sector wages.

In terms of self-employment, about 9% of OIC adults received payments from self-employment last year, 18% of them used a financial institution's account to receive these payments, and 25% received these payments in an account in general. The majority received self-employment payments in cash at 69%, while 9% received these payments via mobile.

As for the payments for selling agricultural products, about 19% of the OIC adults receive payments. Where 76% receive these payments in cash, and 9% receive them through the mobile. 17% receive their payments in an account in common, while 10% receive these payments in a financial institution's account.

6% of the OIC adults received a public sector pension last year, 62% of the pensions recipients received it in an account, whether it was a financial institution's account or other, and 46% opened an account for first time to receive pension, 31% received their pension in cash, while only 3% received their pension through a mobile phone.

Domestic remittances, which are money that people send or receive from relatives or friends, play a notable role in the economy.

During the past year, 34% of OIC adults sent or received domestic remittances, and 24% mentioned that they had received remittances, compared to 20% who sent remittances.

The percentage of domestic transfers sent or received that used a financial institution's account or another was 35%, and 30% sent or received money via a mobile phone, while 35% sent or received money only personally and cash, 8% depends on the money transfer service, and 24% used an over-the-counter service (OTC).

35% of recipients of remittances used an account to receive them, 32% received remittances through a mobile phone, 35% received them in person and cash only, 7% preferred using any money transmission service, while 24% desired an OTC service.

In contrast, 44% of remittance senders sent remittances using an account, 39% sent remittances via a mobile phone, 24% preferred to send money in person and cash only, 8% used the money transfer service, and 24% relied on an OTC service to send money transfers.

3.4 *Saving for the Future*

Saving is one of the general behaviors that people use in order to guarantee their future, whether they use savings to improve their future conditions, or to buy a property, farm, or car, or to set up a project, or to spend on education, emergencies, etc.

The average adult saving rate globally was 21%, compared to 9% in the Middle East and North Africa countries and 10% in countries of sub-Saharan Africa, while in the OIC countries the savings rate was 12%. About 42% of the OIC adults reported that they had kept any money savings during the last year.

In terms of saving patterns, 12% save in financial institutions compared to 16% save in a "savings club" or with someone outer the family, in contrast, the average global saving in financial institutions was 27%, while saving in the savings club was only 13%, which indicates that OIC citizens still prefer saving outside the framework of formal financial institutions (Fig. 5).

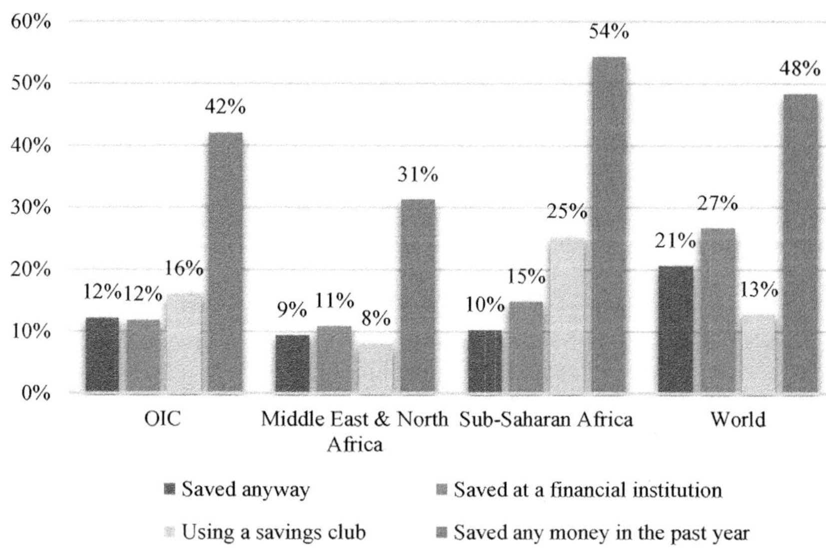

Fig. 5 Methods of Saving in 2017 (%, Age 15+) (*Source* Prepared by the author based on The World Bank Global Findex database [2017])

The individual characteristics of saving patterns in OIC countries show that males, on the contrary, of females are keen on the habit of saving money, as 14% of adult males save compared to 10% for females. The age group (15+) tends to save more than young people (15–24) as 14% of adults save, compared to 8% for youth.

In terms of education, 14% of those with secondary education or higher are saving, compared to 9% of those with primary education or less. Income also has a role in the tendency to save, as 14% of the 60% richest families save, compared to 9% for the 40% poorest of households.

In terms of work, 14% of those involved in the labor force save, while 9% of people outside the work force save. This is a logical result of the lack of a safe and permanent source of income (Fig. 6).

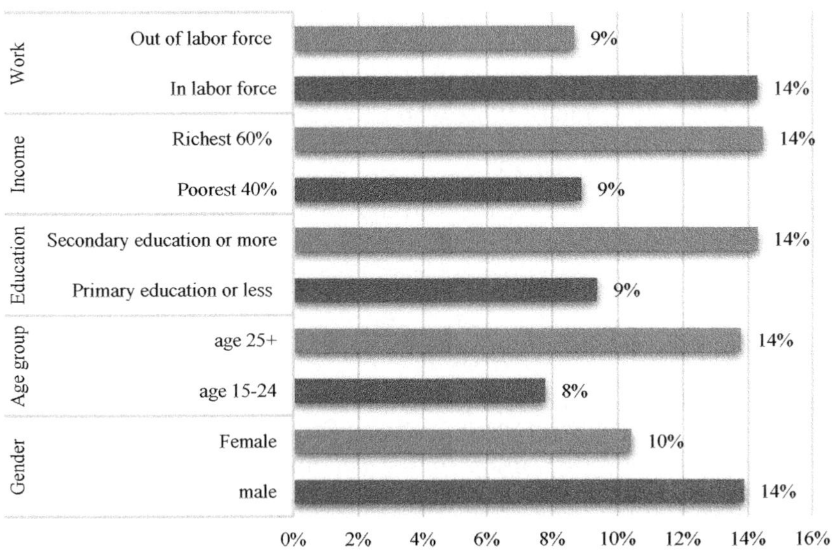

Fig. 6 Saving patterns by individual characteristics in OIC countries 2017 (%, Age 15+) (*Source* Prepared by the author based on The World Bank Global Findex database [2017])

3.5 *Borrowing Money*

Many people in developing countries are forced to borrow to meet their livelihood needs, and in the OIC, there are 45% of adults who borrowed any money last year. The motivation for borrowing differs. 8% resorted to a loan for housing, 13% borrowed to meet medical and health needs, and 8% borrowed for business purposes.

Informal borrowing is prevalent among OIC citizens, as 29% borrowed from relatives or friends and 6% borrowed from the savings club, compared to 9% from official financial institutions, and 13% from other financial institution or from the bank using credit cards.

3.6 *Accessing Money in Emergencies*

In terms of the ability to cope with financial risks, the Findex measures the individual's ability to obtain an amount equivalent to "1/20 of gross national income (GNI) per capita in local currency within the next month." The proportion of those who have access to emergency funds in OIC is 50%. Relatives and friends are the core suppliers of emergency funds with 40% of adults who can raise funds, followed by obtaining money from work with 29%, then savings by 19%, then selling assets by 5%, and 4% depended on receiving loans from the employer, a bank, or friends, and other suppliers represent 3% (Fig. 7).

4 Financial Inclusion Challenges in OIC

There are many challenges that hinder the integration of many OIC citizens into the official financial system, as the lack of financial knowledge which prevents them from using appropriate financial products and profiting from financial services that suit their specific needs, the spread of illiteracy that prevents understanding of bank documents and how to deal with financial technology tools as the illiteracy rate among adults in OIC is 27.5% (OICStat, 2019), in addition to the absence or lack of financial awareness concerning the importance of saving, how to make financial decisions, and so on.

One of the main factors that prevent individuals from accessing basic financial services is their lack of official identity documents, the lack of

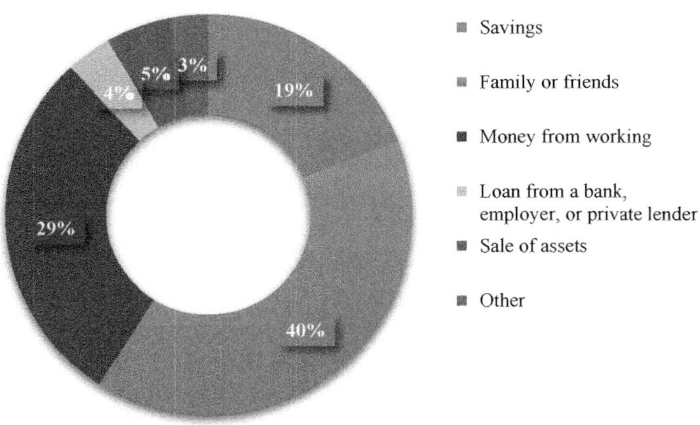

Fig. 7 The main source of emergency funds in OIC 2017 (%, Age 15+) (*Source* Prepared by the author based on The World Bank Global Findex database [2017])

confidence among consumers regarding the safety and reliability of financial institutions, the high costs of opening a bank account or transferring funds and high loan interest.

The poor in rural and remote areas in general also face many obstacles when trying to access financial services, as many people do not have enough funds to open an account, especially with the unemployment rate, reaching 7.03% (OICStat, 2019), and there is no need to use financial services for low income and extreme poverty.

There is also a lack of the necessary infrastructure for digital financing, as the proportion of the population covered by cellular networks for the second generation is 94.02%, from the third generation 74.61%, and from the fourth generation 49.54%. Fixed broadband MB/s in OIC is 2.46, and the number of Internet subscribers per 100 people is 4.17% (OICStat, 2019).

Financial institutions are also reluctant to offer financial services to poor people for several reasons, as a lack of financial guarantees and their failure to repay previous loans.

Financial Inclusion index data show that there are several obstacles for individuals to integrate into the formal financial system, as 55% of the adults in OIC do not have an account due to several reasons according

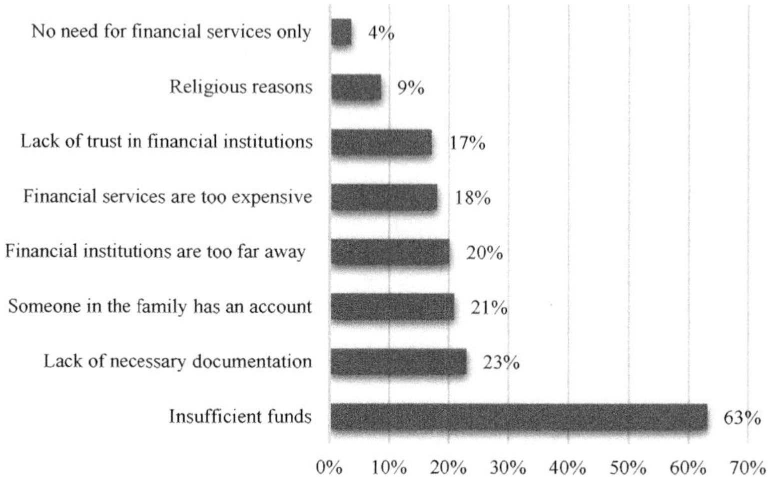

Fig. 8 Reasons for no financial account in OIC 2017 (%, Age 15+) (*Source* Prepared by the author based on The World Bank Global Findex database [2017])

to respondents to the survey of the "Global Financial Inclusion Index" database (Fig. 8).

The first barrier for not having an account is insufficient funds; as 63% of respondents said that they have not enough money to have an account, 23% have no account due to lack of necessary documentation, 21% said they don't need an account as one of the family members has an account. Distance is another barrier as 20% said that there is no financial institution nearby, while 18% can't open an account due to high costs. Among those without an account, 17% think they should not trust a financial institution, 9% have no account due to faithful reasons, finally, 4% said that they do not need to open an account (Demirgüç-Kunt et al., 2018).

5 Financial Inclusion Opportunities in OIC

There are many opportunities for enhancing financial enclosure in the OIC countries, but in this study, we will focus on the importance of Islamic Finance and Sharia-based blockchain technologies.

5.1 Islamic Finance and Financial Inclusion

Data refer that millions cannot benefit from the current traditional financial and banking services as most financial services currently available are interest-based; hence, they are not compatible with Sharia, which leads to the reluctance of many Muslims to benefit from these services.

A study of the International Finance Corporation (IFC) stated that about a third of small and medium projects in the Arab world do not benefit from official financial services due to the absence of financial products compatible with Islamic Shariah (Makhlouf, 2017, p. 7).

Another study indicated that about 40% of Muslims around the world rejected loans because it isn't compatible with Sharia, i.e., about 700 million people.

Therefore, Islamic Finance appears as one of the significant options to enhance financial enclosure not only among citizens of the OIC countries but also for Muslims all over the world.

Islamic Finance has been recognized as part of global financing thanks to the growing Islamic assets, the widening customer base, and their geographical spread.

5.2 Islamic Finance Outlook

The "Islamic Financial Services Industry Stability Report 2019" indicates that the size of Islamic Finance sector assets amounted to $ 2.19 trillion in the second quarter of 2018, compared to $ 2.05 trillion at the end of 2017 with a growth rate of 6.9%, with expectations to reach 3 trillion in 2020 (Islamic Financial Services Board, 2019, p. 7).

Islamic Finance includes 3 main areas: the Islamic banking sector, the Islamic capital market, and the Takaful sector.

The Islamic banking services sector represents the largest sector with 71.7% of the total Islamic financial services, followed by the Islamic capital market, which includes both Sukuk and Islamic Funds by 26%, and finally the Takaful sector by 1.3% (Fig. 9).

As for the Islamic banking sector, it grew by 0.9% between 2017 and 2018, to reach 1.57 trillion dollars, while the Islamic capital market sector grew by 26.9%, to reach 591.5 billion dollars, compared to Takaful Contributions which reached 27.7 billion dollars with growth rate of 4.3%.

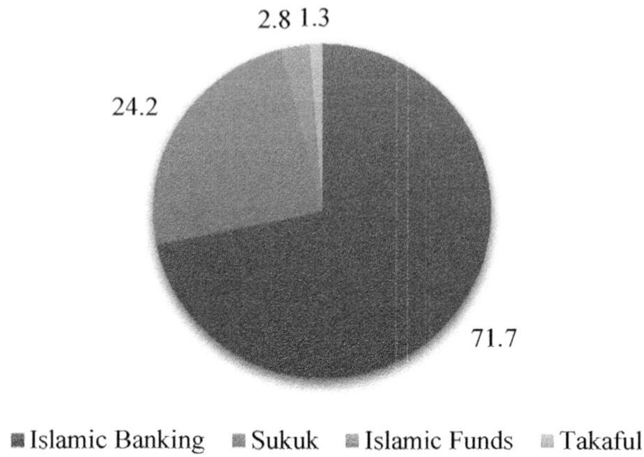

Fig. 9 Islamic Financial services by sector in 2018 (*Source* Prepared by the author based on Islamic Financial Services Industry Stability Report [2019])

The Arab Gulf region (GCC) still controls the largest share of Islamic financial assets by 42.3%, followed by Asia with 28.2%, then the Middle East countries with 25.1%, while Africa's contribution did not exceed 0.8%, and other countries' share is 3.5% (Fig. 10).

Table 1 indicates the geographical and sectoral classification of the volume of Islamic Financial Services Industry (IFSI) for the year 2018.

In terms of countries, Iran is at the forefront of the OIC, as it contributes 32.1% of the IFSI in 2018, followed by Saudi Arabia with a share of 20.2%, then Malaysia with 10.8%, then the United Arab Emirates with 9.8%, and Kuwait with 6.3%, The top five countries collectively hold 79.2% of the total international Islamic banking industry.

Corresponding to the OICStat, the total Islamic Sharia-compliant financing through Islamic banking services is $ 1.1 trillion, while Islamic Sharia-compliant financing through Islamic banking windows is $ 221 billion.

The capital and reserves through Islamic banking services are $ 119 billion, and 2.3 billion through Islamic banking windows.

There are 187 Islamic banks and 81 traditional banks with Islamic windows, and the number of local branch offices for Islamic banks is 34,867 (OICStat, 2019).

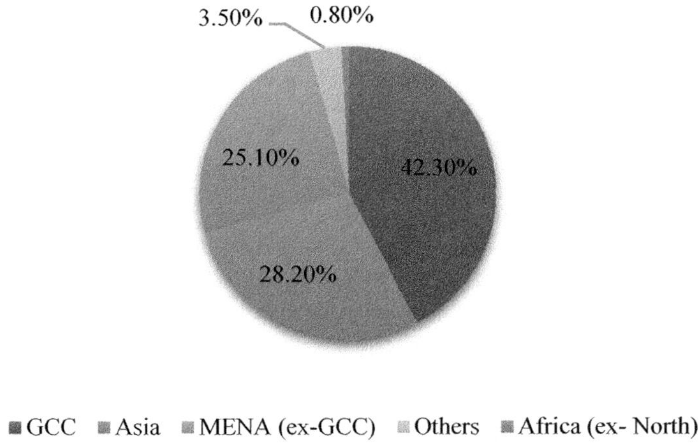

Fig. 10 Islamic financial assets by Geographical regions (*Source* Prepared by the author based on Islamic Financial Services Industry Stability Report [2019])

Table 1 Geographical and Sectoral Classification of IFSI (Billion Dollars, 2018)

Region	*Banking assets*	*Sukuk outstanding*	*Islamic funds assets*	*Takaful contributions*	*Total*	*Share %*
Asia	266.1	323.2	24.2	4.1	617.6	28.2
GCC	704.8	187.9	22.7	11.7	927.1	42.3
MENA (ex-GCC)	540.2	0.3	0.1	10.3	550.9	25.1
Africa (ex-North)	13.2	2.5	1.5	0.01	17.2	0.8
Others	47.1	16.5	13.1	–	76.7	3.5
Total	1,571.3	530.4	61.5	27.7	2,190	100

Source Prepared by the author based on Islamic Financial Services Industry Stability Report (2019)

5.3 *Islamic Finance Role*

Islamic Shariah is based on justice, equality, and seeks to achieve the well-being of citizens by prohibiting unfair practices based on exploitation and deception (Gharar) as well as the prohibition of usury (Riba) and gambling (Maiser), and It prohibits trade and investment in prohibited goods, as also, contracts are characterized by risk sharing (Paldi, 2014).

Islamic Finance plays an important role in increasing Financial Inclusion through financial tools aimed at redistributing wealth, and thus leading to reducing poverty and inequality, and promoting social welfare. Another important feature is integration of the financial sector with real economy as money is not a commodity per se, but rather a means of exchanging commodities (Mohieldin et al., 2011).

There is a great variety in Islamic financial tools such as: Zakat, Sadakat, Endowments (Waqf), Murabaha, Participation (Musharaka), Speculation (Mudarabah), Islamic Loans (Qard Al-Hassan), and Takaful among others. All these sources of financing will help individuals easily obtain financial services and integrate them into the formal financial system.

Islamic Finance also helps expand the diversity of financial products and enable poor people to access them by distributing zakat to those who deserve them, facilitating the provision of interest-free loans to small and micro-businesses, and establishing small firms based on Sharia financing formulas such as Musharaka, Murabaha, and Istisna (Hussain, Shahmoradi, & Turk, 2015).

It is possible to invest waqf funds in projects that serve the poor and disadvantaged. Islamic Finance is also beneficial in improving agricultural financing and hence improving food security.

There are also Sharia-compliant insurance forms (Takaful) that can provide healthcare services at discounted rates, thus reducing the burden on the poor. Islamic Finance can provide housing through leasing financing (lease-to-own) which is interest-free.

Islamic Finance contributes to increasing savings rates through sukuk and Islamic investment funds, then providing money in emergency situations and using savings to buy real estate assets or for education and welfare.

The expansion of Islamic Finance and the spread of its products meets the need of those who refrain from integrating into the traditional financial system because it conflicts with Islamic law. There are only 14% among the 1.8 billion Muslims, who used banks. Consequently, Islamic Finance can reduce financial exclusion, especially as Islamic Finance services expand to include Muslims and non-Muslims (The World Bank Group, 2015).

5.4 *Sharia-Based Blockchain Technologies*

Blockchain technologies are a pillar of modern FinTech. Blockchain is a shared database of financial transactions that are saved on multiple computers in different locations; its technology is based on several basic concepts:

Business Network: It is a decentralized business method without intermediaries.
The Distributed Ledger Technology (DLT): that records all transactions and copies of each participant are available.
Smart contracts: include digital assets.
Compatibility: where ledger entries are synchronized across all computers in the network.
Confidentiality: the capability to secure information and protect privacy by setting a personal "digital signature."

Blockchain is one of the most promising solutions that can provide financial services to billions of people in the world, especially the marginalized groups. Blockchain technologies are characterized by reducing the cost and time of transferring money across borders and providing crowdfunding and microfinance for small and micro-enterprises, so it acts a vital role in boosting Financial Inclusion.

Blockchain helps in issuing a digital ID and facilitates opening an account remotely to receive financial services and aid, especially in rural and remote areas, where among the reasons for the inability to open a financial account is a person's lack of an identity (Perlman, 2017).

Blockchain also contributes to registering property contracts. Financially excluded people face difficulties in obtaining credit for their lack of guarantees. Through smart contracts, it is possible to register small properties such as land, homes, equipment, cars, or animals, and use them as collateral to obtain credit. It is also easy to obtain insurance services, especially in emergency situations such as droughts, crop shortages, and climatic disasters (Monem, 2019, p. 21).

Recently, there has been an increase in the number of startups in various fields to apply financial technology in Islamic Finance, among them for example blockchain-based halal certification systems or blockchain-based zakat systems.

There are some applications through which Islamic financial services can be expanded to enhance Financial Inclusion, among them Stellar, which is a decentralized payment system based on permissible keys which is compatible with Islamic Sharia. An Islamic cryptocurrency can be created that allows the exchange of commodities through it, as well as the establishment of Islamic microfinance funds, and smart platforms for sukuk.

Smart contracts can automate the implementation of Sharia-based contracts such as Murabaha and Musharaka contracts and thus reduce procedural errors.

Blockchain can contribute to transparency and accountability in Zakat and charity by tracking zakat funds and delivering them to their recipients.

A blockchain-based endowment (Waqf) platform can also be created as a crowdfunding platform. Blockchain techniques are also useful in combating money laundering, terrorist financing, trafficking Haram and harmful goods such as drugs, prostitution, and others. It can protect the consumer/investor, not only protecting financial interests, but also ensuring protection from falling into haram (Islamic Financial Services Board, 2019, pp. 99, 100).

There are many challenges facing Islamic Finance, whether conventional or blockchain-based, the most important of which is the weak infrastructure and regulatory environment needed for Islamic Finance. Despite its growth, Islamic banking services still represent less than 2% of banking assets worldwide, Islamic Finance institutions also face a dearth of qualified personnel (Ben Naceur et al., 2015).

Nevertheless, several countries have made great strides in this field, as Malaysia, Morocco, Saudi Arabia, and Jordan, but the rest of the countries are still in early stages.

6 Conclusion

The study concluded that Financial Inclusion in the OICs is still below the required level, and face many challenges, among them, the reluctance of many to participate in the current traditional financial system because it is not based on Sharia.

Considering the significance of Financial Inclusion in achieving development and advancing the economy, the study focused on the opportunities offered by Islamic Finance and Sharia-based blockchain technologies in improving Financial Inclusion situations.

The study suggests some recommendations to promote financial integration in the OIC countries through Islamic Finance:

Working to reform the infrastructure and regulatory legislation for Islamic Finance and banking, especially those based on blockchain technologies, and this requires the preparation of qualified cadres in Islamic banking.
Encouraging public and private sector initiatives aimed at enhancing Financial Inclusion through Islamic Finance.
Mobilizing financial resources to implement programs to support the poor and provide and microfinance by benefiting from endowment funds, zakat, sukuk, Islamic equity funds, etc., by institutionalizing them, while encouraging Islamic financial innovations.
Spreading a culture of Islamic Finance and raising awareness of its importance and tools.

References

Ben Naceur, S., Barajas, A., & Mas, A. (2015). *Can Islamic banking increase financial inclusion?* (IMF Working Paper WP/15/31).

Demirgüç-Kunt, A., Klapper, L., Singer, D., Ansar, S., & Hess, J. (2018). *The Global Findex database 2017: Measuring financial inclusion and the fintech revolution*. World Bank.

European Commission. (2008). *Financial services provision and prevention of financial exclusion*. Author. Retrieved from https://www.bristol.ac.uk/media-library/sites/geography/migrated/documents/pfrc0807.pdf

Hussain, M., Shahmoradi, A., & Turk, R. (2015). *An overview of Islamic finance* (IMF Working Paper WP/15/120), 1–34. Retrieved from https://www.imf.org/external/pubs/ft/wp/2015/wp15120.pdf

Islamic Financial Services Board. (2019). *Islamic Financial Services Industry Stability Report 2019*. Author.

Makhlouf, M. (2017). *Islamic banking opportunities across small and medium enterprises in MENA: executive summary*. World Bank Group. Retrieved from http://documents.worldbank.org/curated/en/997581487153582013/Islamic-banking-opportunities-across-small-and-medium-enterprises-in-MENA-executive-summary

Marketline. (2017). *Islamic finance—High growth potential but serious challenges persist*. Author.

Mohieldin, M., Iqbal, Z., Rostom, A., & Fu, X. (2011). *The role of Islamic finance in enhancing financial inclusion in Organization of Islamic Cooperation (OIC) countries* (Vol. Policy Research Working Paper WPS5920). The World Bank.

Monem, H. A. (2019). *Using blockchain in financial services.* Arab Monetary Fund.

OIC Statistics (OICStat) Database. (2019). Retrieved from http://www.sesric.org/oicstat.php

Paldi, C. (2014). Understanding Riba and Gharar in Islamic Finance. *Journal of Islamic Banking and Finance, 2*(1), 249–259.

Perlman, L. (2017). *ITU-T focus group digital financial services: Distributed ledger technologies and financial inclusion.* International Telecommunications Union (ITU). Retrieved from https://www.itu.int/en/ITU-T/focusgroups/dfs/Documents/201703/ITU_FGDFS_Report-on-DLT-and-Financial-Inclusion.pdf

The World Bank Group. (2015). *Islamic finance.* Retrieved from https://www.worldbank.org/en/topic/financialsector/brief/islamic-finance

United Nations. (2016). Retrieved from sustainable development goals knowledge platform https://sustainabledevelopment.un.org/sdg8

World Bank. (2018a). *Financial inclusion.* Retrieved from https://www.worldbank.org/en/topic/financialinclusion/overview

World Bank. (2018b). *UFA2020 overview: Universal financial access by 2020.* Retrieved from https://www.worldbank.org/en/topic/financialinclusion/brief/achieving-universal-financial-access-by-2020

Key Determinants of Financial Inclusion: An Empirical Evidence from Western Balkan Countries

Nikola Stakić, Lidija Barjaktarović, and Dharmendra Singh

1 Introduction

Financial inclusion (FI) has become one of the most important economic topics of the twenty-first century that needs to be addressed with systematic and holistic approach, by involving all relevant institutional and private stakeholders. Increasing importance has come from various reasons, primarily due to rising global population, followed by deterioration in economic inequality. Identification and measurements of FI indicators on the global level have given the possibility to policymakers, national and international organizations, and academic community to adequately assess and propose the most effective measures that will further benefit fundamental economic and social indicators. At the same time,

N. Stakić (✉) · L. Barjaktarović
Singidunum University, Belgrade, Serbia
e-mail: nstakic@singidunum.ac.rs

L. Barjaktarović
e-mail: lbarjaktarovic@singidunum.ac.rs

D. Singh
Modern College of Business and Science, Muscat, Oman
e-mail: dharmendra@mcbs.edu.om

Ananda S. and D. Singh (eds.), *Financial Inclusion in Emerging Markets*,
https://doi.org/10.1007/978-981-16-2652-4_3

new financial technology and digital-based economies should create positive impact by improving financial inclusion measures, especially those related to operating efficiency, access and penetration usage of diverse financial services. FI means that individuals and businesses have access to useful and affordable financial products and services that meet their needs—transactions, payments, savings, credit, and insurance—delivered in a responsible and sustainable way (World Bank, 2020).

Financial inclusion is a building block for both poverty reduction and opportunities for economic growth, with access to digital financial services critical for joining the new digital economy. Digital finance alone could benefit billions of people by spurring inclusive growth that adds $3.7 trillion to the projected GDP (gross domestic product) of emerging economies within a decade, along with 95 million of newly created jobs. Nearly two-thirds of the additional GDP would likely come from improved productivity enabled by digital payments. Businesses, financial-services providers, and government organizations all reap large efficiency gains in the shift from cash to digital payments and from paper to electronic record keeping. One-third of the GDP estimate would come from increased investment as individuals and businesses are brought into the formal financial system, shifting informal savings into digital accounts and unlocking more credit that can be used for investment in businesses and durable goods (McKinsey Global Institute, 2016).

International organizations and governing bodies address financial inclusion with the profound level of importance. It is positioned as an enabler of other developmental goals in the 2030 Sustainable Development Goals, where it is featured as a target in eight of the seventeen goals. Widespread emphasis on financial inclusion implies its significant impact on the more fundamental, socioeconomic factors like eradication of poverty, ending hunger with achieving food security, profiting health and well-being, and reducing inequality (UN SDGs, 2015). World Bank, along with its partners, focuses strongly on the promotion of financial inclusion through the Universal Financial Access (UFA) 2020 initiative. The UFA 2020 initiative, as a basic step, envisions that adults worldwide will be able to have access to a transaction account or an electronic instrument to store money, send payments, and receive deposits as a basic building block to manage their financial lives, by committing itself to enable 1 billion people to gain access to a transaction account through targeted intervention. Since the inception of the initiative, results are promising—officially included banked adults have increased from 51 to

69% in the 2011–2017 period, which accounts for more than 1.2 billion people (World Bank, UFA, 2020).

Most of the initiative related to financial inclusion focus on the emerging economies, predominantly in the Asian, African, and Latin-American countries, which exhibits highest levels of financial exclusion, manifested through the lack of access to the broad range of financial services that those in developed countries take for granted. As a result, the majority of people in emerging economies rely on informal financial solutions that are often less flexible and more expensive than formal alternatives—and frequently fail to deliver when needed the most.

Apart from those regions, Eastern Europe with countries aiming to become EU members is also facing considerable challenges with respect to financial inclusion. More specifically, Western Balkan (WB) countries (Albania, Bosnia and Herzegovina, Kosovo*, Montenegro, North Macedonia, and Serbia) should address multifaceted aspects of financial inclusion in a more proactive manner, given its poorer indicators, lagging other emerging economies in the EU and especially developed ones. For instance, in the institutional aspect of financial inclusion, limited access to finance is one of the main obstacles for firms in doing business and has serious implications for economic growth and hampers the transmission of monetary policy. Other aspects of FI also deserve stronger focus in order to contribute to more sustainable economic growth and development.

This paper is organized as follows: second part reviews some of the past studies of financial inclusion and its impact on socioeconomic indicators, followed by its overall assessment in the WB countries, with respect to both individual and banking-oriented indicators. Methodological approach in constructing the index of FI, as well as pooled regression model, is analyzed in subsequent part. Based on the empirical findings, authors discuss concluding remarks and policy implications related to financial inclusion.

2 Literature Review and Analysis of Related Work

FI and its relationship with macroeconomic and social determinants has been a subject of extensive body of research in the previous decade. This is particularly visible upon the composition of aggregated dataset of indicators for both supply-side and demand-side factors, whose focus is on the institutional and individual usage. International Monetary Fund's Financial Access Survey and World Banks' Global Findex database complements each other as the two most comprehensive sources of information.

Multidimensional nature of FI has been initially presented through different types of indicators, aggregated in the comprehensive index of FI. In order to compare levels of financial inclusion across economies at a particular time point, and monitor the progress of policy initiatives for FI over a period of time, Sarma (2008) considered three basic dimensions of an inclusive financial system: banking penetration, availability of the banking services, and usage of the banking system. Similarly, Chakravarty and Pal (2010) have proposed composite indices of FI that incorporate various banking sector variables to reflect the level of accessibility, availability, and usage of banking services. Amidzic et al. (2014) constructed composite index of FI by using factor analysis and weighting methodology with three-dimensional selection on the aggregate index.

One of the pioneering research examining relationship between financial inclusion and economic development was done by Sarma and Pais (2011), where they have shown that levels of human development and financial inclusion in a cross-country analysis move closely with each other. Furthermore, other socioeconomic variables like income, literacy, and inequality were strongly associated with levels of financial inclusion.

There is also an empirical evidence of linkages of FI with not only economic growth, but with financial and economic stability and inequality as well (Sahay et al., 2015). Findings have shown that financial inclusion increases economic growth up to a point after the marginal benefits for growth wane as both inclusion and depth increase. FI can have positive effect on financial development, conditioned on existence of proper supervision, especially when it comes to access to credit. The pace of financial development also matters. If the pace is too fast, it can lead to financial and economic instability, due to lack of regulatory and prudential supervision that should follow it (Stakic et al., 2019). In contrast to credit access, increasing other types of access to financial services does not impact financial stability adversely.

In the previous decade nexus between financial inclusion and other macroeconomic and development variables has been extensively studied through regional and national context as well. This is particularly visible for the regions and countries facing with the lowest levels of indicators, like South Asia, MENA, sub-Saharan Africa (Ghosh, 2011; Mehrotra et al., 2009; Neime & Gaysset, 2018; Sharma, 2016; Singh & Stakic,

2020; Thomas et al., 2017). In parallel with the new financial technology and start of Internet and mobile banking, FI has been upgraded to account for new determinants, which are of profound importance in developing regions facing geographic remoteness and lack of adequate physical infrastructure. Utilization of mobile phones and the Internet to provide financial services has become a new way to offer unbanked people more opportunities to participate in the formal financial system at a reasonable cost. Both mobile and Internet banking help to build an inclusive financial system in a country by providing an easy way to access banking products and services. In addition, there is clear evidence that the wide use of mobile phones spurs economic growth through FI (Aker & Mbiti, 2010; Andrianaivo & Kpodar, 2012; Ghosh, 2016; Lenka & Barik, 2018).

When it comes to financial inclusion in WB countries and its main determinants, so far there has been no adequate research showing their nexus. Very few available researches are based on the descriptive assessment of inclusion, provided by data from Global Findex report (Kokorovic Jukan et al., 2017, World Bank, 2019). Apart from that, there is extensive empirical research by Moder and Bonifai (2017), analyzing access to finance constraints in the WB countries by using firm-level survey data. Lack of academic research body, with respect to FI and its positive merits, is also present at the national levels of each country. One of the reasons for such status lies in the fact that none of the WB countries has national FI strategy which should raise the awareness among key stakeholders, in order to provide additional support for reaching the standards of developed economies.

2.1 *Assessment of Financial Inclusion in the WB Region*

In the previous decade, the WB region has shown significant progress in various inclusions' indicators, initiated by national governments, central banks, as well as commercial and development banks. Measures undertaken have had the predominant goal of reaching to unbanked groups of societies, in order to be effectively included in the formal financial system. On aggregate (61.17%), the whole region has managed up to keep with:

1. Global average levels in the year 2017, in terms of percentage of adults who own account in the financial institution, 68% vs. the global average of 67%.

2. ECA (European and Central Asia) average level in the year 2017, in terms of percentage of adults who has an account, 65.1%.
3. Average level of developing countries in the year 2017, in terms of percentage of adults who has an account, 63%.

In addition, the high growth trend has been achieved, compared with Findex Reports from 2011 and 2014, where 52.33% and 59.17% of adults, respectively, were formally included. It is important to stress that the WB FI level is relatively higher than the region's income level suggests, but large behind new European Union (EU) member countries (ECB, 2017; WBG, 2016). The levels of FI significantly vary across country despite their overall economic development in the past decade: adults accounts (% age 15 +) of Albania are far less than the regional mean, with only 39.3%, whereas North Macedonia and Serbia have achieved above-average penetration of 76.6% and 71.4%, respectively (Fig. 1). Also, it is worth mentioning that the WB region has the highest migration rate in ECA, 25% (WB, 2019).

Regional progress has been mainly driven by coordinated activities of central banks, association of banks, and commercial banks. Central banks

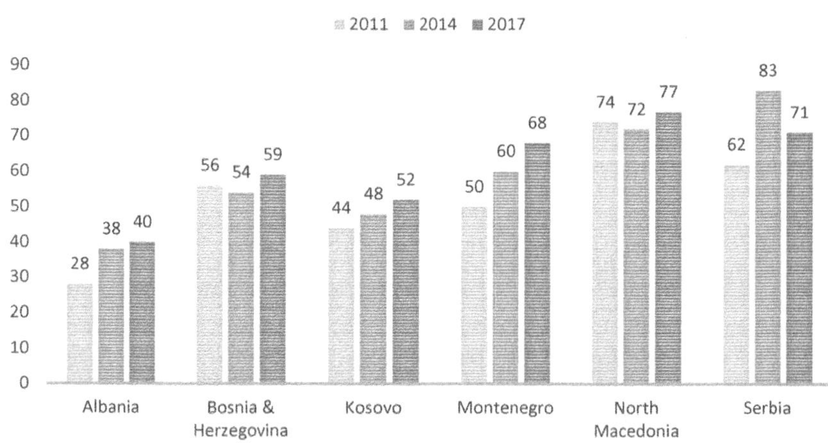

Fig. 1 Account penetration of adults in WB Region[1] (*Source* Global Findex Data Base, WB [2018]

[1] The colour print should be used for this figure.

and association of banks are mainly focused on financial education of youth and their teachers, in accordance with individual characteristic of specific country. Therefore, they have taken the necessary activities to promote Global and European Money Week. In the Republic of Serbia, the Ministry of Education of the Republic of Serbia and VISA concluded an agreement for cooperation on pilot project—FINPIS: "Including financial literacy in education and upbringing system of the Republic of Serbia," where special focus is on teachers (MESTDRS, 2017; FinPis, 2018).

It is important to emphasize that financial sector of the WB is primarily bank-based or bank-centric, which have influence on way of financial inclusion. In terms of size, the regions' financial sector assets are equal to 93% of GDP (on average). The regional banking sector is mainly foreign-owned (managed) and dependent on external developments. Accordingly, top 5 leading banks (Barjaktarović & Ječmenica, 2011; Barjaktarović, 2013), which are predominantly foreign-owned, hold 80–90% of total banking assets and predominantly have headquarters in capital cities (ECB, 2017; WBG, 2016). Aims of commercial banks are to: (1) acquire as much as possible customers, (2) optimize cost to income structure with improving efficiency and introducing cheaper alternative channels for selling banking products, (3) be competitive with new-coming players on the market which comes from fintech industry, (4) perform business in accordance with United Nations Global Compact, (5) offer customers favorable credit lines in cooperation with European Union for FI.

Despite positive results in terms of formal financial penetration, there are considerable disparities in account penetration with respect to:

1. Gender (ECB, 2017). This is particularly related to Albania and Bosnia and Herzegovina where 38% and 55% of female adults in each country, respectively, have opened an account in any of the financial institutions. However, there are visible positive trends in Serbia, Montenegro, and North Macedonia, where 70, 68, and 73% of female adults in each country, respectively, have opened an account in any of the financial institutions. Furthermore, in Serbia and Montenegro is low gender gap comparing to the global average level. In the case of North Macedonia, gender gap is on the global average level.
2. Age. Young adults (15–24 years), in the average 37.8% owned accounts, while older adults (25+ years), in the average 67.8% has

an opened account (world's average level is 56%). So, there is space for further inclusion of young adults (world's average level is 72%). Furthermore, it has impact on preferred way of executing payment transactions and cash withdrawal (i.e., older adults prefer to visit banks' branches due to cultural and security-related reasons).

It can be noticed that usage of accounts in the WB region is on satisfactory level, i.e., lower level of inactive accounts comparing world's average level, 8.2 vs. 20%. In terms of way of attracting unbanked citizens and increasing usage of electronic payment, for the WB countries Internet is very important tool, but below global average (Table 1). It is espe-

Table 1 Individual usage indicators in the WB countries in 2017 (in %)

Indicators	*Albania*	*Bosnia and Herzegovina*	*Kosovo**	*Montenegro*	*North Macedonia*	*Serbia*	*World*
FI account	39.3	58.8	52.3	68.4	76.6	71.4	67
Debit card ownership	22	40	n.a	36	53	60	48
Borrowed from the FI in the last year	12.5	14.7	14.7	23.7	20.5	19.7	11
Deposited in the last year (% of FI accounts)	65	85	n.a	85	73	88	69
Made digital payment in the past year	2	8	n.a	7	10	78	45
Received wages in the past year	16	24	n.a	36	25	37	20
Saved at the FI	8.7	9.8	8.7	10.1	17.3	12	27

Source Compiled from Global Findex Database [2017]

cially obvious in the Republic of Serbia, which averages are above global standards, with 78% versus 45%.

Foreign-owned bank on the Western Balkan region has strategy to issue debit cards which are connected to the opened account, and it is at the same time identification card in the case of physical presence in the branch or in the case of issuing payment check in the store.

Usage indicators, with respect to borrowing and depositing activates, are mostly below global averages. Reasons for such a financial exclusion can be attributed to societal and behavioral factors, in addition to traditional supply-side and demand-side factors. Accordingly, the most important barriers for FI are that someone in the family has opened an account and insufficient funds. Secondly, an important reason is that financial services are too expensive. Thirdly, relevant significant factors are lack of necessary documentation and trust in financial institutions. Location of financial institution is significant factor for financial exclusion as well. Fourthly, lack of need for financial services is important reason. Finally, the least important factor is religious reasons, i.e., in fact it is important only for Albanians (Table 2). It is important to stress that comparing to results in Findex 2014, citizens have changed their opinion, because barrier category "no need for financial services" is at the bottom of significant factors for financial exclusion. However, in the following period citizens of the WB region should get education why it is good to have an account with financial institution and be part of financial included, i.e., banked customers, instead of relying on someone else's account.

In the previous period, different research used different indicators to measure the extent of financial inclusion, and various banking-related indicators had been used in previous studies. For this study, it is relevant to follow the three-dimensional approach by Sarma (2008), both supply-side and demand-side factors were analyzed on the individual and composite level to assess nexus between FI and different economic parameters (Sarma & Pais, 2011; Sharma, 2016; Sethi and Acharya, 2018). In this research, for metrics for FI were used with seven indicators: (1) Number of ATMs per 1,000 km^2, (2) Number of ATMs per 100,000 adults, (3) Number of branches of commercial banks per 1,000 km^2, (4) Number of branches of commercial banks per 100,000 adults, (5) Borrowers at commercial banks per 1,000 adults, (6) Outstanding deposits with commercial banks (as % of GDP), and (7) Outstanding loans with commercial banks (as % of GDP).

Table 2 Reasons for financial exclusion among WB countries in 2017 (% of all adults)[2]

Reasons	*Albania*	*Bosnia and Herzegovina*	*Montenegro*	*North Macedonia*	*Serbia*
Someone in the family has an account	22	33	54	46	34
Insufficient funds	50	22	19	13	14
Financial services are too expensive	27	3	5	5	3
Lack of necessary documentation	14	6	6	3	8
Lack of trust in financial institutions	11	4	4	4	4
Financial institutions are too far away	17	3	3	2	2
No need for financial services	1	3	5	2	8
Religious reasons	4	0	0	0	0

Source Compiled from Global Findex Database [2017]

[2] Kosovo* is excluded in this part of the analysis due to unavailability of data. However, it will be included in the empirical part of the paper with different indicators.

Factors from (1) to (4) assess penetration indicators whereas the last three indicators are usage indicators. When it comes to the WB countries, results are reasonable diverse, especially for the geographical penetration of Montenegro, Kosovo*. and Albania, in comparison with the other countries, due to its dispersity and small area. Overall, Albania has the lowest results with the growth of accession to financial services that has been very slow since 2005. FI average values for the 2005–2018 periods are presented in Table 3.

3 Research Methodology and Data

The study is focused on providing FI determinants in WB countries. In that regard, the effort has been made to measure the effect of natural log of GDP per capita, fixed broadband subscriptions (per 100 people),

Table 3 Average values for financial inclusion' indicators for 2005-2018 in WB countries[3]

Country/ Indicator	*(ATMs) per 1,000 km2*	*(ATMs) per 100,000 adults*	*Branches of commercial banks per 1,000 km2*	*Branches of commercial banks per 100,000 adults*	*Borrowers at commercial banks per 1,000 adults*	*Outstanding deposits with commercial banks (% of GDP)*	*Outstanding loans with commercial banks (% of GDP)*
Albania	24.52	29.28	17.60	20.91	120.18	65.97	34.19
Bosnia and Herzegovina	22.34	38.26	18.67	30.90	272.33	41.30	52.35
Kosovo*	34.47	28.31	27.18	21.74	86.86	41.46	31.56
Montenegro	22.16	61.27	14.57	39.40	235.06	43.32	56.15
North Macedonia	31.04	46.81	15.79	23.46	250.83	47.83	41.23
Serbia	27.82	41.26	24.88	35.68	345.77	37.34	42.43

Source IMF, Financial Access Survey

[3] Borrowers at commercial banks per 1,000 adults for Kosovo* data exists from 2010.

mobile cellular subscriptions (per 100 people), real interest rate and unemployment (% of total labor force) on the FI index. Annual data for the WB countries (Albania, Bosnia & Herzegovina, North Macedonia, Montenegro, Serbia, and Kosovo) from 2005 to 2018 has been used in the study. The required data have been collected from Financial Access Survey of International Monetary Fund, for financial inclusion indicator, and from World Development Indicators of the World Bank database, for control variables. In this study seven variables of financial inclusion have been used which are further divided into indicators of FI access and FI usage indicators. Total three indices were constructed for WB countries—FI comprehensive index, FI Access index, and FI usage index. In the second part of the analysis, pooled regression model has been used to measure the impact of selected variables on FI index.

Single, comprehensive *index of FI* is calculated using all seven, previously described indicator. Furthermore, two separate sub-indexes of access and usage side were calculated and displayed in Table 4. For calculating the FI index, principal component analysis (PCA) technique has been used. In PCA, normalized data for all the seven indicators were used to

Table 4 FI index values for 2005–2018 in WB countries

Countries	*Year*	*FI access index*	*FI usage index*	*FI comprehensive index*
Albania	2005	12.41	8.05	3.65
	2006	16.73	19.10	28.88
	2007	22.98	29.61	45.06
	2008	31.98	63.94	82.61
	2009	35.28	63.72	85.86
	2010	36.13	76.18	94.90
	2011	36.76	84.05	101.17
	2012	36.86	92.34	106.89
	2013	36.17	85.82	100.85
	2014	34.81	91.26	102.89
	2015	34.98	84.85	97.88
	2016	33.97	91.57	101.24
	2017	31.83	77.96	89.21
	2018	30.84	78.35	88.11
Bosnia & Herzegovina	2005	25.99	194.65	179.21
	2006	28.09	201.44	185.91
	2007	34.00	209.60	199.30
	2008	41.18	222.36	217.03
	2009	51.37	217.31	221.04
	2010	44.70	215.30	213.17
	2011	48.00	222.40	221.42
	2012	50.14	230.55	229.14
	2013	52.99	244.87	241.83
	2014	55.31	235.43	236.73
	2015	56.10	233.85	234.64
	2016	55.44	236.58	235.18
	2017	55.87	239.35	237.32
	2018	61.70	256.81	255.16
Kosovo*	2005	13.48	28.22	44.14
	2006	13.95	31.68	47.64
	2007	15.60	47.53	61.52
	2008	19.40	56.39	71.94
	2009	23.75	47.28	68.54
	2010	26.94	47.87	72.08
	2011	28.59	62.30	84.78
	2012	29.22	56.19	80.50

(continued)

Table 4 (continued)

Countries	*Year*	*FI access index*	*FI usage index*	*FI comprehensive index*
	2013	28.99	43.62	70.24
	2014	28.65	48.88	73.01
	2015	31.06	47.27	74.04
	2016	29.77	47.90	73.53
	2017	26.48	112.74	117.84
	2018	24.75	163.81	153.60
Montenegro	2005	28.53	190.54	171.89
	2006	39.67	200.43	190.50
	2007	56.23	225.60	232.33
	2008	71.63	260.66	277.44
	2009	78.54	225.40	255.76
	2010	79.37	199.99	234.10
	2011	81.34	184.34	221.33
	2012	84.30	175.72	216.48
	2013	87.11	181.33	223.67
	2014	86.21	179.25	220.16
	2015	91.13	176.29	221.48
	2016	93.39	175.14	222.13
	2017	95.36	178.06	225.21
	2018	100.52	192.30	240.55
North Macedonia	2005	16.37	4.30	22.89
	2006	24.00	10.96	35.45
	2007	34.93	41.29	68.16
	2008	47.49	201.41	199.35
	2009	50.86	214.91	212.58
	2010	52.40	222.99	219.52
	2011	51.60	228.22	222.12
	2012	50.61	233.60	225.72
	2013	53.93	244.69	236.80
	2014	55.11	254.34	244.98
	2015	58.77	264.38	255.83
	2016	58.41	259.92	251.81
	2017	58.28	264.79	255.63
	2018	57.74	268.78	257.42
Serbia	2005	27.56	128.10	132.30
	2006	36.36	131.01	142.90

(continued)

Table 4 (continued)

Countries	*Year*	*FI access index*	*FI usage index*	*FI comprehensive index*
	2007	47.66	138.29	159.74
	2008	55.46	144.29	174.67
	2009	57.49	142.93	174.92
	2010	57.95	156.20	185.21
	2011	57.11	157.08	183.99
	2012	55.52	345.56	319.77
	2013	52.05	398.18	352.44
	2014	49.92	409.72	357.96
	2015	50.56	440.61	380.46
	2016	54.29	452.18	391.24
	2017	49.85	450.35	385.36
	2018	51.38	432.81	373.22

Source Authors' calculations

calculate weightings for different indicators. The Z-score of all the indicators was used for calculating the first component coefficients (PCA) which are used as weight in index calculation.

The line graph of FI comprehensive index, FI access index, and FI usage index is in the following Figs. 2, 3, and 4, respectively.

It is visible that Serbia has gained recently since 2012 in its FI status and Kosovo is at the bottom among all the Balkan nations.

In terms of access to banking products and services, Montenegro is doing exceptionally well followed by Serbia and North Macedonia. Also, in case of access to banking services, Kosovo is at the bottom among all the WB countries.

In usage part the ranking is same as in comprehensive FI index, and Serbia has taken the lead since 2012 and is way ahead of other countries. After year 2008, a fall in usage of banking services is seen in case of Montenegro, whereas North Macedonia has shown consistent improvement in usage of banking services and products after 2008.

The pooled panel data regression analysis has been adopted to measure the impact of Internet on FI along with other macroeconomic variables, such as GDP per capita, unemployment, and real interest rate. Fixed broadband subscriptions (per 100 people) have been considered as a proxy for Internet connections, mobile cellular subscriptions (per 100 people) as a proxy for mobile connections and total percentage of total

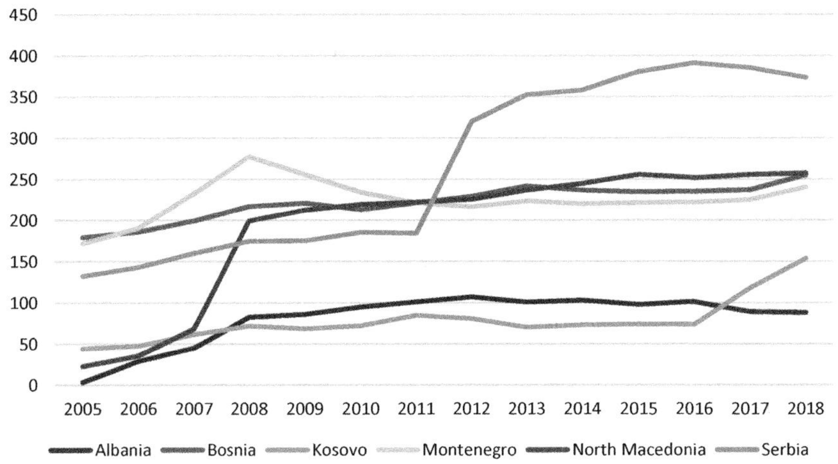

Fig. 2 FI Comprehensive Index for WB countries for 2005–2018 period (*Source* Authors' calculations)

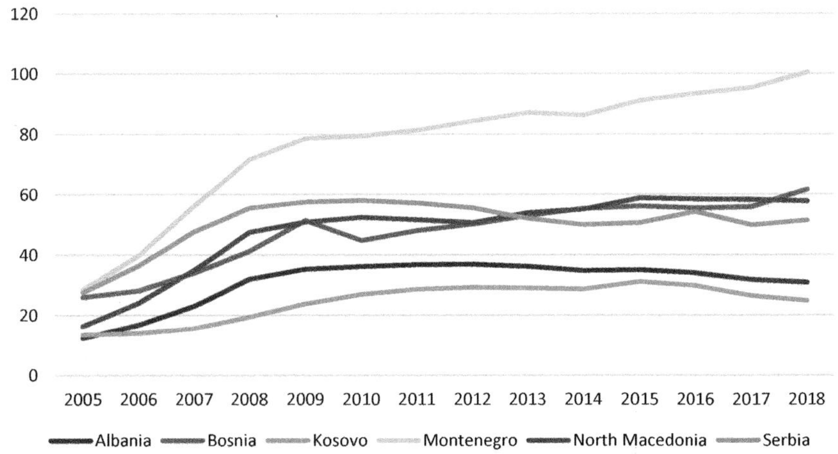

Fig. 3 FI Access Index for WB countries for 2005–2018 period (*Source* Authors' calculations)

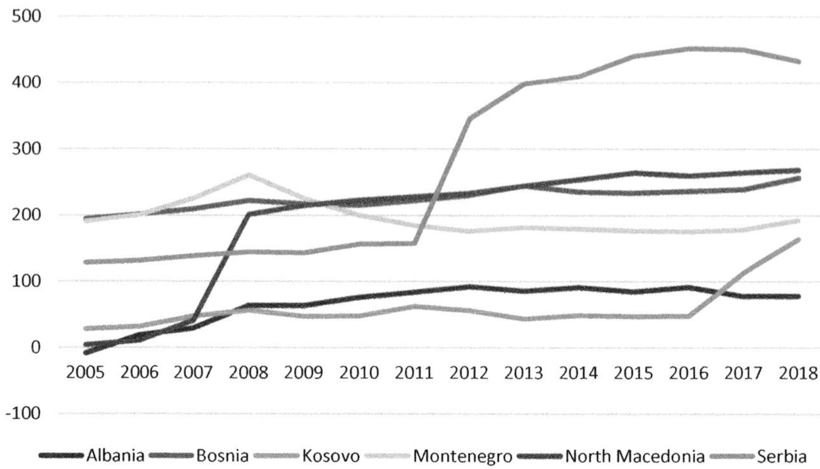

Fig. 4 FI Usage Index for WB countries for 2005–2018 period (*Source* Authors' calculations)

labor force has been considered as a proxy for unemployment. The basic model used in the analysis has been shown in Eqs. 1 and 2.

$$\text{FIit} = \alpha 0 + \beta 1\text{GDPit} + \beta 2\text{INTERNETit} + \beta 3\text{REALRATEit} + \beta 3\text{UNEMPLOYMENTit} + \mu\text{it} \quad (1)$$

$$\text{FIit} = \alpha 0 + \beta 1\text{GDPit} + \beta 2\text{MOBILEit} + \beta 3\text{REALRATEit} + \beta 3\text{UNEMPLOYMENTit} + \mu\text{it} \quad (2)$$

where subscripts i and t are the representatives of countries and periods, respectively.

Before running the regression all the variables were tested for unit root, and all the variables except 'unemployment' were found to be stationary at level. That is why OLS was selected as the next analysis to measure the impact on FI index. The first difference of unemployment was used in the regression, as it was stationary at the first level. Two regression models were developed with the same dependent variables (FI Index); in the first model Internet was used along with GDP, real interest rate, and unemployment. In the second model, mobile subscription was used along with other independent variables. Internet and mobile are considered separately due to high correlation with each other.

4 Results

The results of the first pooled panel data regression model have been displayed in Table 5. The FI comprehensive index, which includes both access and usage indicators, is significantly affected by all the variables considered and the model has R-square of 0.65. GDP per capita, Internet, real interest rate are all significant at 1% level of significance. GDP per capita and Internet subscriptions are positively affecting FI in Western Balkan countries whereas real interest rate and unemployment are negatively affecting FI comprehensive index. Internet subscription and GDP are positive determinants of FI implying that increase in GDP per capita and Internet subscription will lead to more FI in WB countries.

Unemployment is significant at 10% and is showing negative coefficient like real interest rate. This signifies that rise in rate of interest lowers down banking activities or usage of banking products and services.

The results of the second pooled panel data regression model with mobile as an independent variable in place of Internet are shown in Table 6. The model has R square value as 0.57 and all the variables are

Table 5 Regression results for FI Index and Internet subscriptions

Variables	*Coefficient*	*t-statistics*	*P-value*
GDP	20.75	4.77	0.0000
Internet	8.22	6.22	0.0000
Real interest rate	− 5.21	− 2.88	0.005
Unemployment	− 3.22	− 1.72	0.09

Source Authors estimation

Table 6 Regression results for FI Index and Mobile subscriptions

Variables	*Coefficient*	*t-statistics*	*Probability*
GDP	23.15	4.57	0.0000
Mobile	1.069	4.57	0.0000
Real interest rate	− 3.39	− 1.74	0.087
Unemployment	− 8.06	− 4.57	0.0000

Source Authors estimation

significant. Similarly, GDP per capita and mobile subscriptions are most significant variables (1%), with GDP having highest positive impact on FI index, followed by mobile subscriptions. Increase in GDP per capita will lead to increase in disposable income which may also increase the usage of banking products and services. Similarly, increase in mobile subscriptions will also help in using banking services in a more cost-efficient and convenient way. Identically like in the first model, real interest rate and unemployment are having negative impact on FI index. Perennial higher interest rate environment discourages primarily individual borrowers, and institutional to lesser extent, to have any formal relationship with the banks and other financial service providers, which subsequently affects overall level of FI. Unemployment will result into lesser usage of banking services, where unofficial channels of payments within the informal economy will have more significant impact.

5 Conclusion

Results have shown that there is strong relationship, primarily between economic growth, Internet, and mobile usage with the level of FI in the WB region, which is in accordance with presented facts in the assessment of FI in the WB region. The most important barriers for FI are insufficient funds and expensiveness of financial services. In that regard, increased GDP per capita in the region will increase number of banked citizens, i.e., they will have sufficient funds to be financially included. Having in mind that there are considerable disparities in account penetration with respect to age in the region, Internet is adequate and important tool for attracting young adults (15–24 years). Young adults prefer to use online digital tools and social networks, which should ultimately increase Internet usage of banking products in the WB region. Values of FI comprehensive index, FI access index, and FI usage index per country in the WB region are in accordance with individual-oriented data of FI compiled by World Bank. Serbia and North Macedonia are leaders in the region, Bosnia and Herzegovina, and Montenegro are the followers whereas Kosovo and Albania are lagging behind.

Empirical findings have also revealed negative relationship between FI and real interest rate and unemployment in the region. It is in accordance with the long-standing business practice in this region, where many working people are not officially registered as employees (they are officially recognized as unemployed) and they do not have an appropriate labor contract. Consequences are such that they do not receive salary on the banking account; rather they receive it in cash. Furthermore, the WB financial market is banco-centric, with limited offer of investable financial instruments, exerting low levels of liquidity and transparency. Despite historically low interest rate environment, households still prefer to deposit their savings in commercial banks. Traditional views can be explained, among other things, with poor financial literary, inadequate knowledge about other investment alternatives and high-risk aversion. However, in the following period citizens of the WB region should get proper education about merits of financial institution which will contribute to rising living standard. Future studies will include analysis of FI for different financial intermediaries (especially related to the group of connected companies) and fintech new competitors in the WB region.

References

Aker, J. C., & Mbiti, I. M. (2010). Mobile phones and economic development in Africa. *Journal of Economic Perspectives, 24*(3), 207–232.

Amidzic, G., Massara, A., & Mialou, A. (2014). *Assessing countries' financial inclusion standing—A new composite index*. WP/14/36, IMF.

Andrianaivo, M., & Kpodar, K. (2012). Mobile phones, financial inclusion, and growth. *Review of Economics and Institutions, 3*(2), 30.

Barjaktarović, L., & Ječmenica, D. (2011). Optimism vs pessimism of competitiveness of Serbian banking sector. *Industrija, 2*, 137–150.

Barjaktarović, L., Filipović, S. & Dimić, M. . (2013). Concentration level of banking industry in CEE countries. *Industrija, 41*(3), 39–53.

Chakravarty, S., & Rupayan, P. (2010). *Measuring financial inclusion: An axiomatic approach*. Indira Gandhi Institute of Development Research (Working Paper No. 2010/003).

European Central Bank /ECB/. (2017). *Access to finance in the western Balkan* (Occasion Paper Series No 197/2017).

FinPis. (2018). *Pilot project "Including financial literacy in education and upbringing system of the Republic of Serbia"*. http://finpis.mi.sanu.ac.rs/

Ghosh, S. (2016). Does mobile telephony spur growth? Evidence from Indian states*Telecommunications Policy, 40*(10–11), 1020–1031.

Ghosh, S. (2011). Does financial outreach engender economic growth? Evidence from Indian states. *Journal of Indian Business Research, 3*(2), 74–99.

International Monetary Fund /IMF/. (2019). *Financial access survey—IMF data access to macroeconomics & financial data*. http://data.imf.org/?sk=E5DCAB7E-A5CA-4892-A6EA-598B5463A34C

Kokorovic Jukan, M., Babajić, A., & Softic, A. (2017). Measuring financial inclusion in Western Balkan countries—A comparative survey. https://doi.org/10.14706/icesos1715.

Lenka, S. K., & Barik, R. (2018). Has expansion of mobile phone and internet use spurred financial inclusion in the SAARC countries? *Financial Innovation, 4*(5), 1–19.

McKinsey Global Institute. (2016). *Digital finance for all: Powering inclusive growth in emerging economies.*

Mehrotra, N., Puhazhendhi, V., Nair, G., & Sahoo, B. B. (2009). *Financial inclusion-an overview*. Department of Economic Analysis and Research, National Bank for Agriculture and Rural Development (NABARD), Occasional Paper.

Ministry of Education, Science and Technological Development of the Republic of Serbia /MESTDRS/. (2017). *Ministry and VISA has concluded an agreement for cooperation on pilot project—FINPIS.* http://www.mpn.gov.rs/ministarstvo-i-visa-potpisali-protokol-o-saradnji-na-realizaciji-pilot-projekta-finpis/

Moder, I., & Bonifai, N. (2017). Access to finance in the Western Balkans. ECB Occasional Paper, (197).

Neime, S., & Gaysset, I. (2018). Financial inclusion and stability in MENA: Evidence from poverty and inequality. *Finance Research Letters, 24*, 230–237.

ProCredit Bank Belgrade. (2020). *Business ethics and environmental standards.* https://www.procredit-holding.com/about-us/business-ethics-and-environmental-standards/

Sahay, R, Cihak, M., Barajas, B, Kyobe, A. J., N'Diaye, P. M., Mitra, S., Reza Yousefi, S., & Mooi, Y. N. (2015). *Financial inclusion: Can it meet multiple macroeconomic goals*. IMF Staff Discussion Notes 15/17, International Monetary Fund.

Sarma, M. (2008). *Index of financial inclusion, Indian council for research on international economic relations* (Working Paper No. 215).

Sarma, M., & Pais, J. (2011). Financial inclusion and development. *Journal of International Development, 23*(5), 613–628.

Sethi, D., & Acharya, D. (2018). Financial inclusion and economic growth linkage: some cross country evidence. *Journal of Financial Economic Policy, 10*(3), 369–385. https://doi.org/10.1108/JFEP-11-2016-0073.

Sharma, D. (2016). Nexus between financial inclusion and economic growth: Evidence from the emerging Indian economy. *Journal of Financial Economic Policy, 8*(1), 13–36.

Singh, D., & Stakic, N. (in press). *Financial inclusion and economic growth nexus: Evidence from SAARC countries*. South Asia Research.

Stakić, N., Ahmad Fida, B., & Singh, D. (2019). *Nexus between financial development and economic growth in Oman, diversification of Oman economy for sustainable development: Strategic issues and imperatives*, vol. 1, pp. 1–17.

Thomas Asha, E., Bhasi, M., & Chandramouli, R. (2017). *Financial accessibility and economic growth-evidence from SAARC countries*. Contemplations on New Paradigms in Finance, Directorate of Public Relations and Publications, CUSAT, 32–52.

United Nations. (2015). *The 2030 agenda for sustainable development*. https://sustainabledevelopment.un.org/

World Bank. (2018). *The Global Findex Data Base 2017*. https://globalfindex.worldbank.org/

World Bank Group /WB/. (2019). *Migration and Brain Drain: Europe and Central Asia—Office of the chief economist fall 2019.*

World Bank Group /WBG/. (2016). *Financial sector outlook: Financial systems in the Western Balkans—Present and future, World Bank Group Finance & Markets*.

World Bank. (2020). *UFA 2020 overview: Universal financial access by 2020*. http://www.worldbank.org/en/topic/financialinclusion/brief/achieving-universal-financial-access-by-2020

Banking Products and Services

Business Correspondents' Perspective on Financial Inclusion Initiatives: An Empirical Analysis

H. N. Shylaja and H. N. Shivaprasad

1 Introduction

Financial exclusion is a situation where a certain section of society is not able to have access to suitable financial products and services at an affordable cost which otherwise are available to the affluent section of the society. With the objective of bringing such financially excluded section of the society under the ambit of being able to access financial services, a lot of initiatives starting from nationalization of banks till the very recent PMJDY have been introduced from time to time. FI implies that the poor get access to timely credit and also various other financial services like insurance, mutual funds, remittances, pension, etc. Along with timely access they also should be available at affordable yet market-driven cost. Access to a no-frills savings bank account would serve as the first step in ensuring access to all the above-mentioned services.

H. N. Shylaja (✉)
Post Graduate Programs in Management, School of Commerce and Management Studies, Dayananda Sagar University, Bangalore, India

H. N. Shivaprasad
Dr. D Veerendra Heggade Institute of Management Studies and Research, Dharwad, India

Ananda S. and D. Singh (eds.), *Financial Inclusion in Emerging Markets*,
https://doi.org/10.1007/978-981-16-2652-4_4

Pradhan Mantri Jan Dhan Yojna is an initiative which was introduced in the year 2014, which is a comprehensive financial inclusion plan pan India with the sole objective of covering all hitherto excluded households into the purview of banking services and thereby ensuring that all get access and will be able to use the benefits and facilities provided by the formal banking sector. This scheme envisages the provision of not only the access but also the usage of the banking services which covers citizens over a certain distance.

Access to one simple no-frills account by each household would not only ensure access to all the necessary financial services. With exposure to the basic banking services, the newly banked would also gain information and knowledge about various initiatives by the central government, viz. no minimum balance requirement, financial literacy, access to credit, insurance, direct benefit transfer, interest on deposit, life insurance cover, etc.,

The plans have been executed in two different phases with 15th August 2014 to 14th August 2015 being the phase 1 and 15th August 2015 to 14th August 2018 being the second phase.

There are a lot of hopes that this scheme would bring in 100% inclusion and ensure that all who hitherto were excluded would participate in the mainstream financial sector. The scheme will be rolled out by utilizing the existing infrastructure of institutions like post offices, through PPP. The existing system of BCs would be restructured and strengthened and thereby the model made more viable. Expansion of bank branches and the ATMs, creation of swabhimann villages, mapping the sub-service areas, coverage of SSAs, focusing more on urban financial inclusion, strengthening the existing model of BCs, mobile banking, and national unified USSD platforms are some of the implementation plans of PMJDY.

However, with all the initiatives and efforts that the concerned have put in there is a need to pause and check the progress made such that the lacunae if any in the plans could be plugged in and further changes made. The proposed study aims not only to check the progress made but also to analyze the perspectives of the business correspondents too.

2 Review of Literature

Literature review suggests that most of the operational definitions about FI or exclusion is either context-specific which is developed out of country-specific problems and also the economic and social conditions.

Specific dimensions of FI or exclusion play a very important role from the perspective of the development of public policy. However, a careful look into the development of definitions clearly reveals that during the development stages, the focus was largely on the availability of physical access which lately covers the access to, knowledge about the products and usage of the same.

As per the definition given by the Committee on FI in India, 2008, C. Rangarajan,

> "...FI is the process of ensuring access to financial services and timely and adequate credit where needed by vulnerable groups such as weaker sections and low-income groups at an affordable cost." (Report of the Committee on FI in India, 2008)

Ansley (2010), in the study, opines that there are three key aspects for the definition of FI: access to financial services and products, financial capability, and financial literacy. However, it has been observed time over and again that most of the definitions put more emphasis on the indicators than the other elements.

Kumar, Nitin (2012), in his article goes on to suggest that India being an emerging economy, has placed a lot of importance on FI. Also, he observes that financial exclusion being widely pertinent in rural and less populous regions when compared to that of urban and developed regions. Through this study it has been noted that the number of bank branches in hitherto less branches regions has increased and so is the case in the regions which has higher income too They conclude the study by making an observation that there is evidence of positive impact of different inclusion initiatives taken by the regulatory bodies.

Singh, Anurag & Tandon, Priyanka (2013) suggest that the banks need to restructure their policies to accommodate the needs of low-income groups in terms of services that they would need and also to ensure that the entire process of financial inclusion be viewed as both business opportunity and social obligation.

CRISIL Inclusix Report, (2012) in the Inclusix report on Indian FI status bought out the information that there is an increase in the FI score from 35.4 in 2009 to 42.8 in the year 2012 which clearly indicates that the status of FI in the country has definitely improved.

Garg, Sonu & Agarwal, Parul (2014), opines that by leveraging the information communication and technology, the banks could easily reach out to the last mile customer in tier 3 and tier 6 cities. The customers could also be served by offering innovative products by leveraging on technology. With access to the financial inclusion being ensured, the newly banked would soon get converted into business opportunities to the banks too.

Mishra, Satyabrata (2015) opined that FI targets to bring all unbanked under the umbrella of the formal financial sector would certainly enhance their social and economic conditions and help the poor to escape from the vicious circle of poverty. Financial inclusive education will make the vulnerable section of the society to be aware of public policies, FI mission, rules and regulations regarding various aspects of financial services. It is also opined that awareness camps need to be organized to make poor people aware of banking facilities.

Park, C. & Mercado, R. (2015) opine that to ensure inclusive growth, financial inclusion needs to be ensured and only when there is inclusion in terms of access to financial services, one would start taking part in economically befitting activities like investment decisions, etc. This would further be followed by usage of various other services.

According to Kokate, C. N. & Nalawade, N. Kavishwar (2015), FI would have far-reaching impact and would help poor to come out of their abject poverty. They go on to say that the formal banking institutions not only provides formal identity, access to payment system, and deposit insurance to the underprivileged, they go on and suggested that the banks, the government, and other agencies are required to bring in the coordinated effort such that the poor and underprivileged get access to banking services.

Barua, Abheek, Kathuria, Rajat & Malik, Neha (2016), opine that in India, financial inclusion has been given prominence and that the focus has shifted from mere access to savings products to that of access to credit, insurance, and pension products too. With the intervention of effective and suitable technology measures, the delivery of financial resources could be ensured to the households.

Pal, Ranapratap (2016), proposes that with the increased emphasis on the business facilitator and business correspondent models and also upon the model of micro-finance, the rural unbanked can easily gain access to the basic banking services. He also goes on to say that there should be an increase in the number of bank branches established in rural India.

With the different initiatives introduced by both the Government of India and the RBI, there have been improvements in the number of people having a savings account bank but what was the need of the hour was to get the newly included to use the services. With an objective of providing the much-needed push in this direction of providing holistic services, a very ambitious and a coveted policy initiative "Pradhan Mantri Jan-Dhan Yojana" was declared by our honorable Prime Minister, Shri. Narendra Modi, on 15th August 2014. "Sab Ka Sath Sab Ka Vikas"—this philosophy forms the core of the scheme too.

3 Research Methodology

The study draws heavily from primary as well as secondary data. The primary data is collected with the help of a structured questionnaire. The data is collected from the individuals working as BCs with a minimum of two to three years of experience from the period September 2014 to December 2014 in the first phase. For the second phase, the data is collected after the implementation of PMJDY from the same set of BCs from August 2018 till December 2018. About 100 BCs who had a minimum of about 2 to 3 years of experience only were selected as they would be able to give clear observations related to the inclusiveness of the beneficiaries. The secondary data is collected from PMJDY Web site for further analysis.

The CAGR is calculated for evaluating the progress in terms of financial inclusion wherein the two samples of BCs responses are analyzed using two-sample paired t-test.

3.1 Objectives of the Study

The intent of the study is to analyze the progress made in terms of the expansion of banking services through the PMJDY. The business correspondents being the primary link between the last mile customer and the bank, an attempt is also made to understand the demographic profile of the BCs. The perspective of business correspondents and their opinions on the various aspects of banking post-implementation of PMJDY is another important objective of the study. An attempt is also made to give suggestions to make the model of BC stronger.

4 Results of the Study

With the mission mode introduction and implementation of the PMJDY across the country, the kind of growth in terms of the number of bank branches, number of beneficiaries who got access to banking services, growth in the number of deposit accounts, growth in the money deposited in the deposit accounts and such other things, has increased manifold. The following presents the progress made in terms of PMJDY since its launch in the year 2014.

4.1 Report on Progress in PMJDY Since the Launch in August 2014

The following Table 1 gives detailed information related to the progress in the Pradhan Mantri Jan Dhan Yojana since the date it was incepted (Fig. 1).

Since the launch of PMJDY, there is a growth in the number of beneficiaries of the rural and semi-rural section by about 26% in four years' time. Also, the number of beneficiaries of the urban and metro centers has also increased by 27% over the last four years. While the growth in the number of beneficiaries' accounts across the country is about 26% of the deposit deposited in such accounts has grown over 63% in the last four years. The number of RuPay card issued to the beneficiaries (in crores) has increased from 129,917,010 in the year 2015 to 291,470,537 in the year 2019 by around 22% in the last four years.

4.1.1 Status of Bank Branches at Rural, Semi-Urban, Urban and Metro Centers

With all the efforts toward improving the banking status across the country, there has been a significant progress which can be seen in the following Table 2. The following Table 2 gives information related to the household coverage across different states in the country as on October 2019.

Table 3 shows the progress with reference to the access to formal banking services. With the robust push given by the government and the RBI to cover all the unbanked households, the percentage of unbanked in the country has reduced from 46% in the year 2011 (NSSO 11th round report) to 19% (World Bank report, 2017) in the year 2017.

Table 1 Table showing the progress in PMJDY since the launch in August 2014

	2015	**2016**	**2017**	**2018**	**2019**	**CAGR** %
Beneficiaries at urban and metro center bank branches (numbers in crores)	8,67,72,337	13,17,07,034	16,86,63,484	19,01,89,607	21,68,79,196	25.73
Beneficiaries at rural/semi-urban center bank branches (numbers in crores)	5,85,95,703	8,25,68,440	11,30,14,787	13,23,10,158	15,10,64,059	26.71
Total beneficiaries (numbers in crores)	14,53,68,040	21,42,75,474	28,16,78,271	32,24,99,765	36,79,43,255	26.13
Deposit in accounts (Rs. In lakh)	14,64,064.61	35,67,200.72	62,97,242.81	80,67,482.19	1,02,41,542.78	62.63
RuPay card issued to beneficiaries (numbers in crores)	12,99,17,010	17,75,29,672	21,99,38,757	24,26,68,879	29,14,70,537	22.39

Source Progress Report, PMJDY, as on 28 September 2019

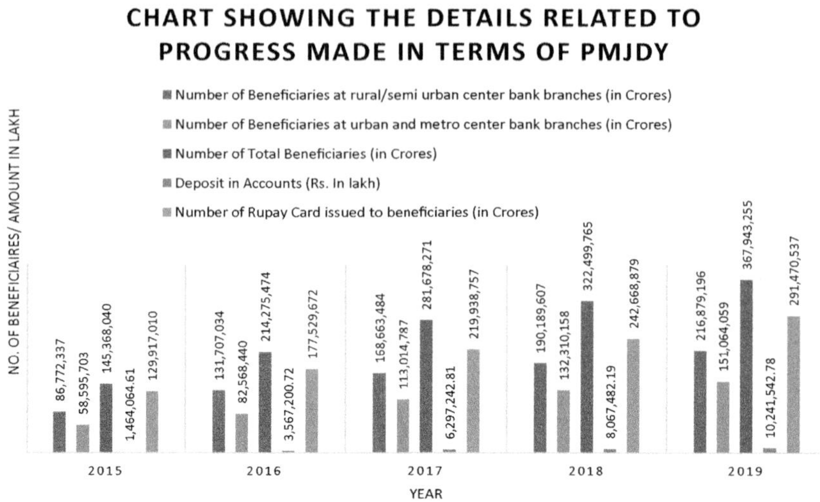

Fig. 1 Chart showing the details related to progress of PMJDY (*Source* PMJDY Progress report, 2019)

4.2 Business Correspondent Model or Bank Mitr Model of Financial Inclusion

The BC model or Bank Mitr model of financial inclusion has been given a lot of importance in the PMJDY as could be seen in the implementation plans and the strategies devised. It is in this context that the following study is made. The present section of the study focuses on knowing the experiences of the BCs post the implementation of PMJDY. Only those BCs who have more than four years of experience been selected. A set of 26 key questions were designed for which the answers were sought from the selected BCs. The BCs were interviewed in two phases. Initially, they were interviewed during the first phase when the PMJDY was just announced and the work had just started rolling. Secondly, they were interviewed almost two years after the implementation of PMJDY and their answers recorded. The same is tabulated and presented herewith.

Table 2 Table showing the number of bank branches, RuPay cards issued

S.No	State Name	Beneficiaries at rural/semi-urban center bank branches	Beneficiaries at urban/metro center bank branches	Total beneficiaries	Balance in beneficiary accounts (in crore)	No. of RuPay cards issued to beneficiaries
1	Andaman & Nicobar Islands	33,127	16,764	49,891	23.63	41,225
2	Andhra Pradesh	50,68,433	51,57,489	1,02,25,922	1,973.41	83,17,274
3	Arunachal Pradesh	1,97,380	1,23,486	3,20,866	121.53	2,76,650
4	Assam	1,20,11,645	38,07,151	1,58,18,796	3,704.08	1,22,88,615
5	Bihar	2,66,68,968	1,55,24,537	4,21,93,505	10,845.42	3,44,89,653
6	Chandigarh	45,245	2,10,263	2,55,508	113.24	1,87,574
7	Chhattisgarh	93,80,789	51,67,462	1,45,48,251	3,245.11	1,03,92,069
8	Dadra & Nagar Haveli	98,474	24,888	1,23,362	53.13	82,724
9	Daman & Diu	24,529	29,850	54,379	21.39	42,154
10	Delhi	5,50,677	39,61,857	45,12,534	1,881.20	38,35,774
11	Goa	1,20,981	42,710	1,63,691	94.31	1,23,342
12	Gujarat	75,00,648	70,17,679	1,45,18,327	4,519.14	1,19,81,540
13	Haryana	36,67,293	36,86,471	73,53,764	3,362.44	61,77,544
14	Himachal Pradesh	11,02,341	1,47,554	12,49,895	671.47	9,91,602
15	Jammu & Kashmir	19,51,633	3,23,795	22,75,428	969.72	17,26,352
16	Jharkhand	93,85,105	35,62,106	1,29,47,211	3,504.14	1,03,08,318
17	Karnataka	81,91,223	65,64,004	1,47,55,227	3,793.28	1,02,95,417
18	Kerala	20,63,417	21,43,935	42,07,352	1,343.19	30,08,522
19	Lakshadweep	4,417	986	5,403	8.56	5,164
20	Madhya Pradesh	1,49,06,183	1,71,40,444	3,20,46,627	5,355.46	2,50,74,815
21	Maharashtra	1,29,19,449	1,32,40,099	2,61,59,548	6,274.75	1,87,14,489
22	Manipur	4,05,026	5,26,437	9,31,463	196.31	7,11,301
23	Meghalaya	3,88,792	70,534	4,59,326	193.9	3,21,800
24	Mizoram	1,19,838	1,88,956	3,08,794	101.45	85,023
25	Nagaland	1,22,017	1,72,458	2,94,475	60.14	2,43,136

(continued)

Table 2 (continued)

S.No	State Name	Beneficiaries at rural/semi-urban center bank branches	Beneficiaries at urban/metro center bank branches	Total beneficiaries	Balance in beneficiary accounts (in crore)	No. of RuPay cards issued to beneficiaries
26	Odisha	1,09,54,745	39,87,087	1,49,41,832	4,641.89	1,23,74,426
27	Puducherry	69,628	85,979	1,55,607	41.49	1,16,195
28	Punjab	39,62,786	29,27,628	68,90,414	2,550.24	55,94,069
29	Rajasthan	1,56,00,208	1,07,15,367	2,63,15,575	7,949.09	2,06,01,442
30	Sikkim	66,259	27,468	93,727	40.52	71,164
31	Tamil Nadu	48,75,623	55,86,950	1,04,62,573	1,986.13	86,16,104
32	Telangana	49,02,827	48,31,100	97,33,927	1,664.41	79,60,666
33	Tripura	6,25,508	2,57,582	8,83,090	674.81	6,87,368
34	Uttar Pradesh	3,42,78,604	2,47,33,606	5,90,12,210	19,275.18	4,76,33,374
35	Uttarakhand	15,71,194	9,58,875	25,30,069	1,187.75	20,08,987
36	West Bengal	2,33,63,233	1,19,89,709	3,53,52,942	12,451.66	2,91,03,974
37	Total	21,71,98,245	15,49,53,266	37,21,51,511	1,04,893.56	29,44,89,846

Source PMJDY progress report, 2019

4.3 BCs and Their Pre- and Post-PMJDY Experiences

Since its inception in 2006, a lot of importance has been given to the business correspondent model of financial inclusion. However beneficial and viable the model was thought initially, it failed to take off as expected. Since then to ensure that the model works there have been various reforms and impetus has been given. At the outset, it appears that there is an improvement in the availability of banking services to hitherto areas where there were no banking services earlier. With an objective of making an assessment of how improved the banking services are, the present research has been conducted. For this a set of 100 BCs who have more than five years of experience working as BCs has been selected and administered a structured questionnaire and their responses recorded twice, the first time being before the implementation of the PMJDY yojana and the second time being three years after the implementation of the same.

Table 3 Table showing the household coverage across different states

State name	*Allotted wards-SSAs*	*Wards-SSAs survey done*	*Wards-SSAs survey pending*	*Total household*	*Covered households*	*Household coverage %*
JAMMU & KASHMIR	604	604	0	3,57,340	3,56,295	99.71%
Himachal Pradesh	2,489	2,489	0	12,98,191	12,98,191	100.00%
Punjab	6,743	6,743	0	47,46,147	47,46,147	100.00%
Chandigarh	136	136	0	1,93,876	1,93,876	100.00%
Uttarakhand	2,769	2,769	0	11,36,431	11,36,431	100.00%
Haryana	4,870	4,870	0	45,96,617	45,96,617	100.00%
DELHI	266	266	0	26,96,322	26,96,322	100.00%
Rajasthan	14,169	14,169	0	1,14,63,959	1,14,63,959	99.99%
Uttar Pradesh	37,424	37,424	0	3,11,59,992	3,11,59,992	100.00%
Bihar	14,640	14,640	0	1,72,81,831	1,72,81,831	100.00%
Sikkim	175	175	0	1,31,086	1,31,086	100.00%
Arunachal Pradesh	236	236	0	1,97,861	1,97,861	100.00%
Nagaland	413	413	0	3,34,034	3,33,762	99.92%
Manipur	576	576	0	5,14,604	5,13,359	99.76%
Mizoram	228	228	0	1,81,946	1,81,946	99.92%
Tripura	767	767	0	7,55,041	7,55,041	100.00%
Meghalaya	539	539	0	4,77,182	4,77,182	100.00%
Assam	4,925	4,925	0	50,13,404	50,11,228	99.96%
West Bengal	13,248	13,248	0	1,92,61,587	1,92,61,587	100.00%
Jharkhand	5,147	5,147	0	54,38,679	54,38,679	100.00%
ORISSA	7,962	7,962	0	74,32,140	74,32,140	99.85%
Chhattisgarh	6,197	6,138	59	51,89,795	51,89,795	99.98%
Madhya Pradesh	18,410	18,410	0	1,47,39,932	1,47,39,932	100.00%
Gujarat	9,831	9,831	0	1,17,09,247	1,17,09,247	100.00%
DAMAN & DIU	24	24	0	22,528	22,528	100.00%
DADRA & NAGAR HAVELI	35	35	0	59,908	59,908	100.00%
Maharashtra	17,722	17,718	4	1,63,74,622	1,63,74,030	100.00%
Andhra Pradesh	11,592	11,592	0	1,18,55,426	1,18,55,366	100.00%

(continued)

Table 3 (continued)

State name	*Allotted wards-SSAs*	*Wards-SSAs survey done*	*Wards-SSAs survey pending*	*Total household*	*Covered households*	*Household coverage %*
Karnataka	11,645	11,645	0	1,11,78,005	1,11,75,204	99.97%
Goa	396	396	0	3,31,457	3,31,457	100.00%
Lakshadweep	29	29	0	10,189	10,189	100.00%
Kerala	5,582	5,582	0	45,85,375	45,85,375	100.00%
Tamil Nadu	19,987	19,987	0	1,43,53,828	1,43,53,794	100.00%
PUDUCHERRY	177	177	0	2,52,105	2,52,105	100.00%
ANDAMAN & NICOBAR	51	51	0	67,287	67,287	100.00%
Telangana	6,193	6,193	0	52,23,218	52,23,218	100.00%

Source Progress Report, PMJDY, 28 September 2019

Paired two-sample t-test is run to find if there exists any difference between the means of two samples. While the data regards to the pre-PMJDY is considered as one sample, the data regards to the post-PMJDY is considered to be the second sample. Also, their means calculated and the hypothesis is tested.

The following section examines the BCs perspective and the hypothesis tested across different parameters.

4.4 Beneficiaries and Their Dependence on the Money Lenders

Ha: The mean difference of pre- and post-PMJDY samples with reference to dependency on local money lenders is not zero.

The non-availability of funds to meet their various requirements drives the people toward availing the loan from that source which is easily available. But post the implementation of PMJDY and the FI initiatives, at the outset, it appears that there has been an improvement in the availability of loans. Upon running the paired two-sample t-test for means, with a significant value less than 0.05, it is statistically proven that there has been a statistically significant difference in the means of pre- and post-PMJDY dependency of the excluded on the money lenders. This clearly indicates that there has been a decreased dependence on local money lenders which implies that the people now are slowly facing formal sources of finance

Table 4 Table showing the t-test results of beneficiaries and their dependence on the money lenders

	Pre-PMJDY	*Post-PMJDY*
Mean	3.06	4.64
Variance	0.966060606	0.293333
Observations	100	100
Pearson Correlation	−0.110814032	
Hypothesized Mean Difference	0	
Df	99	
t Stat	−13.46266961	
P(T < = t) one-tail	2.1147E-24	
t Critical one-tail	1.660391156	
P(T < = t) two-tail	**4.2294E-24**	
t Critical two-tail	1.984216952	

than the informal sources. Thus, the null hypothesis rejected that the means across the two samples is equal (Table 4).

We could see that the PMJDY initiative of FI has a very positive impact on bringing down the dependency of villagers on the local money lenders for their financial requirements.

4.5 *Availability of Loan When Needed*

Ha: The mean difference of pre- and post-PMJDY samples with reference to availability of loan, when needed with complexities is not zero.

Difficult and the sophisticated and technical terminologies used by the banking officers were one of the factors which had kept the deprived section of the society out of availing the banking services, mainly the loan products. Upon running the paired two-sample t-test for means, the significant value is less than 0.05, we reject the null hypothesis and accept the alternate hypothesis and it is concluded that there is statistically significant difference between the means of pre- and post-PMJDY samples of availability of banking services without much hassles (Table 5).

We can see that the PMJDY has impacted the ease of availability of loan to those who need it without much hassles.

Table 5 Table showing the t-test results of availability of loan when needed

	Pre-PMJDY	Post-PMJDY
Mean	2.67	3.64
Variance	0.768787879	1.040808081
Observations	100	100
Pearson Correlation	−0.021229221	
Hypothesized Mean Difference	0	
df	99	
t Stat	−7.136259049	
P(T < = t) one-tail	8.06253E-11	
t Critical one-tail	1.660391156	
P(T < = t) two-tail	1.61251E-10	
t Critical two-tail	1.984216952	

4.6 Saving Habits Among Beneficiaries

Ha: The mean difference of pre- and post-PMJDY samples with reference to improvement in saving habits of people is not zero.

With increased financial awareness and widespread financial literacy programs and the added riders post-PMJDY, it appears that there has been a slight improvement in the saving habits of people when it comes to banking. Upon running the paired two-sample t-test for the pre- and post-PMJDY samples with reference to improvements in saving habits if any, it is statistically proven that there exists a statistically significant difference between the means of pre- and post-PMJDY samples as the significant value is less than 0.05. Thus, we could conclude that there is a definitive improvement in the savings habits of people as per the observations made by the business correspondents who directly interact with the individuals (Table 6).

4.6.1 t-Test Results of Prior and Post-PMJDY

Upon running the paired two-sample t-test for means, significant value is less than 0.05, and therefore there is no evidence to accept the null hypothesis. We therefore reject the null hypothesis and accept the alternate hypothesis and thereby it can be concluded that there is statistically significant difference between the means of pre- and post-PMJDY samples. Thus, we could conclude that there is a definitive improvement in the savings habits of people (Table 7).

Table 6 Table showing the t-test results of availability of loan when needed without complexities

	Pre-PMJDY	*Post-PMJDY*
Mean	1.61	3.67
Variance	0.785757576	1.273838384
Observations	100	100
Pearson Correlation	0.122468431	
Hypothesized Mean Difference	0	
Df	99	
t Stat	−15.29266921	
P(T < = t) one-tail	4.05945E-28	
t Critical one-tail	1.660391156	
P(T < = t) two-tail	**8.1189E-28**	
t Critical two-tail	1.984216952	

Table 7 Table showing the t-test results of people and the usage of banking services

	Pre-PMJDY	*Post-PMJDY*
Mean	3.06	4.64
Variance	0.966060606	0.293333
Observations	100	100
Pearson Correlation	−0.110814032	
Hypothesized Mean Difference	0	
Df	99	
t Stat	−13.46266961	
P(T < = t) one-tail	2.1147E-24	
t Critical one-tail	1.660391156	
P(T < = t) two-tail	4.2294E-24	
t Critical two-tail	1.984216952	

4.7 People and the Usage of Banking Services

Ha: The mean difference of pre- and post-PMJDY samples with reference to the increase in the number of people availing banking services is not zero.

With the mission mode launch of PMJDY and the widespread publicity about the benefits of having an account under PMJDY, there has been a sudden increase in the number of accounts opened across all the banks in the country. However, mere opening of account does not ensure the usage of banking services unless the accounts are operated. Paired two-sample test was performed on the two samples to know if there was any increase or improvement in the usage of banking services and upon running the test it is found that the significant value is less than 0.05, thus there is no evidence to reject the alternate hypothesis. Therefore, we reject the null hypothesis and accept the alternate hypothesis and thereby it can be concluded that there is statistically significant difference between the means of pre- and post-PMJDY samples. Thus, we could conclude that there is a statistically significant improvement in the banking habits of beneficiaries.

4.8 Beneficiaries and the Number of Transactions at the Hand-held Machines of the BCs

Ha: The mean difference of the pre- and post-PMJDY samples with reference to the transactions both deposit and withdrawals conducted at the BC points are not zero.

Providing banking services at the doorstep of every villager at their village and thereby promoting financial inclusivity was one of the objectives of FI. However, initially there was no significant improvement in the number of transactions recorded in spite of various initiatives taken by RBI and concerned banks. With the launch of PMJDY and the associated riders, there appears to be an increase in the banking activities of the beneficiaries. Upon running the test, it is statistically proven that there has been a statistically significant difference in the two means implying that there has been an improvement in the number of transactions which happens through the hand-held devices of BCs (Table 8).

4.9 People Approaching Banks for Loans

Ha: The mean difference of the pre- and post-PMJDY samples with reference to the BCs observations about the number of people approaching a bank for loan products is not zero.

A Paired sample t-test was run to test if the means of both the samples are equal and if the mean difference is zero. Upon running the test, it is found that the mean difference is 1.93 which is significantly more than 0 and also the p-value is significantly lower than 0.05 and therefore, we have no reason to support or accept the null hypothesis. We, therefore, accept the alternate hypothesis and conclude that there is a significant

Table 8 Table showing the t-test results of beneficiaries and the number of transactions at the hand-held machines

	Pre-PMJDY	*Post-PMJDY*
Mean	1.18	4.355
Variance	0.14909091	0.360075758
Observations	100	100
Pearson Correlation	0.22277332	
Hypothesized Mean Difference	0	
Df	99	
t Stat	−49.832862	
P(T < = t) one-tail	3.1609E-72	
t Critical one-tail	1.66039116	
P(T < = t) two-tail	**6.3217E-72**	
t Critical two-tail	1.98421695	

difference between both the means, and we conclude that the number of people approaching banks for loans has increased post-PMJDY (Table 9).

Ha: The mean difference of the pre- and post-PMJDY samples with reference to the BCs observations about the number of people approaching a bank for savings products is not zero.

Post the implementation of PMJDY with the different riders added to the RuPay card, it has been observed that the money deposited in the savings bank account has been steadily increasing. To know if actually people are forthcoming in using the saving products of banks, this hypothesis was tested. Upon running the paired-sample t-test, it is found

Table 9 Table showing the t-test results of people approaching banks for loans

	Pre-PMJDY	*Post-PMJDY*
Mean	2.17	4.1
Variance	0.243535	0.797979798
Observations	100	100
Pearson Correlation	0.144354	
Hypothesized Mean Difference	0	
Df	99	
t Stat	−20.1849	
P(T < = t) one-tail	3.62E-37	
t Critical one-tail	1.660391	
P(T < = t) two-tail	7.24E-37	
t Critical two-tail	1.984217	

Table 10 Table showing the t-test results of willingness to save at banks

	Pre-PMJDY	*Post-PMJDY*
Mean	1.61	3.67
Variance	0.785757576	1.273838384
Observations	100	100
Pearson Correlation	0.122468431	
Hypothesized Mean Difference	0	
df	99	
t Stat	−15.29266921	
P(T < = t) one-tail	4.05945E-28	
t Critical one-tail	1.660391156	
P(T < = t) two-tail	8.1189E-28	
t Critical two-tail	1.984216952	

that the means of the two samples are not equal but the mean difference is 2.06. Also, the p value is 0.000 which is significantly lower than 0.05 and therefore we do not have much support in evidence of the null hypothesis. Therefore, we reject the null hypothesis and accept the alternate hypothesis and state that there is a statistically significant difference between the means of two samples and we can conclude that the savings habits have increased post-PMJDY (Table 10).

5 Findings

The research has been successful in bringing out the following major findings:

Post the launch of PMJDY, there has been a tremendous increase in the number of accounts opened across the country. But along with the increase in the number of accounts opened, there also has been a significant improvement in the transactions in these accounts. There has been an increase in the number of beneficiaries in rural, semi-urban, urban, and metro center bank branches. There also has been a significant increase in the amount held at banks in these accounts. There also has been an increase in the number of RuPay card loaded with various benefits issued to beneficiaries.

Post the launch of PMJDY, there has been a significant difference in the observations made by the business correspondents in terms of financial inclusion.

Post-PMJDY there has been a considerable decrease in the dependency of money lenders which is a very positive sign in terms of financial inclusion.

From the perspective of BCs post-PMJDY, people are forthcoming in approaching the banks for loans. This by itself is a considerable improvement as far as the landscape of financial inclusion is considered as those who were hesitating to approach the banks for any kinds of loans are now approaching the banks for their various loan requirements. Also, there has been a considerable improvement in the number of people who are availing a different kind of banking services and also there has been an increase in the number of people who are wanting to utilize the banking post-PMJDY.

Beneficiaries who otherwise were shying away from approaching the banks for their various banking services like loan products or savings products are now forthcoming in availing of the services. With the increased awareness that is being created post-PMJDY, there is a definitive increase in the number of people approaching banks for their various needs.

6 Conclusions and Recommendations

6.1 Conclusion

With the mission mode initiatives being taken toward financial inclusion, there is an increase in the number of hitherto excluded who have access to the mainstream financial sector, this no doubt would increase the customer base for the banks and thereby result in increased business opportunity. Primafacie it appears that the there is a decrease in the number of people who are taking loans from the money lenders which otherwise was highly prevalent. With considerable improvement in the number of people who are accessing the banking services the focus should now shift to create awareness about the benefits that one could get by being a part of the formal banking services.

6.2 Implications of the Study

The study has bought out the perceptions of the business correspondents about their opinion about the usage and access of banking services. This in turn gives an opportunity to the bankers to work in close cohesion with the BCs in those areas which requires attention. The BCs could be used in the areas of creating awareness about different schemes and initiatives by the banks as and when they are introduced.

6.3 Limitations of the Study

The major limitation of the study is that the findings and conclusions are drawn based on the answers given by the respondents.

6.4 Scope for Future Work

The scope for future work is that the study could be extended to the beneficiaries and their opinion collected with reference to how the entire process of financial inclusion has bought about any changes in their daily lives if any in terms of not only the access to banking service but also the usage of the same.

References

Aynsely, H. (2010). *Financial inclusion and financial capability: Whats in a name?* Tony Bee Hall. Available at http://www.toynbeehall.org.uk/data/files/Services/FinancialInclusion

Barua, A., Kathuria, R., & Malik, N. (2016). *The status of financial inclusion, regulation, and education in India* (ADBI Working Paper Series No. 568).

CRISIL. (2012). *CRISIL inclusix: An index to measure India's progress on financial inclusion*. Mcgraw Hill.

Garg, S., & Agarwal, P. (2014). Financial inclusion in India—A Review of initiatives and achievements. *IOSR Journal of Business and Management, 16*(6), 52–61.

Kokate, C. N., & Nalawade, K., N. (2015). Financial inclusion In India. *International Journal of Management and Social Science Research Review, 1*(14), 199–202.

Kumar, N. (2012). An empirical analysis of financial inclusion across population groups in India banking: Key driver for inclusive growth. *The IUP Journal of Bank Management, 11*(1).

Mishra, S. (2015). Micro finance: The catalytic agent of financial inclusion in India.*International Journal of Management and Science, 6*(1).

Pal, R. (2016). Financial inclusion: Factor that expedites sustainable economic growth. *International Educational Scientific Research Journal, 2*(8), ISSN No : 2455–295X.

Park, C. Y., & Mercado Jr, R. V. (2015). *Financial inclusion, poverty, and income inequality in developing Asia*. Asian Development Bank Economics Working Paper Series, (426)

Rangarajan, C. (2008). *Report of the Committee on Financial Inclusion, Government of India*. RBI.

Singh, A., & Tandon, P. (2013). Financial inclusion in India: An analysis. *International Journal of Marketing, Financial Services & Management Research, 1*(6), 41–54.

Websites of PMJDY

Assessing the Performance of District Cooperative Banks: An Efficiency-Based Approach

Abhijit Sinha and Amitabha Bhattacharyya

1 Introduction

1.1 Background of the Study

The term 'cooperative society' means a group of people working together for the common objectives or goals. The main objective behind forming a cooperative society is to help each other in the best possible manner so as to derive some amount of benefit out of this. Cooperative societies are formed to support or help each other. Members of a society join a cooperative to have a share of the profit. According to the International Co-operative Alliance, 'a co-operative is an autonomous association of persons united voluntarily to meet their common economic, social and cultural needs and aspirations through a jointly owned and democratically controlled enterprise'. It is the business enterprise which has control over the ownership, but the interests are only for the users. Some values

A. Sinha (✉)
Vidyasagar University, Midnapore, West Bengal, India

A. Bhattacharyya
Balurghat College, Balurghat, West Bengal, India

Ananda S. and D. Singh (eds.), *Financial Inclusion in Emerging Markets*,
https://doi.org/10.1007/978-981-16-2652-4_5

like self-help, self-responsibility, democracy, equality, equity and solidarity form the main bases of cooperatives.

India is a country in which livelihood of almost 55% of the population is dependent on agriculture and allied activities. Though the contribution of the sector has been on a decline, still almost 17% contribution to the country's GDP comes from the agricultural sector. Hence, there is no doubt in saying that farming is still the bread and butter for majority of the Indian households. It is pertinent to note that despite such a high dependence on agriculture, even now a substantial portion of households rely on the informal sector for their financial needs. The demand for finance has been on the rise with technological advancement in agriculture, greater commercialization and use of modern amenities for improving productivity of land and labour. In this economy where agriculture plays such an important role, cooperative banking in the country holds a key feature. The cooperative banking in India has three tiers which include the State Cooperative banks at the state level, District Cooperative Banks (DCBs) at the district level and Primary Agricultural Credit Societies (PACS) in the rural belts of the country. They are well connected to each other and the flow of funds is from the state level banks to the PACS.

In the context of the paper, the role of the DCBs is vital in agricultural operations throughout the districts at the middle level. The main purpose of DCBs is to provide funds to the PACS for agricultural credit. They also expand the rural banking facilities among the people of those areas. These credit institutions also develop the banking habits among the people and mobilize deposits among them. They play a pivotal role in the Short-Term Credit Cooperative Structure (STCCS) and help the Primary Agricultural Credit Societies (PACS) in expanding rural credit. The present study is to assess the efficiency of the DCBs of selected districts in West Bengal through the Data Envelopment Approach.

1.2 Rationale of the Study

The present research is taken up to look at the financial performance of district cooperative banks which primarily focus on the rural economy. The study is pertinent in the Indian context as a huge section of the population is dependent on agriculture and the rural economy forms the backbone of the country. These banks which form the focus of investigation play a vital role in the development and upliftment of the rural economy. In such a scenario, it makes sense to assess the financial position of the district cooperative banks. The study is even more relevant as the recent RBI data talks about the weakening position of these institutions which fall trap to the mis-governance at the local level and non-robust regulatory framework. The data for 2018 appreciates the significant role played by these banks not only in driving the growth of the rural economy but also meeting the needs of rural households. However, at the same time, it alarmingly points to the overall poor position of these credit institutions with almost one-seventh of the total DCBs incurring losses. Moreover, the asset quality is found to be poor with the percentage of non-performing assets at an average of 11% and reaching a high of 20%. The study by Murray (2005) also notes the inability of these banks in delivering adequate and timely credit to the rural poor. With this story in the background, the present investigation is purposively taken to understand the efficiency level of DCBs in West Bengal. Hence, as per experts in the field, there is a need to relate credit disbursement to efficiency. Thus, the research is undertaken to judge the efficiency of banks in respect of West Bengal.

1.3 Problem Statement

The importance of DCBs is evident from various studies. As the banking sector has been facing rapid transformation over the years, the basic focus changed from providing support to the rural economy to operational aspect in terms of profitability. However, a key aspect of performance viz. efficiency is missing in the previous studies. Thus, it is pertinent to look at the efficiency aspect of the district cooperative banks as it will help to gauge the sustainability of these credit institutions.

There are studies in recent times that point to the operational ineffectiveness of these banks which is reflected in the poor profitability (or high losses). In fact, the RBI reports mention the dismal position of almost 15% of the DCBs which are incurring losses. In such a position, it is vital for researchers to look into the overall position of DCBs by assessing the performance not just from the perspective of income/expenses and assets/liabilities but considering them together. The previous literatures show that there is no previous study that appraises these financial institutions from the aspect of efficiency. It is a key to understand the efficiency measure of these banks as it has repercussions on the sustainability of these intermediaries.

2 Review of Literature

2.1 Review of Earlier Studies

It is true that researchers have shown interest in exploring the cooperative sector and looking at the different tiers in the banking system. The discussion gives an idea about the different areas that are covered in the earlier contributions. The research spans the coverage of institutions at different levels which include PACS (Mullah, 2013; Rangamlian, 2017; Yogarani & Padhmanaban, 2019) and cooperative banks (Bharati, 2015; Das, 2015; Gaurav & Krishnan, 2017; Njavallil et al., 2018; Sanjeevi & Babu, 2017). The previous literatures ponder over various issues involving these financial intermediaries. The different problems that are associated with the operational functioning of the PACS are highlighted in the studies of Yogarani and Padhmanaban (2019). The position of PACS in terms of their financial performance parameters, their trend and growth over the years is observed in the research contributions of Rangamlian (2017), Mullah (2013), Das and Chaudhury (2011), Natarajan (2007) and others. The study by Bhattacharyya and Sinha (2019) appraises the PACS of West Bengal from the perspective of efficiency. In a similar study on PACS in the North–Eastern region, the efficiency is the focus of interest (Das, 2017). Venkatesulu (2018) points to the significant role of urban co-operative banks (UCBs) in loan disbursement to Primary Agricultural Co-operative Societies.

There are relatively a greater number of studies on district cooperative banks which is seen from the significantly large number of contributions (Bharati, 2015; Das Tushar, 2013; Gaurav & Krishnan, 2017; Gnanasekaran et al., 2012; Njavallil et al., 2018; Ramachandran & Shanmugam, 2012; Shanthi & Anandan, 2017; Venkatesulu, 2018). With regard to the various issues that are covered by researchers, an easy classification can be done which highlights the key areas. Some of them include assessment of key financial parameters (Bharati, 2015; Das, 2015; Dutta & Basak, 2008; Gnanasekaran et al., 2012; Matkar, 2012; Njavallil et al., 2018; Shanthi & Anandan, 2017; Singh & Sukhmani, 2011; Tandon et al., 2017). The aspect of efficiency is seen in the works of Gaurav and Krishnan (2017), Feroze (2012), and Chander and Chandel (2010). The issues of lending practices and non-performing assets in the DCBs are found in the contributions of Rakshit and Chakrabarti (2012) and Gupta and Suman (2012). Another pertinent issue in banking viz. credit and loan recovery is seen in the contribution of Bhaskaran and Josh (2000).

The other highlighted issues include understanding the operational aspect and related issues (Sanjeevi & Babu, 2017), the development and progress of urban cooperative banks (Ramachandran, 2012) and technological upgradation of the cooperative banks (Sekhar & Sudhir, 2012). Sanjeevi and Babu (2017), Attri and Paul (2015), Babu (2012), and Jagtap (2012) though appreciate the overall financial performance of cooperative banks also highlight the areas of weaknesses that need to be addressed timely which is also seen in the study by Babu and Selkhar (2012). Jain (2001) in theinter-DCB comparison of the three Western states of Maharashtra, Gujarat and Rajasthan recognizes the superior position of Rajasthan in respect of profitability and liquidity. The role of cooperative banks about financing in the rural areas, financing of agricultural requirements is observed in the studies of Devi (2012), Laxman (2012), and Asher (2007). The research contributions of Singh and Sukhmani (2011) and Basak (2009) highlight the key problems that the district cooperative banks confront.

2.2 *Research Gap*

The analysis of earlier academic contributions helps to identify the research gap. It is observed from the reviews of much research evidence that cooperative banking has attracted a lot of interest among researchers. There are few contributions on PACS, the lowest tier in the cooperative banking structure. The focus area in the investigations is on the areas of growth, trend, non-performing assets and ratios. There are contributions that do a detailed analysis of the financial aspect of performance by looking at the key measures of liquidity, profitability and business health. Researchers have also investigated the inter-bank performance analysis in addition to lending and recovery practices. The present study is among the few ones that analyse the performance of DCBs in West Bengal from the perspective of efficiency using Data Envelopment Analysis which thereby will be a further contribution to the existing knowledge.

3 Objectives of the Study

This study has the following objectives:

- To assess the relative efficiency position of the selected DCBs in West Bengal, and

- To assess whether there is significant difference in efficiency in the DCBs of North and South Bengal.

4 Research Design and Methodology

This is a very important area of research as it lays the foundation for any work. The correctness and robustness of the findings depends on the design that is laid. For the present study, the components of the design are as follows:

1. *Sample:* The researchers consider the DCBs of selected fourteen districts of West Bengal. The districts have been chosen on the basis of descending order of size and availability of data for all the seven years.
2. *Data period*: The analysis is based on data for the period 2011–2017.
3. *Nature of the data and source*: The research is based on data available from the reports of the State Cooperative Bank of West Bengal which are released annually at the Central Cooperative Banks' Conference.
4. *Research methods*: In this research, Data Envelopment Analysis, a non-parametric method is used to arrive at efficiency scores which can be categorized into technical efficiency, pure technical efficiency (also called managerial efficiency) and scale efficiency. The computation is based on a two input-two output model under the assumption of variable returns to scale. The inputs are deposits and borrowings whereas the outputs are loans and investment. The following two basic conditions as mentioned by Cooper (2007) have been checked before applying DEA:

   Condition 1: $n \geq p \times q$, where n is the number of DMUs, p is the number of inputs and q is the number of outputs.

   Condition 2: $r > 3\ (p + q)$, where r is the total number of observations.

Furthermore, it is mentioned that the output—oriented technique is followed because in the present competitive environment, like all organizations, DCBs being at the middle level of the 3-tier cooperative banking structure aim to maximize outputs using the given inputs.

Table 1 Descriptive statistics of efficiency

	DCBs	*Bankura*	*Burdwan*	*Dakshin Dinajpur*	*Hooghly*	*Howrah*	*Jalpaiguri*	*Malda*
TE	Avg	0.937	0.984	0.869	0.984	1	0.825	0.97
	SD	0.068	0.024	0.093	0.022	0	0.266	0.054
	Min	0.807	0.939	0.73	0.942	1	0.319	0.869
	Max	1	1	1	1	1	1	1
PTE	Avg	0.942	1	0.971	0.988	1	0.852	0.973
	SD	0.067	0	0.073	0.02	0	0.239	0.048
	Min	0.813	1	0.805	0.951	1	0.409	0.882
	Max	1	1	1	1	1	1	1
SE	Avg	0.994	0.984	0.895	0.996	1	0.952	0.997
	SD	0.007	0.024	0.068	0.005	0	0.079	0.006
	Min	0.981	0.939	0.8	0.988	1	0.781	0.985
	Max	1	1	1	1	1	1	1

Source Computed by authors

5 Results of the Study

This section of the paper discusses the findings about relative efficiency levels. The discussion is made under different sub-sections for easy understanding by readers.

5.1 Descriptive Statistics

The discussion in this sub-section gives an idea about the characteristics of the data. The mean, standard deviation, minimum and maximum values of different forms of efficiency are highlighted in the two Tables 1 and 2.

5.2 Efficiency Results

5.2.1 Technical Efficiency

The scores below give the relative overall efficiency score. A score of one implies 100% relative efficiency whereas any score less than one implies inefficiency in the system. In the latter case, there is scope for improvement depending on the efficiency result. Table 3 gives the result in this regard.

The technical efficiency of a unit refers to the relative overall efficiency with reference to the group that is considered for the study. The

Table 2 Descriptive statistics of efficiency

	DCBs	*Mugberia*	*Murshidabad*	*Nadia*	*Purulia*	*Raiganj*	*Tamluk-Ghatal*	*VCCB*
TE	Avg	0.953	0.923	0.97	0.798	0.611	1	0.885
	SD	0.035	0.12	0.037	0.082	0.238	0	0.094
	Min	0.905	0.69	0.917	0.715	0.306	1	0.755
	Max	1	1	1	0.939	0.953	1	1
PTE	Avg	0.967	0.943	0.976	1	0.635	1	0.901
	SD	0.027	0.098	0.034	0	0.228	0	0.086
	Min	0.94	0.737	0.92	1	0.39	1	0.785
	Max	1	1	1	1	0.971	1	1
SE	Avg	0.985	0.976	0.994	0.798	0.951	1	0.981
	SD	0.017	0.034	0.008	0.082	0.074	0	0.025
	Min	0.956	0.921	0.98	0.715	0.785	1	0.933
	Max	1	1	1	1	0.953	1	1

Source Computed by authors

score ranges from zero to one. The former implies zero percent efficiency (theoretically) whereas the latter means that the unit lies on the envelope. In the table above, it is obvious that among the outperformers we have the DCBs of Howrah, Tamluk-Ghatal, Burdwan and Hooghly with the first two being the leaders in the group. Among the laggards, the DCBs of Raiganj, Purulia and Jalpaiguri (in that order) with efficiency levels of 61.1%, 79.8% and 82.5% respectively find a place. Though the efficiency of the group ranges from 61.1% to 100%, an interesting observation is the rapid improvement record of Raiganj during the period which still has a scope of raising its output by 38.9% to be positioned on the frontier. About the mean performance over the years, though there are ups and downs in the efficiency level, the figures lie within a narrow range of 85.7% (in 2014) and 96.9% (in 2016).

5.2.2 *Pure Technical Efficiency*

The next efficiency aspect that is judged is the pure technical efficiency (also called managerial efficiency) of DCBs. The results help to identify the scope of improvement for the different decision-making units. Table 4 gives the results.

The above table shows that there is enough scope for many of the banks to improve their operations through better managerial decisions which will lead to an increase in the outputs using the same inputs

Table 3 Technical efficiency of DCBs

DCBs	*2011*	*2012*	*2013*	*2014*	*2015*	*2016*	*2017*	*Avg*	*SD*	*Coeff. of Variation*
Bankura	1.000	0.979	1.000	0.914	0.927	0.934	0.807	0.937	0.068	7.204
Burdwan	1.000	1.000	0.964	0.982	0.939	1.000	1.000	0.984	0.024	2.441
Dakshin Dinajpur	0.893	0.839	0.791	0.873	1.000	0.955	0.730	0.869	0.093	10.674
Hooghly	0.966	0.942	0.985	1.000	1.000	1.000	0.994	0.984	0.022	2.254
Howrah	1.000	1.000	1.000	1.000	1.000	1.000	1.000	1.000	0.000	0.000
Jalpaiguri	1.000	1.000	0.600	0.319	0.872	0.983	1.000	0.825	0.266	32.270
Malda	0.919	1.000	1.000	1.000	0.869	1.000	1.000	0.970	0.054	5.528
Mugberia	0.951	0.905	0.935	0.933	0.944	1.000	1.000	0.953	0.035	3.727
Murshidabad	0.690	0.975	1.000	1.000	0.825	0.981	0.990	0.923	0.120	13.004
Nadia	0.975	0.917	0.979	0.919	1.000	1.000	1.000	0.970	0.037	3.815
Purulia	0.844	0.741	0.939	0.759	0.715	0.850	0.739	0.798	0.082	10.209
Raiganj	0.306	0.614	0.480	0.500	0.511	0.953	0.912	0.611	0.238	38.965
Tamluk-Ghatal	1.000	1.000	1.000	1.000	1.000	1.000	1.000	1.000	0.000	0.000
VCCB	1.000	0.878	1.000	0.795	0.755	0.907	0.857	0.885	0.094	10.588
Avg	0.896	0.914	0.905	0.857	0.883	0.969	0.931			
SD	0.191	0.115	0.166	0.208	0.142	0.045	0.104			
Coeff. of Variation	21.288	12.619	18.340	24.234	16.141	4.667	11.130			

Source Computed by researchers

Table 4 Pure technical efficiency of DCBs

DCBs	*2011*	*2012*	*2013*	*2014*	*2015*	*2016*	*2017*	*Avg*	*SD*	*Coeff. of Variation*
Bankura	1.000	0.998	1.000	0.922	0.928	0.935	0.813	0.942	0.067	7.132
Burdwan	1.000	1.000	1.000	1.000	1.000	1.000	1.000	1.000	0.000	0.000
Dakshin Dinajpur	1.000	1.000	0.990	1.000	1.000	1.000	0.805	0.971	0.073	7.528
Hooghly	0.969	0.951	0.996	1.000	1.000	1.000	1.000	0.988	0.020	2.026
Howrah	1.000	1.000	1.000	1.000	1.000	1.000	1.000	1.000	0.000	0.000
Jalpaiguri	1.000	1.000	0.623	0.409	0.933	1.000	1.000	0.852	0.239	28.048
Malda	0.928	1.000	1.000	1.000	0.882	1.000	1.000	0.973	0.048	4.946
Mugberia	0.983	0.947	0.940	0.943	0.953	1.000	1.000	0.967	0.027	2.792
Murshidabad	0.737	0.977	1.000	1.000	0.896	1.000	0.991	0.943	0.098	10.429
Nadia	0.987	0.935	0.991	0.920	1.000	1.000	1.000	0.976	0.034	3.478
Purulia	1.000	1.000	1.000	1.000	1.000	1.000	1.000	1.000	0.000	0.000
Raiganj	0.390	0.641	0.491	0.505	0.519	0.971	0.932	0.635	0.228	35.891
Tamluk-Ghatal	1.000	1.000	1.000	1.000	1.000	1.000	1.000	1.000	0.000	0.000
VCCB	1.000	0.941	1.000	0.808	0.785	0.910	0.863	0.901	0.086	9.592
Avg	0.928	0.956	0.931	0.893	0.921	0.987	0.957			
SD	0.170	0.094	0.161	0.194	0.132	0.029	0.074			
Coeff. of Variation	18.316	9.875	17.316	21.685	14.358	2.902	7.717			

Source Computed by researchers

measure. The outperformers in the set include the DCBs in Burdwan, Howrah, Purulia and Tamluk-Ghatal with their managerial efficiency showing a relative efficiency of 100% in all the years. In fact, the DCB of these two districts show wide variability. The position of the remaining banks is good with low coefficient of variation.

5.2.3 *Scale Efficiency*

This is the third component of efficiency that arises from the scale at which the operations take place. It is important to note that this efficiency helps to assess whether the decision-making unit is operating at the optimum scale (Table 5).

The result shows that on average only two of the sample banks (Howrah DCB and Tamluk-Ghatal DCB) operate at the most productive scale size. Of the remaining, excepting Dakshin-Dinajpur and Purulia

Table 5 Scale efficiency of DCBs

DCBs	*2011*	*2012*	*2013*	*2014*	*2015*	*2016*	*2017*	*Avg*	*SD*	*Coeff. of variation*
Bankura	1.000	0.981	1.000	0.991	0.999	0.999	0.992	0.994	0.007	0.727
Burdwan	1.000	1.000	0.964	0.982	0.939	1.000	1.000	0.984	0.024	2.441
Dakshin Dinajpur	0.893	0.839	0.800	0.873	1.000	0.955	0.906	0.895	0.068	7.573
Hooghly	0.997	0.991	0.988	1.000	1.000	1.000	0.994	0.996	0.005	0.481
Howrah	1.000	1.000	1.000	1.000	1.000	1.000	1.000	1.000	0.000	0.000
Jalpaiguri	1.000	1.000	0.963	0.781	0.934	0.983	1.000	0.952	0.079	8.301
Malda	0.991	1.000	1.000	1.000	0.985	1.000	1.000	0.997	0.006	0.617
Mugberia	0.967	0.956	0.995	0.989	0.990	1.000	1.000	0.985	0.017	1.745
Murshidabad	0.936	0.998	1.000	1.000	0.921	0.981	0.999	0.976	0.034	3.435
Nadia	0.988	0.980	0.988	1.000	1.000	1.000	1.000	0.994	0.008	0.818
Purulia	0.844	0.741	0.939	0.759	0.715	0.850	0.739	0.798	0.082	10.209
Raiganj	0.785	0.958	0.977	0.991	0.985	0.982	0.978	0.951	0.074	7.767
Tamluk-Ghatal	1.000	1.000	1.000	1.000	1.000	1.000	1.000	1.000	0.000	0.000
VCCB	1.000	0.933	1.000	0.985	0.962	0.997	0.993	0.981	0.025	2.555
Avg	0.957	0.955	0.972	0.954	0.959	0.982	0.972			
SD	0.069	0.076	0.053	0.084	0.076	0.040	0.071			
Coeff. of Variation	7.211	7.905	5.467	8.849	7.882	4.076	7.337			

Source Computed by researchers

Table 6 Returns to scale

DCBs	*2011*	*2012*	*2013*	*2014*	*2015*	*2016*	*2017*
Bankura	CRS	IRS	CRS	DRS	IRS	IRS	IRS
Burdwan	CRS	CRS	DRS	DRS	DRS	CRS	CRS
Dakshin Dinajpur	IRS	IRS	IRS	IRS	CRS	IRS	IRS
Hooghly	DRS	IRS	DRS	CRS	CRS	CRS	DRS
Howrah	CRS	CRS	CRS	CRS	CRS	CRS	CRS
Jalpaiguri	CRS	CRS	IRS	IRS	IRS	IRS	CRS
Malda	DRS	CRS	CRS	CRS	DRS	CRS	CRS
Mugberia	IRS	IIRS	DRS	IRS	I IRS	CRS	CRS
Murshidabad	IRS	IRS	CRS	CRS	DRS	IRS	DRS
Nadia	IRS	DRS	DRS	IRS	CRS	CRS	CRS
Purulia	IRS	IRS	IRS	IRS	IRS	IRS	IRS
Raiganj	DRS	IRS	IRS	IRS	DRS	IRS	IRS
Tamluk-Ghatal	CRS	CRS	CRS	CRS	CRS	CRS	CRS
VCCB	CRS	DRS	CRS	DRS	DRS	DRS	DRS

Note DRS: Decreasing returns to scale, IRS: Increasing returns to scale, CRS: Constant returns to scale
Source Computed by researchers

DCBs, all the others attain an efficiency of more than 90%. The position of Purulia DCB is dismal with an inefficiency level of 20.2%.

5.2.4 *Returns to Scale*

The results point to the level of operation and help to take decision about whether to decrease or increase the level of operation. The change is required to arrive at the most productive scale size (MPSS) to reduce the inefficiency arising from poor scale of operation. The terms CRS, IRS and DRS denote constant returns to scale, increasing returns to scale and decreasing returns to scale, respectively. The CRS points to a position of 'optimum' scale. The IRS implies that there is a need to upscale the size of operation so that scale efficiency can be improved. The DRS, on the other hand, suggests a cutting-down of scale size to improve the overall result. The results are given in Table 6.

5.2.5 *Distribution of Districts on the Basis of Mean Efficiency Score*

This section summarizes the above results to categorize the DCBs based on their relative performance (Table 7).

Table 7 Distribution of districts based on mean efficiency score

Avg. efficiency being less than 90%	*Avg. efficiency above 90%*
Overall efficiency	
Dakshin Dinajpur, Jalpaiguri, Purulia, Raiganj, VCCB	Bankura, Burdwan, Hooghly, Howrah, Malda, Mugberia, Murshidabad, Nadia, Tamluk-Ghatal
Pure technical efficiency	
Jalpaiguri, Raiganj	Bankura, Burdwan, Dakshin Dinajpur, Hooghly, Howrah, Malda, Mugberia, Murshidabad, Nadia, Purulia, Tamluk-Ghatal, VCCB
Scale efficiency	
Dakshin Dinajpur, Purulia	Bankura, Burdwan, Hooghly, Howrah, Jalpaiguri, Malda, Mugberia, Murshidabad, Nadia, Raiganj, Tamluk-Ghatal, VCCB

Source Prepared by the researchers

5.2.6 *Testing for Mean Difference*

In this section, the mean difference on overall efficiency is tested to find whether there is any difference among the banks of South and North Bengal. Since the number of banks in the two groups is different, the Welch test is applied instead of the t-test. The results are given in Table 8.

The above table points to the fact that there is no significant difference among the banks of South and North Bengal. However, interestingly, it is clear from the effect size that the gap which was wide in the earlier years of the study period shows a significant decline during the later part of the period.

6 Conclusions and Implications

6.1 Conclusions

The study focuses on the lowest tier of the structure of cooperative banking in India. There are many studies on the cooperative sector and district cooperative banks. This empirical study is an interesting one and comes up with important findings. For the purpose of the investigation, fourteen districts are chosen from south and north Bengal on the basis of descending order of business. The research is interesting as it enquires

Table 8 Mean-difference test using Welch test

Year	*Is null hypothesis rejected?*	*Conclusion*	*Effect size*
2011	No (0.348)	There is no significant difference	0.841
2012	No (0.854)	There is no significant difference	0.110
2013	No (0.338)	There is no significant difference	1.071
2014	No (0.358)	There is no significant difference	0.712
2015	No (0.471)	There is no significant difference	0.301
2016	No (0.880)	There is no significant difference	0.065
2017	No (0.984)	There is no significant difference	0.009

Figures in the parentheses represent the *p*-value
Source Computed by the researchers

into the efficiency level of the DCBs based on the application of the Data Envelopment Analysis, a non-parametric method of analysis which makes it a unique study. The understanding is gathered on three efficiency measures namely technical (overall), managerial and scale efficiency. A look into the efficiency of DCBs of West Bengal shows that the overall position of the banks is good though there are exceptions. Other than the case of technical (or overall) efficiency, more than 70% of the banks show an efficiency score of more than 90%. In respect of the operation size, the returns to scale point to operation at a non-optimal scale thereby calling for scale adjustment to reach the optimum level.

6.2 *Implications*

The findings can help managers in understanding the position of DCBs in terms of efficiency. The inferences of the study can facilitate corporate decision-makers in deciding ways to improve the efficiency level of banks. The efficiency level in the three aspects can help to identify the better and poor district cooperative banks which can thus help the bank-level managers to adopt measures to reach the 'envelope' and attain relative perfect efficiency levels. The findings, therefore, imply that they will help to develop guidelines on the means to generate maximum outputs from minimum inputs.

6.3 *Limitation*

The limitation of the research is that the data on non-performing asset of the banks are not available and hence could not be considered for analysis purpose.

6.4 *Scope for Further Study*

In the future endeavour in this issue, research can consider the application of productivity analysis using bootstrapping method that will further give useful insights into another aspect of performance. Moreover, if data is available, efforts can be given to explore the causal relationship.

References

Asher, M. G. (2007). Reforming governance and regulation of urban cooperative banks in India. *Journal of Financial Regulation and Compliance, 15*(1), 20–29.

Attri, K. K., & Paul, M. (2015). Growth and performance of co-operative banks in India. *Sai Om Journal of Commerce & Management, 2*(5), 9–15.

Babu, K. V. S. N. J. (2012). Performance evaluation of urban co-operative banks in India. *IOSR Journal of Business and Management, 1*(5), 28–30.

Babu, K. V. S. N. J., & Selkhar, B. M. (2012). The emerging urban co-operative banks (UCBs) in India: Problem and prospects. *IOSR Journal of Business and Management, 2*(5), 1–5.

Basak, A. (2009). Performance appraisal of urban cooperative banks: A case study. *The IUP Journal of Accounting Research and Audit Practices, VII*(1), 31–44.

Bharati, R. (2015). Analysis of the financial performance of co-operative banks in Bijapur District (Karnataka State): A comparative study. *International Multidisciplinary E-Journal, IV*(VIII), 120–142.

Bhaskaran, R., & Josh, P. (2000, December). Non-performing assets in co-operative rural financial system: A major challenge to rural development. *Bird's Eye View*, I–XXIV.

Bhattacharyya, A., & Sinha, A. (2019). Performance assessment of primary agricultural credit societies in West Bengal: An efficiency approach. *Asian Journal of Multidimensional Research, 8*(2), 353–361.

Chander, R., & Chandel, J. K. (2010). Financial viability and performance evaluation of co-operative credit institutions in Haryana (India). *International Journal of Computing and Business Research, 1*(1), 1–22.

Das, R. (2015). Liquidation of cooperative banks in India: Implications of performance indicators for liquidation. *ACRN Oxford Journal of Finance and Risk Perspectives, 4*(4), 1–22.

Das, S. (2017). Performance of the primary agricultural cooperative societies: Special Reference to short term cooperative credit structure in North Eastern Region. *Amity Journal of Agribusiness, 2*(2), 22–29.

Das, S., & Chaudhury, D. S. (2011). A study of state coopertive banking system in the north eastern region of India. *International Journal of Consumerism, 1*(1), 54–63.

Das Tushar, B. (2013). *Net interest margin, financial crisis and bank behaviour: Experience of India Banks*. Retrieved April 2, 2014 from http://www.rbi.org.in/scripts/PublicationsView.aspx?id=15418

Devi, R. U. (2012). The role of credit co-operatives in the agricultural development of Andhra Pradesh, India. *International Journal of Cooperative Studies, 1*(2), 55–64.

Dutta, U., & Basak, A. (2008). Appraisal of financial performance of urban cooperative banks—A case study. *The Management Accountant, 43*(3), 170–174.

Feroze, P. S. (2012). Technical efficiency and its decomposition in district co-operative banks in Kerala: A data envelopment analysis approach. *South Asian Journal of Marketing & Management Research, 2*(3), 21–36.

Gaurav, S., & Krishnan, J. (2017). How efficient are India's cooperative banks? Evidence from DCCBs. *Economic and Political Weekly, 52*(12), 115–124.

Gnanasekaran, E., Anbalgan, M., & Nazar, N. A. (2012). A study on the urban cooperative banks success and growth in Vellore district—Statistical analysis. *International Journal of Advanced Research in Computer Science and Software Engineering, 2*(3), 434–437.

Gupta, J., & Suman, J. (2012). A study on cooperative banks in India with special reference to lending practices. *International Journal of Scientific and Research Publications, 2*(10), 1–6.

Jagtap, K. N. (2012). Special services rendered by cooperative bank—An overview. *Golden Research Thoughts, 2*(4), 1–4.

Jain. (2001, April–June). Comparative study of performance of District Central Co-operative Banks (DCCBs) of Western India i.e. Maharashtra, Gujarat & Rajasthan for the year 1999–2000 from the point of view of net profit/loss. *NAFSCOB Bulletin*.

Kadam, N. L. (2012). An evaluation of performance of Sangli District Central Cooperative Bank Ltd. Sangli in respect of agricultural finance. *Indian Streams Research Journal, II*(VII). https://doi.org/10.9780/22307850. http://old isrj.lbp.world/UploadedData/1201.pdf

Matkar, A. (2012). A glance in financial performance and retail banking products of Maharashtra state cooperative bank. *Abhinav, 1*(3), 142–156.

Mukherjee, S. (2011). Microfinance through cooperatives: Performance and prospects. *International Journal of Research in Commerce, Economics & Management, 1*(7), 102–106.

Mullah, K. (2013). Status of primary agricultural co-operative societies: An aggregate and state wise analysis. *Journal of Agricultural Finance in India, 2*(2), 309–317.

Murray, E. V. (2005). Revival of Cooperative Credit Institutions - Recommendations of the Vaidyanathan Committee. Retrieved from https://www.researchgate.net/publication/265167607_Revival_of_Cooperative_Credit_Institutions_-_Recommendations_of_the_Vaidyanathan_Committee.

Natarajan, D. P. (2007). PACS in Kerala-in search of profitability. *Indian Cooperative Review, 5*(2), 234–244.

Njavallil, C. J., Thoomkuzhy, J. J., & John, M. E. (2018). Evaluation of the financial performance of co-operative bank in Kerala-Upputhara Service Co-Operative Bank. *Research Review International Journal of Multidisciplinary, 3*(8), 698–705.

Rakshit, D., & Chakrabarti, S. (2012). NPA management of rural cooperative banks of West Bengal: An overview. *Business Spectrum, I*(3), 1–39.

Ramachandran, A. (2012). A study on the progress of the scheduled urban cooperative banks in India with respect to major indicators of financial performance. *RADIX International Journal of Banking, Finance and Accounting, 1*(9), 1–21.

Ramachandran, A., & Shanmugam, D. S. (2012). An empirical study on the financial performance of selected scheduled urban co operative banks in India. *Asian Journal of Research in Banking and Finance, 2*(5), 1–24.

Rangamlian, K. (2017). PACs as an instrument for sustainable development and growth of Kamrup (Rural) District of Assam. *Indian Co-Operative Reviews NCUI, 54*(3), 165–174.

Sanjeevi, P., & Babu, P. (2017). Operational and financial performance of urban cooperative banks in India. *Journal of Advance Management Research, 5*(5), 173–185.

Sekhar, B. M., & Sudhir, B. (2012). Core banking solutions in urban cooperative banks-issues and challenges. *International Journal of Scientific & Engineering Research, 3*(8), 1–8.

Shanthi, R., & Anandan, M. (2017). Financial performance of co-operative bank in Tamil Nadu. *International Journal of Management and Development Studies, 6*(4), 1–6.

Singh, G., & Sukhmani. (2011). An analytical study of productivity and profitability of district central cooperative banks in Punjab. *Journal on Banking Financial services and Insurance Research, 1*(3), 128–142.

Tandon, M. S., Sharma, N. N., & Bhulal, V. K. (2017). A comparative study of financial performance with special reference of co-operative banks. *Asian Journal of Management, 8*(3), 711–717.

Venkatesulu, A. (2018). A study on urban co-operative banks in India—Issues and prospects. *International Journals of Advanced Research in Computer Science and Software Engineering, 8*(4), 315–319.

Yogarani, M., & Padhmanaban, K. (2019). A study on the working performance of primary agricultural co-operative societies in India. *Journal of the Gujarat Research Society, 21*(5), 157–165.

Micro Insurance and Credit Societies

Role of Non-governmental Organizations in Micro Health Insurance Schemes: A Case Study from India

Savitha Basri

1 Introduction

India faces the challenge of providing enough funding for health care or adequate and effective health financing mechanisms such as insurance because of the existence of a large informal economy which neither comes under the purview of accountable economic activities that can be taxed nor can avail social health insurance coverage of the formal economy. The government health care expenditure is just 1.13% of GDP, resulting in a high level of out of pocket expenses (62%) (MoHFW, 2017). Moreover, private health insurance cannot be afforded by the poor population working in the informal sector. Consequently, the poor report to hardship financing that includes dissavings, borrowing from usurious lenders, selling productive assets, discontinuation of children's schooling, and substitution of labour. Considering the impoverishing effect of health risk on the income and financial well-being of low-income populations, several international agencies have advocated micro health insurance (MHI) as a

---

S. Basri (✉)
Manipal Institute of Management, Manipal Academy of Higher Education, Manipal, Karnataka, India

Ananda S. and D. Singh (eds.), *Financial Inclusion in Emerging Markets*,
https://doi.org/10.1007/978-981-16-2652-4_6

viable option to protect the poor from iatrogenic poverty and to improve access to health care services.

1.1 Micro Health Insurance

Rapid developments in the microfinance sector and self-help group (SHG) activities make the outreach of micro health insurance a reality. As a health financing mechanism, MHI removes financial barriers to get timely access to hospitals and prevents them from falling below the poverty line in the process of availing medical care. MHI is any not-for-profit insurance scheme that is aimed primarily at the informal sector and formed based on a collective pooling of health risks, in which the members participate in its management. The benefit package of these custom-designed health insurance products usually covers limited illnesses and has a lower sum insured owing to the unaffordability of high premiums by the target population. The benefits package (coverage and sum insured) cannot be negotiated between individuals and the insurers, and the premium calculation depends on community risk rating (not individual or household rating). Non-government organizations (NGOs) or microfinance institutions (MFI) usually act as distribution intermediaries due to the trust, knowledge of the target market, and deeper penetration of these entities in the rural and informal markets. MHI as known in India is referred to as community health funds (CHF), revolving drugs funds, or mutual health organizations (MHO) in the African subcontinent (Preker et al., 2002).

MHI broadly covers financing schemes that have three key features: community control, voluntary membership, and prepayment for health care by community members. These schemes target low-income households living in the same district or the members of micro-finance groups. The membership is usually voluntary, unlike social health insurance. MHI lowers out-of-pocket expenditure (OOPE), catastrophic health expenditure (CHE), hardship financing in the form of borrowing from usurious sources or sale of assets. It brings about changes in health-seeking behaviour from home medicine to medical care at health facilities and improves utilization of inpatient medical services while balancing the local requirements and affordability (Preker et al., 2002). Due to considerable flexibility in the contract with the insurance companies and the hospitals, scaling up of MHI is easier.

MHI deals with the information asymmetry problems with efficacy through certain design features and implementation mechanisms. Due to the constant flow of information among the people in rural communities, information asymmetry will be less prevalent and much lesser the possibility of adverse selection. Furthermore, over-utilization by some member's results in higher premiums and cost-shifting to other members who would disallow moral hazard practices. Generally, NGO initiated MHIs connect the community and formal insurance companies and hence, improve participation and efficiency. However, a small risk pool, the insufficient sum insured, lack of external financial assistance, non-financial impediments to utilize health services, lower level of awareness and knowledge on insurance, and shortage of trained management personnel pose formidable challenges to the success of (Ranson, 2002).

Bamako scheme started in Africa in 1987 has motivated many countries to adopt MHI as a viable policy initiative to ensure universal access to health care. Social health insurance in Germany and Japan was created on the principles of MHI, however, currently, it is seen only in some of the developing countries. Sampoorna Suraksha Programme (SSP), Voluntary Health Service (VHS), Bharat Agro Industries Foundation (BAIF), Development of Human Action (DHAN), Rajgarh Ambikapur Health Association (RAHA), Self Employed Women's Association (SEWA), Action for Community Organization, Rehabilitation and Development (ACCORD), Karuna and Yeshasvini scheme, and Navsarjan are some of the successful MHI schemes (Table 1). The partner–agent model is the dominant type of health insurance model although there are other two types; type I (HMO design) and type II (insurer design) (Devadasan et al., 2006). This model enables access to the existing target market, educate and encourage preventive measures, collect the premium, disburse the claim amount, use the existing distribution channels and combine credit/savings activities with insurance to realize economies of scale and scope.

These schemes stipulate individual as the unit of enrolment and focus on the poor in the informal sector. The coverage is restricted to inpatient services, and other risks such as life, assets, and natural calamities are also covered. The majority of the scheme provides cashless benefits at any network hospital. MHI membership reduces out-of-pocket payment expenditure (OOPE), increases utilization of health care facilities (in the form of outpatient visits or hospitalization), increases access to medical care, better access to drugs, and primary care, and decreases hardship financing.

Table 1 Comparisons of micro health insurance schemes in India

Name, acronym, location, year	*Target population*	*Type of MHI*	*Unit of enrolment*	*Premium per person (INR)*	*Coverage (% of target population)*	*Ceiling on benefit (INR)*	*Provider payment*	*Benefit package*
Student Health Home, West Bengal (1952)	Full-time students	Provider	School or college	4 per student	5 lakh students	Unlimited	Third party	Inpatient
VHS, Tamil Nadu (1972)	Population of catchment area	Provider	Family	Sliding scale 80	12%	Unlimited	Third party	Inpatient
RAHA, Chhattisgarh (1980)	Poor living in catchment area	Insurer	Individual	20	58%	1200	Third party	Inpatient
ACCORD, Tamil Nadu (1992)	Scheduled tribe	Provider	Individual	22	36%	1500	Third party	Inpatient
SEWA, Gujarat (1992)	SEWA Union members	Linked	Individual	100	10%	2000	Insurance company	Inpatient
DHAN Foundation, Tamil Nadu (2000)	Members of community banking scheme	Insurer	Individual	100	40%	10,000	KKVS reimburses patients	Inpatient
BAIF, Maharashtra (2001)	Members of community banking scheme	Linked	Individual	225	58%	5000	Insurance company reimburses	Inpatient

Name, acronym, location, year	*Target population*	*Type of MHI*	*Unit of enrolment*	*Premium per person (INR)*	*Coverage (% of target population)*	*Ceiling on benefit (INR)*	*Provider payment*	*Benefit package*
Karuna Trust, Karnataka (2002)	Scheduled tribes and scheduled caste	Linked	Individual	30	31%	2500	Third party payment	Inpatient
Yeshasvini, Karnataka (2003)	Members of co-operative societies	Insurer	Individual	120	48% in 2009	200,000	Cashless treatment	Surgery Outpatient
SSP, Karnataka (2004)	SHG members of SKDRDP	Linked	Family	350	32% in 2011	5000	Cashless treatment	Inpatient

1 US$ = 74.29 INR, 19 November 2020

Source Devadasan et al. (2006) and Savitha and Kiran (2012)

1.2 Health System Goals and the Role of Micro Health Insurance

Universal coverage of health services is the main agenda of many nations' development programmes including India, which requires access to affordable health care to all without regard to one's ability to pay. This idea of equity in access and financing stipulates the health care system in any country to achieve better health status and health equality, to be responsive to people's non-medical expectations, and to ensure fairness in financial contribution (WHO, 2000). This broad objective can be broken down into equity in utilization, financial protection, and sustainability. Equity is interpreted about both income and gender equality of access to health care. The Health system performs four main functions namely (i) provision of health services, (ii) resource generation (investment and training), (iii) health financing (risk pooling), and (iv) government stewardship (governance and oversight) to achieve these objectives (WHO, 2000).

Among these main functions, the health-financing sub-function requires priority in India due to its impoverishing effects, especially on the poor. MHI ensures the provision of financial resources to facilitate timely treatment in public and private health care services. The functions of MHI include revenue collection, fund pooling, and strategic purchasing (WHO, 2000). In the revenue collection function, the determination and mobilization of financial resources from households depends on enrolment and the ratio of prepayment. The enrolment depends on the affordability of premiums, the unit of enrolment, timing of the collection of premiums, quality of the care offered, and geographical location of the household (Carrin et al., 2005). The pooling function allows the sharing of financial resources between healthy and sick that involves the accumulation and management of contributions of members to spread the risk of illness among all the members. Strategic purchasing requires a continuous search to buy the best health services by contracting with quality service providers and using effective payment methods and contracting arrangements (WHO, 2000).

By performing these functions, MHI aims to achieve three independent goals namely mobilization of resources, protecting the households from financial consequences of illness, and the inclusion of the poorest by making them active participants in the health care system which ultimately contributes to the objectives of the health system. Resource mobilization denotes cost recovery ratio, amount of resources raised through community-financing arrangements as a share of the country's total health revenues and indirectly by efficiency and quality of health care and moral hazard (Ekman, 2004). Financial protection is the reduction in annual health expenditure as a percent of total annual household income. It denotes a reduction in OOPE, access to health care, and utilization of health care. The size of the poorest members in a scheme measures social inclusion (Jakab & Krishnan, 2001). Also, demand-side factors (income, size of family, education, the gender of head of the household) and supply-side factors (scheme design and implementation) determine enrolment/social inclusion.

The performance of functions of MHI to achieve its objectives depends upon the design of the schemes in terms of technical, management, organizational, and institutional characteristics (Preker et al., 2002). Technical characteristics namely benefit packages, the structure of premium, purchasing of health services, and allocation mechanisms determine revenue collection, risk pooling, and enrolment. The level of pre-payment, type of contribution (compulsory or voluntary), the degree to which contributions are progressive, tools to address adverse selection, flexibility in the payment of premium, and provision of subsidies affect the revenue collection (Preker et al., 2004). Size of the insurance scheme, trust, and confidence in the management of MHI, and moral hazard control mechanisms affect the risk pooling. Provider payment mechanism, referral systems, waiting period provisions, contents of the benefits package, and provider contract specifications are factors that determine the extent of strategic purchasing (Carrin et al., 2005). Management characteristics include staff (leadership, the extent of the capacity building), culture (management style, structure), and access to information (financial, health information, resources, and behaviour). Organizational characteristics include organizational forms, incentive regime (degree of autonomy, accountability, financial responsibility), and linkages with providers. Institutional characteristics are stewardship (government and donor support), governance, insurance markets, and factor and product markets (Preker et al., 2002). Figure 1 depicts the broad conceptual framework of the study.

1.3 Effect of Features of MHI on Its Performance

Resource mobilization (RM), reduction in impoverishment (financial protection), and equitable utilization (social inclusion) measure the

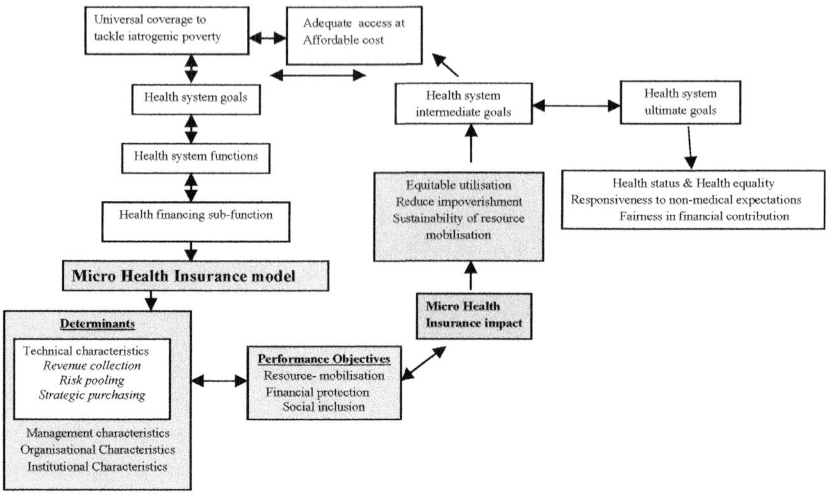

Fig. 1 Micro health insurance characteristics, performance, and health system goals (*Source* Author's compilation)

performance of MHI in realizing universal coverage. Fair (financial) contribution denotes distribution of the cost of illness based on ability to pay. In the literature, due to the absence of any relevant validated instrument, financial protection acts as a proxy. It is measured by a decrease in CHE, OOPE, access to health care, and utilization of health care measures financial protection. In addition to these measures, risk coping strategies represent a comprehensive measure of financial protection. The design of the schemes in terms of technical, management, organizational, and institutional characteristics determines the performance of MHI in realizing the objectives of financial protection, resource mobilization, and social inclusion (Preker et al., 2002). Successful implementation and achievement of goals of MHI depend on effective design and management that improves participation, cost recovery rates, and social inclusion of the poorest members of the society (Ahmed et al., 2005; Jakab & Krishnan, 2001).

Factors that determine success are the mechanisms incorporated in the scheme to deal with adverse selection, accommodation of non-cash stream of income of members, ownership of the community, and trained and competent management (Preker et al., 2002). The success of the scheme also depends on the organizational linkages between the scheme and providers, donor support, and government funding (Jakab & Krishnan, 2001). Moreover, provider-based schemes have a moderately positive effect on resource mobilization and financial protection (Ekman, 2004). The partner–agent model is the best method of providing insurance to the poor (Dercon et al., 2004). Designing a scheme requires the consideration of benefits package, premium, information asymmetry problems in the insurance market, accounting and management, and participation of members (Wiesmann & Jutting, 2001). Survival of the scheme depends on the extent of risk-pooling and resource mobilization it achieves (De Allegri et al., 2006) and mechanisms to control the problems of information asymmetry (Wiesmann & Jutting, 2001). Literature on technical, management, organizational, and institutional characteristics and their role in scheme show the importance of scheme characteristics in shaping the performance of MHI.

1.3.1 Technical Characteristics

Technical expertise in the management of the scheme in the form of design of benefit packages, revenue collection, pooling, and purchasing mechanisms is essential to improve the efficiency of MHIs (Preker et al., 2004). It also depends on the adequacy of the benefits package, policies on co-payment, ceilings, deductibles, and reimbursement procedures adopted by the scheme (Zhang et al., 2010). Revenue collection appears to be more successful when the contribution scheme considers the nature of the membership population's revenue (Jakab & Krishnan, 2001). In rural areas, cash flow occurs after harvesting of crops, hence annual contributions collected during the harvest season are the most common practice in MHI. Flexibility in the payment of premium in terms of amount or kind and the time of payment would contribute to better scheme performance (Wiesmann & Jutting, 2001). Certain technical design features such as affordability of premiums, unit of enrolment, the timing of collection of premium, and quality of care offered by the providers influence the enrolment in a scheme (Carrin et al., 2005).

The ratio of prepaid contributions to health care costs determines revenue collection and thereby, resource mobilization. While calculating prepaid contributions, all stakeholders that contribute including central and local governments, corporations, and donors are to be included (Carrin et al., 2005). The extent of financial protection offered by

MHI varies on its risk coverage, whether the package includes comprehensive high-cost services including outpatient and inpatient or limited services with higher co-payment. Moreover, family enrolment as a unit of membership and waiting period provisions can curtail adverse selection. A Referral system is another component of strategic purchasing that can curtail moral hazard and improves efficiency (Carrin et al., 2005). The practice of strategic purchasing can improve the quality of the services (WHO, 2000) through negotiating the cost of services with providers, inspecting the line of treatment, and quality of care provided to their members before sanctioning and releasing the claim money. A review on the MHI impact concluded that out of 62 schemes for which information was available, ten schemes had some form of strategic purchasing (Baeza et al., 2002). It was noted, with great concern, that MHOs do not negotiate with providers or check their prescriptions owing to a lack of required medical and pharmaceutical skills.

Payment and reimbursement methods for hospitals are a part of strategic purchasing. The most common method of payment is a line item and global budgets in low and middle-income countries. Direct payment of claims to hospitals enhances efficiency by reducing administrative cost ratio and is recognized as one of the superior methods of reimbursement (McCord & Osinde, 2005). Fee-for-service payment is another method, which is retrospective and provides a strong incentive for quality in the sense that they encourage the production of additional services, but it may lead to the overproduction of services. Payments systems influence the quality of care. Retrospective rather than prospective and variable rather than a fixed payment method allows for the greatest flexibility for purchasers to incorporate quality standards in purchasing arrangements (Waters et al., 2004).

1.3.2 Management Characteristics

The second important characteristic is the management of schemes that include staff (leadership, the extent of the capacity building), culture (management style, structure), and access to information (financial, health information, resources, and behaviour) (Preker et al., 2004). Strong management of the scheme is necessary due to the possibility of misuse or overuse of insurance claims by members. Also, local management, accountability, and monitoring are crucial in implementing equitable and accountable community health financing schemes (Polonsky et al., 2008).

Top-down interference with the design and management of the schemes has a negative effect on their function and sustainability. Efficient management and development of an insurance product depend on the bias or priority of management and the board. Management capacity is another important factor that helps in running the scheme effectively and making necessary adjustments. Major hindrances to the success of the scheme were lack of skills in fixing the rate of premium and benefits packages, marketing and distribution, contracting with providers, accounting, monitoring and evaluation, and collecting dues.

Any improvement in revenue collection, cost containment, membership, and quality of services requires the active participation of the community in scheme management, the absence of which would result in provider capture and monopoly pricing (Jakab & Krishnan, 2001). Schemes providing better information would improve subscribers' confidence and enrolment rates and involvement in decision-making has a significant impact on subscribers' values (Ouimet et al., 2007). Hence, members should participate in decision making for better performance of the scheme.

1.3.3 Organizational Characteristics

Organizational characteristics include linkages in the form of vertical and horizontal integration, strategic alliances, administrative capacity, and enlarged risk pools. Besides, organizational forms, incentive regimes (degree of autonomy, accountability, financial responsibility), and linkages with providers determine the success of the scheme (Preker et al., 2004). Vertical integration depends on the stipulations regarding the nature and scope of the services offered by health care providers. Organizational linkages such as those between schemes and providers and between schemes themselves (including national government health system and/or social security system) are a critical determinant of the performance of MHIs (Jakab & Krishnan, 2001).

1.3.4 Institutional Characteristics

The key institutional characteristics namely the degree of congruence between the scheme's operating rules and participating population's normal behaviour patterns and health care providers' experience with third-party payments determine the magnitude and quality of involvement and management of the scheme by the target population (Preker et al., 2004). Additional institutional characteristics include stewardship (government and donor support), governance, insurance markets, and factor and product markets. Strength and the quality of these overseeing structures shape governance. A strong management board with knowledgeable people and a balance of priorities is essential for the long-term sustainability of MHI schemes (McCord & Osinde, 2005).

Community-financing schemes compete in the factor markets with other organizations involved in financing and providing health care. Negotiation skills to conclude the contract with providers and other market players determine the performance. In any health market, government plays a stewardship role by creating an enabling legal environment, transferring resources in terms of subsidies to the poor members of the scheme (Bennett, 2004), and regulating and monitoring MHI that determines the scheme performance. However, minimal government regulation of MHI has been advocated sighting adverse effect of government subsidies in the form of cream-skimming and adverse selection (Pauly et al., 2006). When local political structures and MHI administration support each other and also bureaucrats' enthusiasm and loyalty, public subsidies get embedded in these schemes, MHI would be successful (Mladovsky & Mossialos, 2008).

2 Relationship Between Features of SSP on Financial Protection, Enrolment, and Resource Mobilization

2.1 Sampoorna Suraksha Programme

Sampoorna Suraksha, meaning total security (*Kanishta Nirvahane, Garishta Bhadrate*) was started in 2004 to provide financial risk coverage to the self-help group (SHG) members of Sri Kshetra Dharmasthala Rural Development Program (SKDRDP), staff and their families in case of unforeseen consequences of ill health and maternity. The programme also provides credit in case of excessive inpatient medical expenses to insured families. The benefits package includes cashless treatment for hospitalization and delivery expenses, death compensation, and sickness allowances. Enrolment of members takes place through SHGs and field staff in February of every year. The sum insured is INR 10,000 per person on a family floater basis and the premiums (INR 350 per person) are pooled for a group policy issued by insurance companies.

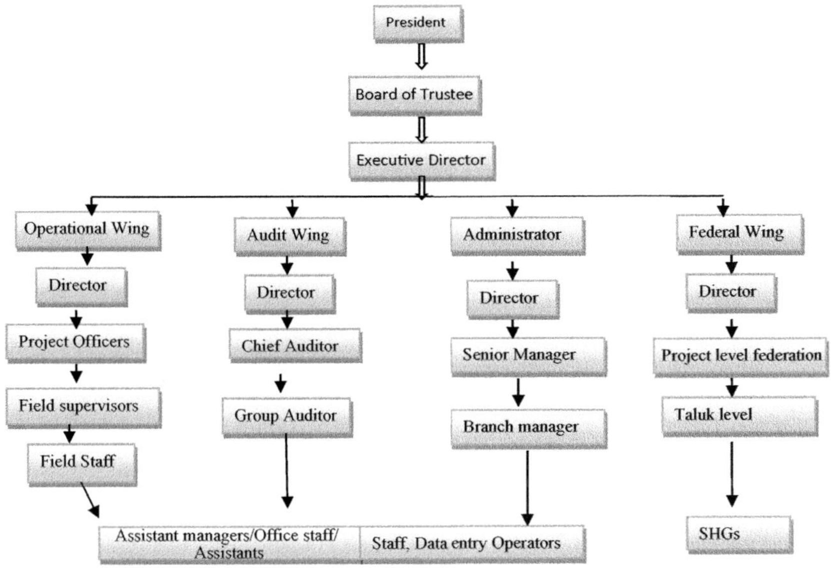

Fig. 2 Organization structure of SSP (*Source*: Author's compilation)

SSP acts as a community-based aggregator and a TPA. It assumes the role of agent or insurance intermediary as it uses existing infrastructure and established channels of micro-credit and micro-savings to offer insurance products to the SHGs. The objective of SSP is to provide financial assistance to meet the unexpected medical expenses to the stakeholders and their family, to facilitate access to the best hospitals, and to provide medical facilities at a lower cost (Sampoorna Suraksha Brochure, 2011). The organization map of SSP depicts a hierarchy structure (Fig. 2). SSP features are depicted in (Table 2).

2.1.1 Enrolment and Benefits

The field staffs (called in the local language as *sevanirathas*) have to create awareness of the benefits of SSP before the enrolment month. Their responsibilities include filling the registration forms, collecting the premium from the members, and issuing SSP cards to the members. Supervisors have to monitor the enrolment in their villages and submit consolidated accounts of the subscription and premium to the Project Officer of respective *valaya*, who in turn would send it to SSP head

Table 2 Key features of Sampoorna Suraksha Programme

Ownership and governance	*Shree Kshetra Dharmasthala Rural Development Project (SKDRDP) Trust and Insurance Companies*
Micro health insurance Model	Partner–agent model for hospitalization benefit and full-service model for special benefit cover
Insurance company	United Insurance Company Ltd., Oriental Insurance Ltd., Company Ltd, New India Assurance Company Ltd., National Insurance Company Ltd. in 2011–2012
Target population	Self Help Group (SHG) members of SKDRDP and their families
Enrolment	265,028 households; 926,581 members in 2018–2019
Insurance partners	Oriental Insurance, National Insurance, New India Assurance, and United India Insurance
Eligibility	Age group from 5 to 85 years, only for SHGs of SKDRDP
Benefit package	Life, Health and assets; INR 10,000/ for hospitalization per person in a family
Process of reimbursement	Third-party payment
Method of reimbursement to the hospital	Paid by Real Time Gross Settlement
External funding	None
Nature of relationship with the provider	Contract basis
Role of government	None
Community involvement in scheme design and management	Feedback given at the annual or monthly meetings is used to improve the scheme design
Role of health care provider	Provision of health care services, no involvement in management or designing benefit package
Political context	No government involvement
Structure and performance of health care system	Multi-tier structure, private sector dominates

office. The office pays the premium to the insurance company for the term beginning from 1st March to 28th February. Since 2011–2012, the maximum number of family members per policy was restricted to seven.

The benefits of Sampooran Suraksha covered in 2011–2012 were medical benefits (health treatment) and special benefits (delivery allowances, death consolation, domiciliary treatment, rest allowance, and consolation of natural calamities).

Medical Benefits

Health benefits are provided as cashless treatment at network hospitals up to the sum assured (INR 10,000/ per individual) and cover over 100 diseases. The scheme offers a family floater cover with a maximum of INR 70,000/. Outpatient treatment is excluded from coverage. Unlike private-for-profit companies, SSP does not exclude pre-existing diseases. Besides, there is no waiting period and co-payment or deductibles to be paid by the policyholders. The coverage is provided only for general ward admissions in the network hospitals, however, non-network hospital admissions are considered for reimbursement in special cases.

Special Benefits

The members of the programme can avail of special benefits like consolatory benefits to overcome liquidity constraints due to the risk of ill health, natural calamity, or loss of life.

2.1.2 Accessing Medical Care and Claims Adjudication and Settlement

Insured members can get medical treatment in any of the state-wide more than 100 network hospitals, even without the referral letter from any doctor. Within 24 hours of admission, the insured individual has to produce the SSP card to the hospital registration section. The hospital has to send the pre-authorization request to the SSP head office at Dharmasthala using an online system. The medical officer will verify the line of treatment, probable diagnosis, investigation planned, and probable total costs. The accounting section will check the unclaimed balance and the previous claim record of the member. If approved, the office will send an online authorization letter with the sanctioned limit to the hospital. Sampoorna Suraksha's assistant staff visits the hospital to verify the admission of the member. This mechanism prevents moral hazard and impersonation.

Within ten days of discharge, the hospital has to send the claim form A with the pre-authorization number given by the SSP office along with a photocopy ID card, discharge summary, investigation reports, laboratory reports, and the total bill along with separate bills for the diagnostic and laboratory investigation. SSP office sends the sanctioned amount by RTGS (Real Time Gross Settlement) to the hospital. In case of treatment in non-network hospitals, the insured can submit form B for reimbursement.

The network hospital has to send medical bills, discharge summary, reports (investigation and diagnostic such as X-ray, CT scan, MRI, laboratory) within ten days after the discharge of insured patient. Medical officers of SSP in the head office scrutinize pre-authorization forms, claim applications, investigation reports, and discharge summaries. Office staff verifies the name, address, and other details and unclaimed total amount of benefit. The settlement of the sanctioned claim takes place within 30 days of receipt of the claim application using the RTGS system.

Form C submission is required to claim special benefits. The Supervisors and Project Officers in the region verify and endorse it and send it to the SSP head office at Dharmasthala. The insurance company conducts audits and inspections, project officers of respective regions, and the medical team from the SSP office to ensure quality medical care to members of the scheme and to prevent supplier and member moral hazard.

A Memorandum of Understanding among SKDRDP, insurance company, and network hospitals specifies the role and responsibilities of each party. The insurance company issues a group health policy for a one time consolidated premium to SHGs who enroll in the programme. SSP issued a membership card to each policy holding family. The role of SSP in providing medical benefits are the registration of members, collection of the premium, maintenance of subscription records, handing over-subscription amount along with registration forms, and consolidated statement to insurance companies. It has to forward the approved claim forms to the insurance companies, and coordinate the pre-authorization with insurance companies and settle cashless claims with network hospitals. SSP office sends a debit note to the insurance company (Fig. 3).

2.2 *Features of SSP and Its Effect on Financial Protection, Enrolment, and Resource Mobilization*

Various characteristics of SSP (technical, management, organizational, and institutional) affect the performance of SSP in terms of resource mobilization (RM), social inclusion (SI and enrolment), financial protection (FP), financial sustainability (FS), and viability of the programme. The data collected by interviewing SSP administrators, project officers, and

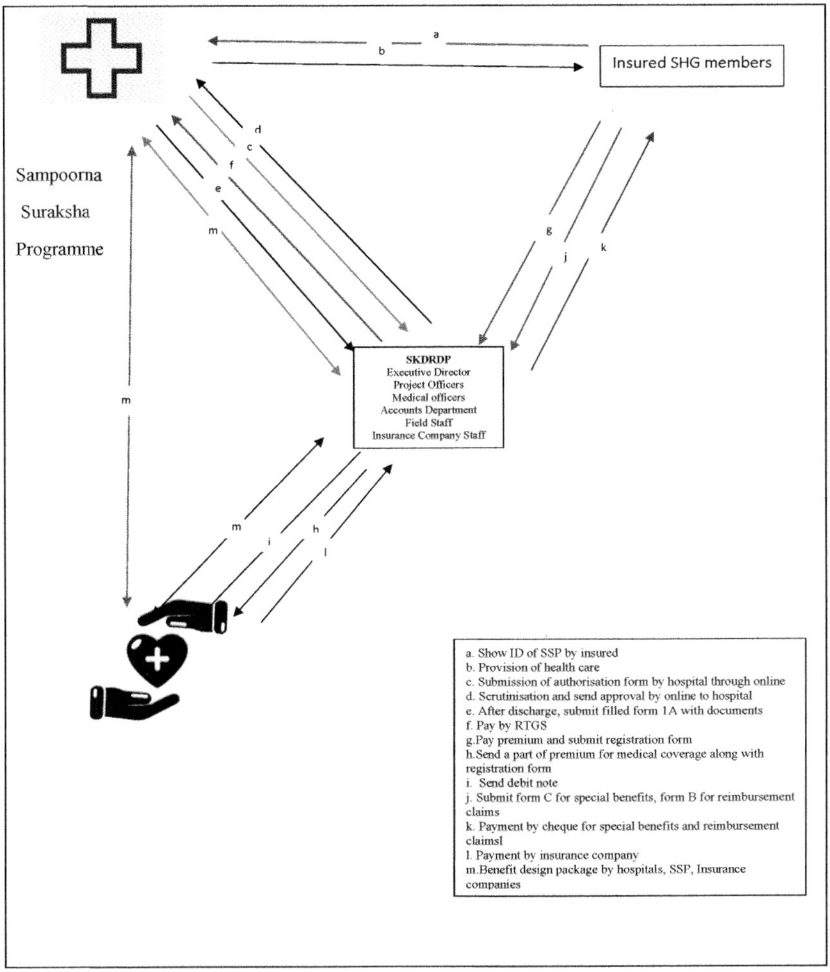

Fig. 3 Access to medical care and claim management process (*Source* Author's compilation)

field staff, and secondary data were collected from the brochures, annual reports, and promotion materials of SSP.

Technical characteristics such as revenue collection, risk pooling, and strategic purchasing affect the performance of MHI in terms of FP, enrolment, and RM (Preker et al., 2004). Certain technical design features affect the enrolment thereby revenue collection. Management characteristics namely staff (leadership and capacity in terms of management skills), culture (style of management and structure), and access to information (on financial resources, health information, and behaviour) determine the RM and enrolment. Forms of organization (economies of scale and scope, contractual relationships), incentive regime (extent of decision rights, market exposure, financial responsibility, accountability, and coverage of social functions), and linkages (extent of horizontal and vertical integration or fragmentation) are organizational characteristics that influence RM and financial sustainability. Certain institutional characteristics such as stewardship (strategic and operational decisions, regulations), governance (ownership arrangements), insurance markets (rules on revenue collection, pooling, and transfer of funds), and factor/ product markets determine the viability and performance of SSP (Preker et al., 2004). This section focuses on the role of these characteristics on the outcome of SSP in terms of RM, FP, enrolment, and financial sustainability.

2.2.1 Technical Design Characteristics

Revenue Collection

The effectiveness of SSP depends on the resources mobilized which in turn depends on (a) coverage of target population, (b) the level of prepayment compared with out of pocket expenditure, (c) whether contributions are compulsory or voluntary, (d) degree of progressivity of contributions, and (e) subsidies for the poor (Preker et al., 2004).

Coverage of Target Population

The attractiveness of SSP is indicated by the percentage of the population covered, which was 53.4% in 2004 but was reduced to 47.7% in 2005, later increased by 5.5% to 42.2% in 2006. Since then, a decline in membership has been observed (31.6% in 2016, 22.3% in 2018, and 22.6% in 2019). Although a gradual increase in enrolment (both microcredit and SSP) has been observed since inception in absolute numbers, the rate of increase has been declining over the years. Declining membership has adversely affected the enrolment in SSP and RM. As shown in Table 3, membership has gradually decreased from 2014 to 2019,

Table 3 Enrolment in SSP and the claims settled

Year	*No of families enrolled*	*No of members enrolled*	*Total claims*	*Amount settled (in INR lakhs)*
2004–2005	54,000	186,000	11,810	351
2005–2006	77,078	195,600	13,299	332
2006–2007	146,722	403,828	22,759	675
2007–2008	223,389	721,203	42,172	1208
2008–2009	252,542	932,682	67,861	2138
2009–2010	294,374	1,177,325	98,402	3320
2010–2011	419,979	1,662,089	136,980	4699
2011–2012	420,302	1,660,370	123,123	4685
2012–2013	366,722	1,272,019	71,825	4268
2013–2014	293,134	1,089,541	66,254	4032
2014–2015	310,458	1,177,094	61,273	3710
2015–2016	370,593	1,325,578	75,104	5356
2016–2017	324,584	1,194,822	54,999	3750
2017–2018	236,479	833,186	43,508	3802
2018–2019	265,028	926,581	22,090	1969
Total	4,055,384	14,757,924	911,459	44,295

Source Sampoorna Suraksha Program (2019)

the steepest decline was in 2017–2018 (305) and 2012–2013 (23.4%). However, an increase of 11% was observed in 2018–2019.

Ratio of Prepaid Contributions to Health Care Costs

Higher prepaid contributions would generate sufficient revenue that enables the programme to provide better and sustainable financial protection to insured members. The ratio of premium to health care costs covered by the programme varied from 0.47 in 2004–2005 to almost 0.88 in 2005–2006. It declined to 0.72 in 2009–2010 and 0.61 in 2013–2014 and 0.55 in 2017–2018. This denotes higher financial protection as the prepayment was less than claims. Nevertheless, the financial consequence of SSP was drastic. Insurance companies had to suffer heavy loss and SSP had to obtain funds from the MFI wing of SKDRDP to meet the deficit. If the programme continues to incur losses, it would dissuade insurance companies from issuing group policies to the members of SSP.

Financial sustainability improves by increasing the revenue collection or by curtailing the expenditure. Since the claim benefits and administrative expenses consume the revenue earned, there is a need to curb the claim benefits and cost of administration. Hence, to understand the viability of SSP, the study assessed the expenses involved in providing special benefits coverage. The administrative costs borne exclusively by SSP to provide insurance coverage was high in the initial two years (6.2% in 2004–2005, 6.1% in 2005–2006), but it declined by half in 2006–2007 (3.1%) and 2007–2008 (3.1%). It was 4.5% in 2010–2011. It reached a high level of 4.9% in 2013–2014, 5.5% in 2017–2018 owing to the higher cost of various resources. A reduction in administrative cost is highly needed given the low level of revenue collection and high claims ratios.

Nature of Contribution

SSP membership is voluntary for SHG members and their families. SSP did not coerce or put pressure on the SHG members to enroll in the programme. However, it insisted on the cash payments for the premium. Voluntary membership has positive and negative effects. It can encourage the adverse selection among the members as those with the pre-existing illness would join whereas healthy people would stay out. In contrast, compulsory membership would increase RM and FS due to an enlarged risk pool. However, an attempt to curtail adverse selection through compulsory membership for all SHG members' hampers market mechanism by limiting the opportunities available for them in government-sponsored low premium schemes, Universal Health Insurance Scheme, and Yeshasvini.

Subsidies for the Poor

There was no concession in the premium, irrespective of caste, religion, and income. This is regressive, as the poor will have to pay a higher percentage of annual income compared to the non-poor. SSP contracted with public sector insurance companies and removed the distinction between families below the poverty line and above the poverty line while determining the premium amount. Such a policy change might have adversely affected enrolment and RM. As the target population is poor in the informal sector, a regressive premium would discourage many to join SSP or renew their membership.

Technical Design Features Determining Enrolment

Coverage of target population as measured by enrolment depends on the certain technical design factors namely (i) affordability of contributions, (ii) unit of membership, (iii) distance to hospitals, (iv) timing of collection of premium, (v) quality of care, and (vi) trust in the scheme administration (Carrin et al., 2005).

Affordability of Premium
The premium charged by SSP was on average 1.17% of the annual income of the surveyed households. Despite the credit facility to pay the premium, coverage of the target population was low. In this regard, focus group discussion (FGD) held with SHG members had identified a lack of awareness on the borrowing facility in some *karyakshetras* as the primary reason for non-enrolment, in addition to a high level of premium (Savitha, 2017).

Unit of Membership
Another determinant of enrolment is the unit of membership. SSP insisted on family enrolment rather than individual memberships to encourage the participation of the entire household, also, to cross-subsidize the benefits of risk pooling. Larger pooling and cross-subsidization of the risk took place since the high risk as well the low-risk individuals in a family enrolled.

Timing of Premium Collection
Membership in SSP depends on the timing of the collection of premiums (monthly, quarterly, or yearly). SSP enrolment takes place in February of every year; hence, the timing of the collection of the premium is inflexible. SSP offered a credit facility to reduce the negative effect of inflexible schedules and seasonality of income on enrolment. The scheme allowed the borrowers (of loan to pay the premium) to repay along with weekly loan repayments (micro-credit) and savings. This not only brings down transaction costs but also improves the affordability of premiums. However, FGD identified inflexibility to be one of the reasons for non-enrolment. Whatever the impact of inflexibility on enrolment, there was a positive effect on the adverse selection (Savitha, 2017). Usually, the demand for health insurance will be high when an individual falls sick. If the enrolment can take place at any time, the possibility of adverse selection would be high as seen in SSP (Savitha & Banerjee, 2020).

Trust in SSP

SKDRDP enjoys clientele due to the trust in the competence of its management; hence, SSP could leverage the trust of its parent organization. Supportive field staff that was always available to provide information on the pre-authorization, network hospitals, and sanction of claim benefits strengthened the pre-existing trust. Hence, the staffs' responsiveness to non-medical expectations of members was high. The viability of SSP largely depends on people's confidence and trust in management. Since SSP enjoys the patronage of the religious temple and the trust of its members, it is in a better position to harness information and monitor the behaviour of members that enhances the viability of the programme.

Risk Pooling

Risk pooling is determined by trust in SSP management and the mechanisms of cross-subsidization that facilitate the transfer of income from rich to poor and risk from healthy to the sick. The risk pool of SSP in terms of membership consists mainly of poor families (70% of the target population was below the poverty line). This socially desirable objective has restricted the mobilization of resources and designing of a comprehensive benefits package since the poor cannot afford a high amount of premium.

Trust in the Management of SSP

Trust in the integrity and competence of the management of the programme has greatly contributed to the viability of SSP. Trust was built by providing adequate information on the programme, acting upon the feedback from the members by the management, member-friendly approach of field staff, and good rapport developed due to many years of association with SKDRDP microfinance programme.

Mechanisms to Enlarge the Risk Pool

Financial sustainability improves when the membership base expands. SSP aimed at the larger risk pool from the very start by targeting the population of the entire district rather than specific *taluks* that has not only enhanced risk pool but also gave rise to economies of scale in membership base, cost of administration, and transaction. SSP has penetrated newer markets in two districts where it launched a microfinance programme. However, enrolment in these newer districts seems to be low as SSP was novel to these members.

Adverse selection, moral hazard, and fraudulent activities due to the information asymmetry prevent cross-subsidization and a larger risk pool in any MHI scheme. SSP has implemented various fraud identification mechanisms namely inflexibility in the timing of enrolment, computerized identity card, verification of medical bills, limits on the benefits package, visits the hospitals by Sampoorna Suraksha assistants to verify the admission of members, and scrutiny of the pre-authorization procedure by SSP office. However, lack of screening for pre-existing illness and lack of waiting period to claim benefits increases the scope for information asymmetry. Nevertheless, the waiting period is not justifiable in SSP as the enrolment takes place only once a year. Such a qualifying period is required in schemes that are open throughout the year.

A study by Savitha and Banerjee (2020) reported that illness experience determined enrolment in SSP, risk pool consisted of households either experiencing chronic illness or got treated for an illness. However, it can be argued that adverse selection in SSP is welfare-promoting since the poorest section of the society either postpone health treatment or resort to home remedies and face substantial barriers to access medical care. Therefore, higher utilization denotes equality in access and better health status. This promotes the welfare of the poor individual and society in general. SSP curtailed moral hazard by a unique feature uncommon to other MHI schemes. The designated staff of SSP makes surprise visits to hospitals to check for fraud or prolonged stay in the hospital in addition to the verification of the admission and scrutinization of the identity card. In this way, impersonation to claim the benefit as a third party was difficult.

Strategic Purchasing

The purchasing of health care services is a vital function that includes contracting with the hospitals, deciding the payment mechanism, a system of referrals, and waiting period requirements. SSP practiced strategic purchasing to some extent. In addition to the routine payment of the hospital bills for specified services, SSP had a special contractual relationship with hospitals.

Selection of Network Hospitals

SSP adopted active purchasing based on the quality, accessibility, and cost criterion in selecting the network hospitals. SSP insured were more satisfied with the quality of health services (supplies, doctors, and physical infrastructure) compared to uninsured households (Savitha, 2018).

SSP carefully selects network hospitals based on certain criteria. It sends the information on the benefits package and price of care to the hospitals before the enrolment period. If the hospitals agreed to conditions specified in the agreement, a memorandum of understanding was signed between the project officers and the director of the hospital. The hospitals did not exert monopoly power during price and payment negotiations. If the terms of the contract were not agreeable, they could refuse to be part of network hospitals. The project officers removed the hospitals from the network that inflated medical bills or involved in fraudulent activities and did not take any action despite many reminders. Thus, moral hazard and fraudulent practices were curtailed. However, the lengthy and complex claim procedure would reduce enrolment since the majority of the target population comprises of less-educated individuals.

Claim Disbursement Procedure
Claim disbursement follows a predetermined procedure as shown in Fig. 3. The insurance company and medical team from the SSP office conduct audits and inspections to ensure quality medical care to the members of the scheme and to prevent the supplier and member moral hazard. The absence of a referral system would not result in overutilization of health care facilities due to the opportunity cost (indirect cost) associated with accessing health care. Supplier moral hazard on the part of hospitals was indirectly curtailed by persuading them to restrict the bill amount as per the contractual arrangements.

Benefit Package
Based on the target population's willingness to pay and ability to pay, SSP determined the premium. The benefits package was fixed considering the cost of health care services in the state of Karnataka. SSP provided the coverage of inpatient health services in the benefits package and excluded outpatient (OP) treatment and common ailments. One attractive feature of the benefits package was the inclusion of life risk, health risk, maternity treatment, and death compensation. There was a higher utilization of inpatient services by SSP insured households, and a reduction in OOPE (Savitha & Kiran, 2013) and CHE (Savitha & Kiran, 2015a). SSP brought about changes in health-seeking behaviour from home medicine to medical care at private health facilities (Savitha & Kiran, 2013). However, the real effectiveness of the benefits package was low since the cost of health care services has gone up drastically

whereas the amount of benefit did not change since inception. This was evidenced in the survey as some insured individuals had to rely on other risk coping strategies such as borrowing, sale of assets, and use of savings. However, it was observed that SSP insured borrowed less but no effect on the sale of assets or savings was noted (both amount and number of times) compared to uninsured (Savitha & Kiran, 2015b). Moreover, the borrowing was from non-usurious sources rather than moneylenders or any other usurious interest-bearing credit (Savitha & Kiran, 2016). Nevertheless, increasing the sum insured invariably necessitates a higher premium, which is not affordable by most of the target population. Albeit, SSP sanctions additional amount, higher than the sum insured, if the treatment was enormously expensive such as cancer, heart, and other vital organ surgeries. Also, the insured can get a loan from the '*Pragatibandhu*', the microfinance institution of SKDRDP to meet any expenses that exceed the insured amount. These additional provisions could remove some of the limitations of the benefits package.

2.2.2 *Management Characteristics*

Staff

The religious leader of the Dharmasthala temple (President) leads SKDRDP and the Board of Trustees manages its operations. Although directors and project officers do not have the management qualification, they have experience in implementing various socio-economic development programmes. Field staffs (*Sevanirathas*) motivate SHG members to enroll in SSP by educating them on the importance of health insurance. They monitor moral hazard behaviour due to the proximity to the members. Experienced management implements SSP using the administrative set-up of SKDRDP. The programme had staff with skills required to formulate benefit package, contract with providers, and process claims in addition to collecting premiums and creating awareness. SSP could make use of a pre-existing network of grass-root member households and a large team of field staff with the knowledge of local community and tradition. As SSP expands, complexity in administration and management would arise that necessitates investment in management information systems and professional training of the staff.

Culture

A hierarchical organization structure of SKDRDP has the President and Board of Trustees as the top-level management delegate the authority to four directors who supervise and guide project officers in each *valaya*. Project officers oversee the work of supervisors and field staff. The office staff carries out claims processing, maintaining accounts, and record keeping. Hierarchical structure stresses top-down management with the least participation of insured members in the management. President interacts continuously with staff that helps them to identify with the ideology and values of the SKDRDP such as charity, philanthropy, and mutual aid.

Access to Information

The monthly SHG joint meetings communicate the information on SSP namely benefits package, excluded diseases, claim procedure, nearby network hospitals, and rejection of claims to the members. It was observed that SHG members who were renewing the SSP membership had a higher level of awareness about benefits packages, excluded diseases, and network hospitals compared to newly insured members (Savitha & Kiran, 2012). Frequent information flows among the members and staff of SSP built trust and curtailed moral hazard to a great extent. The '*Jnana Vikasa*' Programme imparts knowledge to all the SHG members on various issues including health that removed non-financial barriers to access care.

SSP has a computerized data recording system at various regions that stores members' basic information and data on utilization of benefits (name of member and hospitals, duration of stay, amount of hospital bill, claims sanctioned and given). However, the *valaya* maintains the records and does not analyze them to assess the performance of the programme. Lack of MIS (management information system) would threaten the viability of SSP in the end when the programme expands to a large number of districts in Karnataka. Management and administration of a large risk pool require quick access to information. Hence, implementation of MIS becomes a necessity. To conclude, SSP has a parent organization that provides stable leadership, management skill, information systems, infrastructure, access to a rural network, and financial resources. This would enhance the viability of SSP.

2.2.3 *Organizational Characteristics*

Forms of Organization

Since SSP is embedded in SKDRDP, it could utilize the workforce, office infrastructure, and established network to provide MHI services resulting in a lower cost of operation. However, SSP had to incur the additional expense of medical staff who handled the pre-authorization procedure and operating/maintenance cost of computers and other office equipment in SSP head office. The economies of scale and scope were possible since the parent organization had a broad range of services namely micro-credit, bundled insurance, and savings. However, economies of scale did not increase resource mobilization and higher enrolment. The scope to increase enrolment is high since SKDRDP has a good clientele that can be motivated to join SSP for better viability and financial sustainability. Contractual agreements with the insurance companies and hospitals are the backbone of SSP in which the programme acts as Third Party Administrator (TPA) and manages the administration and implementation. These agreements make SSP viable as insurance companies absorbed the loss since inception and the hospitals strived to provide better care to insured members.

Incentive Regime

An exploration of the extent of the decision rights reveals that operations were decontrolled from the board. The Executive Director, the Executive Committee consisting of the directors and project officers managed the operations. Field supervisors and field staff were not involved in any major decision making. Office staff handled pre-authorization and claim settlement procedures and kept accurate member records including accounts. There is an audit wing to scrutinize the records of SSP, detect fraudulent activities, and prepare financial statements. A systematic and organized administrative framework made every staff accountable and responsible that has enhanced trust among members.

The main source of funds was the revenue collected from the members. External funding in the form of grants or donations or financial support from the government or other aid agencies was absent. Moreover, SSP did not maintain reserves that exposed the programme to higher financial risk. SSP has incurred a loss since inception, but parent organizations supported it, out of conviction. However, the threat of financial sustainability is impending due to declining enrolment resulting in inadequate resource mobilization and a high level of claims.

Linkages

Vertical integration through a contractual agreement with the providers could provide treatment to members at concessional rates. The Executive director in consultation with the insurance companies, Board of Trustees, and the President sets the contributions and determines the benefits package. The director of SSP guides the implementation through project officers who select the hospitals, contract with providers, and follow-up quality of care, and supervise the implementation.

The revenue of network hospitals increased significantly due to contractual relationships. However, insurance companies had to suffer huge losses due to high medical claims. Insurance companies enhanced the financial sustainability of SSP due to the underwriting of risks. Nevertheless, long-term viability is doubtful if these companies shy away from covering risks owing to lack of profitability.

2.2.4 *Institutional Characteristics*

Stewardship

The management of SSP and insurance companies without the intervention of local, state, or national government took up stewardship function. The government, both central and state, does not play any role in SSP programme design, risk coverage, or implementation. SSP collects the premium amount, transfers a part of it to the insurance companies, records members' data, implements pre-authorization procedure, and makes cashless payment to hospitals whereas insurance companies provide risk coverage, verify the pre-authorization forms, and disburse sanctioned claim amount to SSP. Thus, risk and servicing the clients are shared between SSP and insurance companies.

The top management consisting of the President, Board of Trustees, the executive director, and the SSP director take strategic decisions after consultation with the insurance companies. Project officers and supervisors take operational decisions and field staff implemented them. Regarding the regulation of SSP, IRDA (Micro-Insurance Regulations, 2005) establishes the rules and regulations that are abided by the insurance companies. This Act recognizes SHGs as the distribution agents who can carry out the functions of the premium collection, claims administration, and distribution of policies. Hence, SSP chose the partner–agent model in which SKDRDP acts as an agent for a partner (the insurance companies). Since private insurance companies have to tie up with MFIs or other channels to meet the statutory requirements, SSP seems viable for a long time.

Governance

SSP and insurance companies share the ownership and governance of the programme. Moreover, resource sharing and economies of scope and scale resulted in lower administrative costs. The objective of SSP is to provide financial protection against unforeseen contingencies and improve the access to health care services. The ownership and governance arrangements support the achievement of these objectives.

Insurance Markets

Insurance Regulatory and Development Authority of India (IRDAI) enacted Micro-Insurance Regulations (2005) that mandates insurance companies to mobilize at least seven percent of the net premium underwritten from the rural and informal sectors of India. Insurers have tied up with MFIs and NGOs to meet the statutory requirements to reduce transaction costs. These companies issue a negotiated custom-designed group insurance policy to SSP that include coverage for pre-existing illness. The custom-designed package meets the local needs of the target population and plays an important role in enrolment. Many private insurers or channel partners have not prioritized MHI due to low-profit potential and value addition to existing services. They do not consider it as either a commercial opportunity or as a social responsibility that gives their brands recognition. Even, MFIs hesitate to diversify into non-core activities like insurance. There are high barriers to enter the MHI market, which reduce competition in the current market. At the same time, its commitment to the welfare of the underprivileged people makes the exit from the market difficult.

Factor and Product Markets

Insurance products are less commoditized than in mature markets with a higher service component to the offering in emerging markets. Some of the challenges to be faced in these markets compared to mature markets include achieving adequate returns, incomplete information on risks (smaller pool of policyholders), a narrower range of products, lack of 'experience' databases, less deep financial markets, and less advanced risk management. A few government programmes that target the poor are Yeshasvini, UHS, and Ayushman Bharat Programme. SSP provides a bundled product covering the risks of health, life, and natural calamities and is entrenched in SKDRDP, thereby utilizes the outreach and experience in providing financial services to people. It is one of few MHI schemes in India having a membership base of over 10 lakh individuals. At present, SSP has little competition in the insurance market. Nevertheless, competition from other schemes cannot be ignored. In the factor markets, SSP must compete with other companies, which hire people with basic education. SSP hires local people who have completed 10 years of basic education and trains them.

Since the labour market is abundant with such people in Karnataka, cutthroat competition does not exist. It does not hire professional managers to perform various functions; instead uses internal promotions to fill these positions. SSP does not own hospitals to provide health services to members. Despite that, SSP has significant market power through a contract with providers that specify the quality of care and payment mechanism. Non-compliance with specifications of the contract can lead to the deletion of hospitals from the list of network hospitals. Thus, SSP has an indirect influence on the providers of health care.

3 Conclusion

Effective design and management are critical to the success of MHI schemes. Technical features of SSP such as credit facility to pay a premium, additional loan to insured members to meet medical expenses, bundling of medical and life insurance benefits, cashless treatment, higher benefit compared to other MHIs, and a wide network of network hospitals encouraged higher participation of the target population. Although enrolment in absolute number has increased, the growth in enrolment has declined over the years since inception. Despite the positive role of social capital (mutual help, solidarity, and concern for others) in enhancing enrolment, there was negative growth in the membership base. Certain undesirable design features like an increase in the premium, availability of cheaper options, removal of subsidies for the poorest families, inflexibility in the collection of premium, regressively charged premium and low benefit amount can be attributed to a decline in participation rates. However, the credit facility to pay the premium removed many of the design constraints.

Regressive premium, lack of subsidy coupled with low income resulted in the exclusion of poorest target population from enrolment, especially poor (especially in seasonal occupation) could not afford the premium. SSP members from the poorer households had to spend 2.2% of annual household income to pay the premium. Thus, the design of SSP aimed at rural middle-income class than the poor since certain features like the absence of a sliding scale, exemption policy, payment-in-kind, and flat rate of the premium limited the participation of the poor in SSP.

SSP acted as a strategic purchaser of the health services largely by negotiating the price of care with providers and selecting the hospitals with basic facilities. It monitored the provider's behaviour through pre-authorization requirements that checked the line of treatment, probable cost, the prescriptions, and quality of care provided to their members before effecting payment. This curtailed moral hazard (from members) and fraudulent practices to a large extent. However, it did not attempt to improve the quality of care, except for the selection of the hospitals with basic facilities. Certain strategic mechanisms namely gatekeeping and drug formularies, referral practice, providing financial incentives, and financial incentives to encourage insured to use particular providers were absent. It did not negotiate favourable prices for the essential drugs. Since the primary care and referral system was ignored, members were motivated to be hospitalized even for an acute illness that resulted in high claims.

Lack of gatekeeper mechanism was another factor responsible for high claims. Since SSP does not insist on standard treatment protocols (and drug formularies and physician profiling), has complex claims and administrative processes, and pays on a fee-for-service basis, there was a greater scope for cost escalation and moral hazard in the form of higher incentive to over-service and over-prescribe. However, the adverse effect was curtailed by monitoring service utilization by the members and removing the fraudulent hospitals from the network. It should be recognized that a scheme would not sustain financially if a strict referral system or gatekeeping is not practiced. SSP can use the primary health centre and tier system of the Indian health care system to implement gatekeeping.

The enrolment of members as a percent of the target population has declined over the years; thereby the risk pool has shrunk jeopardizing the financial sustainability and viability of SSP. The insufficient revenue collection resulted in high claims ratio and huge losses since inception. Even with the high claims, financial protection was partial owing to the low benefit package (INR 5000), which was unchanged despite an increase in the cost of medical treatment. Hence, insured members had to incur out of pocket expenses, hardship financing, and adopt risk coping strategies. Increasing the benefits package is not a solution to partial financial protection. This necessitates a higher premium that adversely influences enrolment. If premium increases, people with low health risk would refrain from enrolment giving rise to adverse selection. Besides, the poorest would stay away from the programme. Hence, a tradeoff is required that balances financial sustainability and risk pool. However, SSP has an advantage over other MHI scheme since it is nested within a broader development programme with adequate financial resources that can bail out SSP in times of trouble.

Households as the unit of enrolment, inflexible period of enrolment, and better information flow among members due to proximity reduced selective enrolment of ill persons in the family, especially enrolment after illness and adverse selection. Being embedded in SKDRDP, SSP enjoys clientele due to faith in the integrity and competence of management. Senior management of SSP was committed to the programme and determined to continue it out of conviction, despite financial difficulties. Moreover, SKDRDP increased the income of poor families in its area of operation through micro-finance and other developmental activities. This enhanced the ability and willingness of SHG members to enroll in SSP. Since SSP met their priority needs (health), readiness to participate, and support the programme was high.

The member orientation and strong community networks facilitate the viability of SSP. Some of the management factors that shaped the success of SSP are contracting with providers, determining the appropriateness of care provided and its pricing, accounting and bookkeeping, monitoring and evaluation, peoples' confidence and trust in the management. Relevant information disseminated to members in the monthly SHG meetings conveyed transparency and trust that the premium amount belonged to members' betterment. This positively shaped the renewal and enrolment decisions of members and indirectly increased resource mobilization. However, certain hindrances namely lack of professional management with requisite skills in marketing, and communication, actuarial science, lack of member participation in the management and negotiation with providers for the better quality of care would affect the programme adversely. Besides, the management of data and the creation of an electronic database were insufficient. This would limit the revenue collection, containment of administrative costs, and quality of health services.

Organizational characteristics of the scheme such as contractual linkages between SSP and providers stipulated the nature and scope of the services the providers should offer to the members. Thus, yearly contracts ensured flexibility to change the providers (include or delete from the list of network hospitals) based on their performance. Even the contractual relationship with insurance companies defined the role and responsibilities of the parties concerned. The insurance companies absorbed the loss of the medical component of the benefits package; which ensures the viability of the programme for a long time.

Parent organization SKDRDP facilitated resource sharing and economies of scope and scale. The offering of MHI services through partner–agent and mutual model leveraged the trust that MFI enjoys among SHG members and enhanced the enrolment of the target population. Moreover, bundling the insurance services with credit or savings and using the existing infrastructure to provide service and collect premium reduced administrative cost. Regular auditing of the financial records and preparation of publicly available annual reports helped to build up the credibility.

The premium was the main source of funds. SSP did not seek external financial assistance or aid to cover the losses of a special component of the benefits package. Hence, the threat of financial sustainability looms around the programme due to the high level of claims, inadequate RM, and lack of external funding.

The government did not play a stewardship role by providing subsidies or administrative assistance to SSP. Insurance companies or SSP played the stewardship role by sharing the risk of coverage and servicing the clients. Moreover, the government did not monitor, regulate, and accredit the providers; hence, SSP developed the technical skills to conduct these activities. SSP and the insurance companies jointly had ownership and governance responsibilities. This facilitates resource sharing and economies of scale and scope.

The competition in the job market was not as intense as there was a surplus of labour with the required qualification. Competition in the health care market becomes irrelevant since SSP does not own all the network hospitals to provide health care facilities to the members. The competition in the MHI market was minimal as the high level of entry and exit barriers to the MHI market would prevent a large number of players from entering the industry. However, SSP has to face the threat from the recently introduced schemes of other MFIs and government schemes.

Taken together, these results suggest that SSP is viable owing to (i) Nesting within SKDRDP (ii) Tie up with insurance companies (iii) Dedicated staff and management (iv) High potential for greater penetration. However, the self-financing of SSP is limited due to several features;

limited population coverage, low-cost recovery rates, and membership limited to poorest groups. Unless these issues are addressed, SSP cannot be considered as an exclusive health-financing alternative, rather it can be considered as a supporting mechanism that complements the government efforts to provide health care to all the population. Nevertheless, history is full of examples of religious bodies that have successfully established institutions to develop the target communities in India. SKDRDP must capitalize on its monopoly in many parts of rural Karnataka to make SSP a self-financing MHI scheme.

References

Ahmed, M. U., Islam, S. K., Quashem, M., & Ahmed, N. (2005). *Health micro insurance: A comparative study of the three examples in Bangladesh* (CGAP Good and Bad Practices Case Study No. 13). ILO Social Finance Programme. Available at https://www.ilo.org/employment/Whatwedo/Publications/WCMS_122468/lang--en/index.htm.

Baeza, C., Montenegro, F., & Nunez, M. (2002). *Extending social protection in health through community based health organisations: Evidence and challenge*. International Labour Organisation. Available at https://www.ilo.org/public/english/protection/socsec/step/download/101p1.pdf.

Bennett, S. (2004). The role of community-based health insurance within the health care financing system: A framework for analysis. *Health Policy and Planning, 19*(3), 147–158.

Carrin, G., Waelkens, M., & Criel, B. (2005). Community-based health insurance in developing countries: A study of its contribution to the performance of health financing systems. *Tropical Medicine and International Health, 10*(8), 799–811.

De Allegri, M., Kouyate, B., Becher, H., Gbangou, A., Pokhrel, S., Sanon, M., et al. (2006). Understanding enrolment in community health insurance in sub-Saharan Africa: A population-based case-control study in rural Burkina Faso. *Bulletin of World Health Organization, 84*(11), 852–858.

Dercon, S., Bold, T., & Calvo, C. (2004). *Insurance for the poor?* (QEH Working Paper Series—QEHWPS125, Working Paper Number 125). University of Oxford. http://www3.qeh.ox.ac.uk/pdf/qehwp/qehwps125.pdf

Devadasan, N., Ranson, M. K., Damme, W. V., Acharya, A., & Criel, B. (2006). The landscape of community health insurance in India: An overview based on 10 case studies. *Health Policy, 78*, 224–234.

Ekman, B. (2004). Community-based health insurance in low-income countries: A systematic review of the evidence. *Health Policy and Planning, 19*(5), 249–270.

Jakab, M., & Krishnan, C. (2001). *Community involvement in health care financing: A survey of the literature on the impacts, strengths and weaknesses* (Health, Nutrition, and Population Family [HNP] Discussion Paper Series). World Bank. Available at https://openknowledge.worldbank.org/bitstream/handle/10986/13706/288850Jakab1Community0Involvement1whole.pdf?sequence=1&isAllowed=y.

McCord, M., & Osinde, S. (2005). Reducing vulnerability: The supply of health microinsurance in East Africa. *Journal of International Development, 17*(3), 327–381.

Ministry of Health and Family Welfare. (2017, October). *National health accounts: Estimates for India 2014–15*. https://mohfw.gov.in/sites/default/files/National%20Health%20Accounts%20Estimates%20Report%202014-15.pdf

Mladovsky, P., & Mossialos, E. (2008). A conceptual framework for community-based health insurance in low-income countries: Social capital and economic development. *World Development, 36*(4), 590–607.

Ouimet, M., Fournier, P., Diop, I., & Haddad, S. (2007). Solidarity or financial sustainability an analysis of the values of community-based health insurance subscribers and promoters in Senegal. *Canadian Journal of Public Health, 98*(4), 341–346.

Pauly, M. V., Zweifel, P., Scheffler, R. M., Preker, A. S., & Bassett, M. (2006). Private health insurance in developing countries. *Health Affairs, 25*(2), 369–379.

Polonsky, J., Balabanova, D., McPake, B., et al. (2008). Equity in community health insurance schemes: Evidence and lessons from Armenia. *Health Policy and Planning, 24*(3), 209–216.

Preker, A. S., Carrin, G., Dror, D. M., Jakab, M., Hsiao, W., & Arhin-Tenkorang, D. (2002). Effectiveness of community health financing in meeting the cost of illness. *Bulletin of World Health Organization, 80*(2), 143–150.

Preker, A. S., Carrin, G., Dror, D., Jakab, M., Hsiao, W., & Arhin-Tenkorang, D. (2004). Rich-poor differences in health care financing. In A. S. Preker & G. Carrin (Eds.), *Health financing for poor people: Resource mobilization and risk sharing* (pp. 3–51). World Bank. Available at https://openknowledge.worldbank.org/bitstream/handle/10986/15019/289860PAPER0Health0financing010the0poor.pdf?sequence=1&isAllowed=y.

Ranson, K. M. (2002). Reduction of catastrophic health care expenditures by a community-based health insurance scheme in Gujarat, India: Current experiences and challenges. *Bulletin of World Health Organization, 80*(8), 613–621.

Sampoorna Suraksha Program. (2019). https://sampoornasuraksha.org/

Savitha, B. (2014). Effect of micro health insurance on access and utilization of health services in Karnataka. *Open Medicine Journal, 1*, 96–103. https://doi.org/10.2174/1874220301401010096

Savitha, B. (2017). Why members dropout? An evaluation of factors affecting renewal in micro health insurance. *Journal of Health Management, 19*(2), 292–303.

Savitha, B. (2018). Sources of care selection and health care quality perceptions: Does health insurance matter in patient satisfaction? *Institutions and Economies, 10*(2), 95–120.

Savitha, B., & Banerjee, S. (2020). Education and experience as determinants of micro health insurance enrolment. *International Journal of Health Policy and Management, 10* (4), 192–200. https://doi.org/10.34172/ijhpm.2020.44

Savitha, B., & Kiran, K. B. (2012). Awareness and knowledge of micro health insurance: A case study. *Journal of Health Management, 14*(4), 481–494.

Savitha, B., & Kiran, K. B. (2013). Health Seeking Behaviour in Karnataka: Does Micro Health Insurance matter? *Indian Journal of Community Medicine, 38*(4), 217–222.

Savitha, B., & Kiran, K. B. (2015a). Effectiveness of micro health insurance on financial protection: Evidence from India. *International Journal of Health Economics and Management, 15*(1), 53–71.

Savitha, B., & Kiran, K. B. (2015b). Micro health Insurance and the risk coping strategies for the management of illness in Karnataka: A case study. *International Journal of Health Planning and Management, 30*(1), 145–163.

Savitha, B., & Kiran, K. B. (2016). Illness makes credit sick: Can health insurance rescue the poor from exploitative credit? *The Geneva Papers on Risk and Insurance- Issues and Practice, 41*(2), 184–204.

Waters, H., Morlock, L., & Hatt, L. (2004). Quality-based purchasing in health care. *International Journal of Health Planning and Management, 19*(4), 365–381.

Wiesmann, D., & Jutting, J. (2001). Determinants of viable health insurance schemes in rural sub-Saharan Africa. *Quarterly, Journal of International Agriculture, 40*(4), 361–378.

World Health Organization. (2000). *The world health report: Health systems-improving performance*. World Health Organization. Available at https://apps.who.int/iris/bitstream/handle/10665/42281/WHR_2000-eng.pdf?sequence=1&isAllowed=y.

Zhang, L., Cheng, X., Tolhurst, R., Tang, S., & Liu, X. (2010). How effectively can the New Cooperative Medical Scheme reduce catastrophic health expenditure for the poor and non- poor in rural China? *Tropical Medicine and International Health, 15*(4), 468–475.

Assessing the Performance of Primary Agricultural Credit Societies: A Non-traditional Multi-Dimensional Index Approach

Amitabha Bhattacharyya and Abhijit Sinha

1 Introduction

1.1 Background of the Study

The history of Indian co-operative movement is more than a century old. The cooperative movement had been started in the country for providing mutual help among people and encouraging the people to engage them in agriculture and also help the poor people to release them from the clutches of the informal money lenders who charged exorbitant rates of interest. In India, the first Cooperative Societies Act was passed in 1904 which was based on the English Friendly Societies Act, 1896. According to the Act, only the Primary Credit Societies were permitted to register and disburse credit among the rural people. After independence, there were different Acts and Committees set up to appraise the cooperative

A. Bhattacharyya (✉)
Balurghat College, Balurghat, West Bengal, India

A. Sinha
Vidyasagar University, Midnapore, West Bengal, India

Ananda S. and D. Singh (eds.), *Financial Inclusion in Emerging Markets*,
https://doi.org/10.1007/978-981-16-2652-4_7

sector. The sector, in particular, has tremendous relevance in the development of a country like India where almost 55% of the population is dependent on agriculture and allied activities. Though the secondary and tertiary sectors have been playing a dominating role in respect of their contribution to GDP, agricultural sector still contributes almost 17%.

In this context, it can therefore be easily presumed that majority of the households depend on farming for their regular needs. Moreover, there is a substantial portion of households even today who continue to rely on the informal sector for their financial needs which has been consistently on the rise due to technological advancement in agriculture, greater commercialization and use of modern amenities to improve the productivity of land and labour. In this backdrop, the significance of the sector can be imagined.

1.2 Preliminary Information about PACS

The pyramidal structure of the Short-Term Co-operative Credit Structure (STCCS) in India has three-tiers with the State Co-operative Banks (SCBs) at the top, the District Co-operative Banks (DCBs) in the middle and Primary Agricultural Credit Societies (PACS) at the lowest level. The PACS operate mainly in the rural areas and villages, DCBs work at the district headquarters and the State SCBs located in the state capitals. The Reserve Bank of India (RBI) funds the co-operative banks through NABARD in the form of general lines of credit for lending towards promoting agricultural credit and allied activities in the country. The PACS which is the focus of the study operate in the rural areas provide credit for agricultural purposes to the village people. In the Indian context, the role of the lowest tier is vital for the sustainability in agricultural operations at the ground level. The main purpose of PACS is to provide agricultural credit for the short and medium term.

1.3 Need of the Study

In any credit disbursement system, it is not just credit flow which is important but also the way it is utilized. The present study assesses the relative position of the lowest-tier institutions in selected districts of West Bengal. The investigation is undertaken in the background of several lacunae observed in these institutions some of which include inequity in credit distribution, improper management, excessive government interference, piling up of poor-quality loans and untimely audit of financial statements. With such problems, it is appealing to investigate the relative position of PACS in respect of performance in a state like West Bengal which is still substantially dependent on agriculture for the growth of the state. The findings will help to identify the districts which need focus for improvement of the performance of these financial intermediaries.

1.4 Objectives of the Study

The main objectives of the study are:

- To assess the relative ranking position of the PACS under selected DCBs of West Bengal, and
- To assess whether there is any significant difference in respect of ranking of the PACS operating under North and South Bengal.

2 Review of Literature

It is true that several studies have already been conducted on the co-operative banking sector. However, the contribution to the field of PACS is minimal. The summary of articles reviewed is discussed. The studies cover assessment of financial performance of PACS by looking at the aspects of liquidity, operations, productivity, profitability, stability and recovery performance. Few attempts are also made on the performance of PACS in respect of parameters like working capital, outstanding loans, business turnover, overdues, net worth and loans. It is revealed from the study that the performance of few PACS are good in respect of the above parameters but there is a serious lacuna in the performance of PACS because from the majority of them running into losses (Cahalam & Prasad, 2007; Das, 2013; Kulandaiswamy & Murugesan, 2004; Thirupathi, 2013).The analysis conducted on the financial viability, efficiency, productivity and profitability performance of DCCBs in different areas of India reveals inconsistency in their performance. The two key problems are financial mismanagement and underutilization of resources (Asher, 2007; Chander & Chandel, 2010; Dutta & Basak, 2008; Jain, 2001; Shah, 2007; Singh & Sukhmani, 2011; Selvaraj, 2013). Few studies which are made in the area of financial inclusion and performance prospects of microfinance of rural co-operatives appreciate the good performance of these institutions (Mukherjee, 2011; Rachana, 2011).There are also contributions that look into the aspect of management of non-performing assets of the state cooperative bank and rural cooperative banks in India. The studies reveal unsatisfactory performance of the cooperative banks in this regard and the poor management of poor-quality loans (Basak, 2009; Rakshit & Chakrabarti, 2012; Ratna & Nimbalkar, 2011). The study by Ghosh et al. (2018) looks at the performance of PACS in Nadia district from the perspective of inclusion, efficiency and social responsibility. An interesting contribution on the recovery performance of the loans offered by PACS to the rural customers is seen in the writing of Mazumder et al. (2014) which finds the northern region to be the best performer and North–East as the worst. The study by Mishra (2009) looks at the recovery aspect in addition to identification of the factors that lead to the unstable economic condition of these lowest-tier institutions. The two key factors are the government's share in the capital and the low number of non-borrowing members. Sinha and Bhattacharyya (2019) assess the position of PACS from the aspect of total factor productivity. The prospects of PACS in the country have been studied by Kumar and Mehta (2018) where they mention the key role of these institutions in an agriculture-dependent economy like ours. For a better understanding, the following sub-sections are designed.

2.1 Summarization of the Literature Review

The observations from the previous studies on cooperative banking and PACS are summarized here under:

1. Investigation on the instability of PACS.
2. Analysis of the decadal growth of PACS, State Co-operative Banks and Urban Co-operative Banks in India.
3. Study on the financial performance of PACS in a few selected states of the country.
4. Evaluation of the role of PACS in promoting agri-business of farmers.
5. Study on the Recovery performance of rural credit given by PACS in different regions of India.

2.2 Research Gap

From the above literature reviews, it is evident that there are substantial number of studies and research contributions on the role and performance of cooperative banks. Most of these assess the position in respect of trend in their business and growth of non-performing assets. However, the researchers get scope to investigate the position of PACS as the number of researches is far less than what is seen in the assessment of DCCBs. This study is among the few investigations that use the index method to appraise the performance of these lowest-tier financial institutions and assess their relative position.

3 Research Design

The contribution from any research is dependent to a large extent on the appropriateness of the approach taken by the researchers. Hence, we discuss the different aspects of the research design.

3.1 ***Sample size and sample design***: The present study is based on PACS that operate under thirteen DCBs of West Bengal. The criterion for selecting the sample is based on the extent of business (which is a proxy for size) and whether data is available for all the years of the study period.

3.2 ***Data period:*** The researchers consider a study period of ten years starting from 2008 to 2017.

3.3 ***Data type and source:*** The analysis uses published/secondary data which are available from the various annual reports that are released annually by the State Cooperative Bank during their conference which is held every year.

3.4 ***Research Methodology***: As the focus of the study is on evaluating the performance of PACS, a credit institution, the researchers apply a holistic approach to encapsulate the different performance variables together into a shell so that a better assessment can be done. The investigators apply the weighted index method to determine the weighted score of the PACS of the selected districts for each year of the study period. The methodology applied is like that of the preparation of Human Development Index, though with a minor difference. The difference is that for this empirical study the weights are not arbitrary chosen. Instead, it is the data-driven weight obtained from factor analysis which is then used for computation purpose. For the purpose of this investigation, four dimensions are considered which include:

a. Deposits
b. Loans
c. Investments
d. Membership strength

The Multidimensional index (MDI) is calculated as follows:

$$\begin{aligned} MDI_i = \; & w_1 . \text{ Index for variable } 1 \; + \\ & w_2 . \text{ Index for variable } 2 \; + \\ & w_3 . \text{ Index for variable } 3 \; + \\ & w_4 . \text{ Index for variable } 4 \end{aligned} \quad (1)$$

The index for dimension '1' for PACS of district 'i' is computed as—

$$(\text{Actual value}_{1i} - \text{Minimum value}_1)/(\text{Maximum value}_1 - \text{Minimum value}_1)$$

The index for dimension '2' for PACS of district 'i' is computed as—

$$(\text{Actual value}_{2i} - \text{Minimum value}_2)/(\text{Maximum value}_2 - \text{Minimum value}_2)$$

The index for dimension '3' for PACS of district 'i' is computed as—

$$(\text{Actual value}_{3i} - \text{Minimum value}_3)/(\text{Maximum value}_3 - \text{Minimum value}_3)$$

The index for dimension '4' for PACS of district 'i' is computed as—

$$(\text{Actual value}_{4i} - \text{Minimum value}_4)/(\text{Maximum value}_4 - \text{Minimum value}_4)$$

In Eq. (1), the value of w_i s ($i = 1$ to 4) used for the different variables is obtained by applying factor analysis as mentioned above. Hence, this methodological difference from the earlier makes the approach more objective thereby removing the subjectivity element which is present in the earlier approaches.

4 Findings and Analysis

In this section of the paper, the researchers analys e and discuss the findings in respect of the relative ranking of the PACS in different districts of West Bengal. The index is constructed to determine the rank of the districts in different years which are then used to see whether a similar pattern of ranking follows. For the purpose, the Kendall's tau test is applied. The table for the ranks is given below.

4.1 Analysis of Multivariable Index of PACS Operating Under Different DCBs

The detail of the results of the multi-variable index is given below.

If one looks at the index values, one can understand that the PACS operating under the District Cooperative Banks of Tamluk-Ghatal, VCCB, Burdwan and Nadia are the outperformers. On the contrary, the position of PACS under the DCBs of Raiganj, Purulia, Malda, Jalpaiguri and Dakshin Dinajpur is dismal and they form the poor performers group. It is further revealed from the index value of different districts that most of the PACS under DCBs do not show a major change in the weighted index score (refer to Table 1). In other words, in respect of relative performance, the position remains the same during the entire study period. The change takes place in only a few cases.

4.2 Rank of PACS in Respect of Multivariable Index

On the basis of the index value computed in table 1, the ranking is done following descending order with the highest score being assigned a rank of one, the second highest as rank of two and so on (Table 2).

The table gives an interesting result about the relative position of PACS under the different DCBs. It is clear from the table that the PACS of the following DCBs led in terms of overall performance which include Tamluk-Ghatal District Cooperative Bank, Nadia District Cooperative Bank, Burdwan District Cooperative Bank and Vidyasagar Central Cooperative Bank (VCCB). On the contrary, the ones that stand at the bottom are Jalpaiguri, Dakshin Dinajpur, Purulia and Malda. Another noticeable point is the relatively low change in the ranks of different PACS over the years. Thus, the good ones continue to hold on to that position whereas the poor ones continue to suffer.

Table 1 Multivariable score of different districts of PACS in different districts

Districts	*2008*	*2009*	*2010*	*2011*	*2012*	*2013*	*2014*	*2015*	*2016*	*2017*
Bankura	0.445	0.447	0.386	0.377	0.465	0.468	0.440	0.411	0.314	0.326
Burdwan	0.954	0.942	0.619	0.847	0.937	1.000	0.776	0.930	0.700	0.736
Dakshin Dinajpur	0.033	0.044	0.035	0.022	0.019	0.023	0.018	0.019	0.016	0.015
Howrah	0.426	0.455	0.491	0.515	0.435	0.406	0.398	0.430	0.334	0.338
Jalpaiguri	0.014	0.024	0.031	0.028	0.016	0.016	0.019	0.011	0.008	0.008
Malda	0.207	0.125	0.021	0.186	0.195	0.243	0.225	0.241	0.191	0.222
Mugberia	0.141	0.169	0.186	0.182	0.203	0.268	0.266	0.265	0.274	0.294
Murshidabad	0.476	0.535	0.478	0.460	0.508	0.666	0.655	0.680	0.552	0.618
Nadia	0.630	0.724	0.836	0.739	0.884	0.941	1.000	1.000	0.856	0.972
Purulia	0.114	0.157	0.158	0.120	0.139	0.213	0.130	0.158	0.074	0.079
Raiganj	0.211	0.227	0.253	0.210	0.243	0.249	0.208	0.128	0.145	0.151
Tamluk-Ghatal	1.000	1.000	1.000	1.000	1.000	0.934	0.902	0.888	1.000	1.000
VCCB	0.786	0.831	0.836	0.678	0.779	0.895	0.797	0.824	0.674	0.730

Source Computed by researcher

Table 2 Rank of PACS under DCCBs in terms of multivariable index

Districts	*2008*	*2009*	*2010*	*2011*	*2012*	*2013*	*2014*	*2015*	*2016*	*2017*
Bankura	6	7	7	7	7	6	1	6	7	7
Burdwan	2	2	4	2	2	2	6	4	3	3
Dakshin Dinajpur	12	12	11	13	13	12	12	13	12	12
Howrah	7	6	5	5	5	7	7	7	6	6
Jalpaiguri	13	13	12	12	12	13	13	12	13	13
Malda	9	11	13	9	9	10	10	9	9	9
Mugberia	10	9	9	10	10	9	8	8	8	8
Murshidabad	5	5	6	6	6	5	5	5	5	5
Nadia	4	4	3	3	3	3	2	1	2	2
Purulia	11	10	10	11	11	11	11	11	11	11
Raiganj	8	8	8	8	8	8	9	10	10	10
Tamluk-Ghatal	1	1	1	1	1	1	3	2	1	1
VCCB	3	3	2	4	4	4	4	3	4	4

Source Computed by researcher

4.3 *Kendal's Tau Coefficient*

In this section, the researchers statistically measure the value of correlation using Kendall's tau, the data being ordinal (or ordered data). The value of correlation is found to be 0.939 which is significant at 1% level. Thus, it is evident that the relative position of PACS of different districts remains almost the same. In other words, there is no statistically significant change in the relative position of PACS of the different districts. Hence, from the study, it can be commented that the PACS continue to hold on to their positions. In other words, the weaker PACS continue to remain weak, whereas the good performers continue to dominate.

5 Conclusions

The researchers focus on the lowest-tier of the three-tier pyramidal structure of the cooperative banking system. The study looks at the position of Primary Agricultural Credit Societies by adapting a holistic approach. In this approach, several performance variables are considered which are then used to develop an index for the PACS of each of the districts. This is done to understand the relative position of the PACS so that one can know which the better-performing districts are and also the laggards. The computation of the index value for the districts and their ranking pattern shows that the PACS operating under Tamluk-Ghatal District Cooperative Bank, Nadia District Cooperative Bank, Burdwan District Cooperative Bank and Vidyasagar Central Cooperative Bank (VCCB) show a better overall performance in contrast to the poor show put in by the PACS under the district cooperative banks of Jalpaiguri, Dakshin Dinajpur, Purulia and Malda. Another pertinent point that the research identifies is that there is no significant change in the relative position of the PACS which thereby points to the fact that the poor performing PACS continue to remain weak, whereas the good performers continue to dominate. Hence, this finding is interesting and calls for introspection by the managers of the district cooperative banks to understand how they can better manage the functioning of the primary agricultural credit societies.

5.1 *Limitations of the Study*

The limitation of the study is that the investigation is done on the PACS under thirteen district cooperative banks out of seventeen banks and the

PACS under Balageria Central Cooperative Bank Ltd., Birbhum District Central Cooperative Bank Ltd., Darjeeling District Central Cooperative Bank Ltd. and Hooghly District Central Cooperative Bank Ltd are not considered for the study due to non-availability of data in majority of years.

5.2 *Scope for Further Study*

There is further scope for researchers where they can also investigate the productivity assessment of the selected PACS. That would also be a unique approach towards assessing these rural-based agricultural focused institutions.

References

Asher, M. G. (2007). Reforming governance and regulation of urban cooperative banks in India. *Journal of Financial Regulation and Compliance, 15*(1), 20–29.

Basak, A. (2009). Performance appraisal of urban cooperative banks: A case study. *The IUP Journal of Accounting Research and Audit Practices, VII*(1), 31–44.

Chalam, G. V., & Prasad, A. (2007). An evaluation of financial performance of cooperative societies in Andhra Pradesh (A study of selected PACS in West Godavari district). *Indian Cooperative Review, 45*(1), 42–58.

Chander, R., & Chandel, J. K. (2010). Financial viability and performance evaluation of co-operative credit institutions in Haryana (India). *International Journal of Computing and Business Research, 1*(1), 1–22.

Das, T. (2013). An evaluation of performance of the West Bengal state cooperative bank Ltd.. *International Journal of Research in Commerce & Management*, *4*(2) (February), 131–136.

Dutta, U., & Basak, A. (2008). Appraisal of financial performance of urban cooperative banks—A case study. *The Management Accountant*, *43*(3) (March), 170–174.

Ghosh, P. K., Mitra, A., & Sarkar, S. (2018). An appraisal of performance of Primary Agricultural Cooperative Societies (PACS) in Nadia District of West Bengal. *Economic Affairs, 63*(4), 891–896.

Jain. (2001). Comparative study of performance of District Central Co-Operative Banks (DCCBs) of Western India i.e. Maharashtra, Gujarat & Rajasthan for the year 1999–2000 from the point of view of net profit/loss. *NAFSCOB Bulletin* (April–June).

Kulandaiswamy, V., & Murugesan, P. (2004). Performance of PACS—An empirical evaluation. *Indian Cooperative Review, 42*(2), 122–130.

Kumar, M., & Mehta, V. P. (2018). Performance and Prospects of Primary Agricultural Credit Societies (PACS) in Haryana during 2000–01 to 2014–15. *International Journal of Current Microbiology and Applied Sciences, 7*(4), 20–32.

Mazumder, R., Chakravarty, C., & Bhandari, A. K. (2014). *Recovery performance of primary agriculture credit societies in India: An assessment*. IZA Discussion Paper No. 8294, 1–19.

Mishra, B. S. (2009). Research on performance of credit cooperatives. *Research World, 6*(S6), 5.

Mukherjee, S. (2011). Microfinance through cooperatives: Performance and prospects. *International Journal of Research in Commerce, Economics & Management*, *1*(7) (November), 102–106.

Rachana, T. (2011). Financial inclusion and performance of rural co-operative banks in Gujarat. *Research Journal of Finance and Accounting, 2*(6), 40–50.

Rakshit, D., & Chakrabarti, S. (2012). NPA management of rural cooperative banks of West Bengal: An overview. *Business Spectrum*, *1*(3) (January–June), 1–39.

Ratna & Nimbalkar, K. (2011). A study of NPA's—Reference to urban co-operative bank. *Golden Research Thoughts*, *1*(VI) (December).

Selvaraj, A. (2013). Cooperative bank's performance in Tamil Nadu. *Asia Pacific Journal of Marketing & Management Review*, *2*(6) (June), 95–101.

Shah, D. (2007). Evaluating financial health of credit cooperatives in Maharashtra State of India. *University Library of Munich, Germany*, MPRA Paper-3949 (July).

Singh, G., & Sukhmani. (2011). An analytical study of productivity and profitability of district central cooperative banks in Punjab. *Journal on Banking Financial services and Insurance Research*, *1*(3) (June), 128–142.

Sinha, A., & Bhattacharyya, A. (2019). Productivity growth assessment of primary agricultural credit societies in West Bengal. *Asian Journal of Multidimensional Research*, *8*(6) (June), 275–284.

Thirupathi, T. (2013). An analysis of financial performance of select primary agricultural cooperative credit societies in Mettur Taluk, Salem District. *Research Front, 1*(1), 19–24.

Micro-Financing and Online Banking

Are Indian Microfinance Institutions Efficient? A Two-Stage Double Bootstrapped DEA Based Analysis

Shailja Agarwal and Pankaj K. Agarwal

1 Introduction

Microfinance is an economic conduit targeting poverty alleviation. Inter-alia, it comprises extending small loans to low-income band of the population. In contrast to charity, it aims to assist the poor to work their way out of poverty. It also serves as a tool to achieve objectives of national policies centered on women empowerment, improving lives of the marginalized, bringing people out of poverty and creation of meaningful livelihoods.

However, entities (Microfinance Institutions or MFIs) providing microfinance services cannot achieve these social goals if they are inefficiently run. The quest to bring in more efficiency in MFI has led to; for one; evolution of their organization structure over the years. For example, in the early days of Microfinance in India, most MFIs were cooperative

S. Agarwal
Institute of Management Technology, Ghaziabad, India
e-mail: sagarwal@imt.edu

P. K. Agarwal (✉)
Finance and Accounting, Indian Institute of Management, Jammu, India
e-mail: pankaj@iimj.ac.in

Ananda S. and D. Singh (eds.), *Financial Inclusion in Emerging Markets*,
https://doi.org/10.1007/978-981-16-2652-4_8

societies whereas the modern MFI is more likely to be a Non-Banking Finance Company (NBFC).[1] This phenomenon is not limited to India. Yaron et al. (1997) report that many states started to initiate prudent fiscal and monetary policies, an enabling legislative framework and innovative financing to aid the operations of MFIs (Wijesiri et al., 2015). The famous Microfinance Triangle by Zeller and Meyer (2002) adds "Impact" as the third goal of MFIs in addition to social outreach and financial sustainability.

However, of late, questions are being raised on the governance of MFIs (Servin et al., 2012). A related issue is which MFIs do well and which do not. Many studies have been conducted worldwide to examine how efficiently MFIs have achieved their social as well as financial goals.

In this study, we examine both social and financial efficiency of Indian MFIs in a robust double bootstrapped framework. We also investigate the determinants of financial as well as social efficiency.

1.1 Microfinance in India-An Overview

Starting in 1980, microfinance has now become a global movement to help poor and unbanked access credit. The industry has evolved over the years with structured guidelines, self-regulatory organizations, digitalization and customer centricity coming in place. This has further boosted the loan book and number of borrowers has grown manifold. As per the Microfinance Barometer[2] report 2019, today, the global microfinance industry is worth over INR 8.90 trillion with the loan disbursed amount growing at an average annual rate of 11.5% over the last 5 years. The industry has impacted the lives of 139.9 million borrowers worldwide, 80% of whom are women and 65%, from a rural background.

The Indian story is no different. The total loan book stood at INR 1792 billion at the end of 2019. The sector is dominated by MFIs with presence of four other types of players viz. Banks, Small Finance Banks, NBFC-MFIs and Not-for-Profits. Out of these, while banks have enjoyed stable growth, MFIs have been facing difficulty in accessing

[1] https://www.microfinancegateway.org/sites/default/files/mfg-en-paper-microfinance-in-india-an-overview-2009.pdf background note on microfinance in India accessed on January 16, 2020.

[2] http://www.convergences.org/wp-content/uploads/2019/09/Microfinance-Barometer-2019_web-1.pdf accessed on January 24, 2020.

funds. This has led to sharp rise in the interest rates charged by them. The Small Finance Banks, unencumbered by the stricter regulations on MFIs, have been steadily increasingly the market share and ticket size. Most MFI players in India lend either through Self-Help-Groups (SHG) or Joint-Liability-Groups (JLG). The delinquency of JLGs is quite low in comparison with SHGs (PwC & SIDBI, 2019).

A large chunk of population in India is still in low-income category and deprived of access to finance in the organized sector. In addition, Indian Microfinance is concentrated in a few locations (South India) and a vast geography (East) of this huge country still remains uncovered. This indicates huge potential for Microfinance in India.

Table 1 gives a summary overview of MFI industry in India.

Table 1 An overview of MFIs in India

	Bank	*SFBs*	*NBFC-MFIs*	*NBFC*	*Not for profits*	*Total*
Unique Live Borrowers ('000)	17,849	11,894	25,533	8,047	780	64,103
Active Loans ('000)	22,509	14,914	39,340	8,780	924	86,467
Portfolio Outstanding (INR Million)	599,990	299,900	681,560	185,390	18,630	1,785,470
Market Share in Outstanding Portfolio (%)	34	17	38	10	1	100
Disbursed Amount (INR Billion)	786	317	832	174	22	2,131
Average Ticket Size (INR)	42,086	30,780	25,850	31,722	29,656	31,623
30 + Delinquency	0.50%	1.13%	0.91%	2.73%	0.69%	1.00%
90 + Delinquency	0.22%	0.54%	0.37%	1.35%	0.26%	0.45%

1. SFB = Small Finance Banks 2. NBFC = Non-Banking Finance Company 3. MFI—Microfinance institutions

(*Source* Microfinance Pulse Report by EQUIFAX and SIDBI-Volume-II, 2019)

2 Review of Literature

Prior to 2006, there were only a few studies examining efficiency of MFIs with DEA and most of the work focused on using parametric techniques like Stochastic Frontier Analysis (Haq et el, 2010). However, over the years Data Envelopment Analysis (DEA) is being extensively applied in microfinance around the world. Gutierrez-Nieto et al. (2007) apply DEA to measure the efficiency of 30 Latin American MFIs and carry out a second-stage analysis too. They offer multiple input-out specifications and identify most efficient MFIs in a group of 18. Nghiem et al (2006) study the technical efficiency of 46 Vietnamese MFIs. Bassem (2008) investigates the efficiency of 35 MFIs Microfinance institutions in the Mediterranean zone during the period of 2004–2005. They find that size of the MFIs has a negative effect on their efficiency since the MFIs of medium size are more efficient than the eminent. Gutierrez-Nieto et al. (2009) extend the earlier works by examining social efficiency along with technical one and explore interrelationships between them. In this multi-country study, they study 89 MFIs and employ three inputs (assets, costs and employees) and two social outputs (female borrowers and poverty reach index). Haq et al. (2010) study the cost efficiency of 39 MFIs across Africa, Asia and the Latin America using DEA. They find that the NGO-MFIs particularly, under production approach, are the most efficient and conclude that their result is consistent with NGO-MFI's fulfillment of dual objectives: alleviating poverty and simultaneously achieving financial sustainability. Abdelkader et al. (2012) evaluate the performance of microfinance institutions in The MENA region over the period 2006–2009 using a DEA-Bootstrapping methodology. They find that average efficiency of the most countries of the region decreased over the period under study and efficiency significantly differs by legal status of the MFI. Tahir and Tahrim (2015) employ DEA and Dynamic Malmquist Productivity Index (MPI) to examine the efficiency and productivity of Cambodian MFIs during the period 2008–2011. They found fluctuating efficiency scores over the period and that the major source of efficiency was scale efficiency.

Most of these studies use the conventional DEA methodology which suffers from the limitation that the estimates are biased by construction and remain sensitive to the sampling variation of the estimated frontier (Simar & Wilson, 1998, 2000). In addition, as pointed out by Wijesiri et al. (2015), citing Simar and Wilson (2007) the second-stage analysis of some of the studies uses censored models for determining efficiency estimates, but these estimates are biased and serially correlated. Another notable feature of existing work is that mostly either a multi-country sample has been chosen or the MFIs in the sample had heterogynous business models whereas the DEA formulation assumes homogeneity in the decision-making units.

We attempt to overcome these limitations and use a double boot-strapped procedure following Wijesiri et al. (2015) who examine 36 Srilankan MFIs for the year 2010. To our knowledge this procedure has not been employed before on Indian MFIs before.

3 Methodology

3.1 First-Stage DEA Efficiency Measurement

We use input-oriented DEA model with assumption of Constant Returns to Scale (CRS) given by Charnes et al. (1978). The input-oriented model has been chosen to capture a possible better control of the MFI on inputs than outputs. If (x^j, y^j); $j = 1, 2, 3 \ldots\ldots N$ represent a set of input–output bundles of N firms, then the input-oriented CCR DEA model is represented as:

$$\tau_x\left(x^0, y^0\right) = min\,\theta \tag{1}$$

$$s.t.\ \sum\nolimits_{j=1}^{N} \lambda_j y^j y^0$$

$$s.t.\ \sum_{j=1}^{N} \lambda_j y^j \geq y^0$$

$$\sum_{j=1}^{N} \lambda_j x^j \leq \theta x^0$$

$$\lambda_j \geq 0\,(j = 1, 2, 3, \ldots\ldots\ldots N);\ \theta\ unrestricted$$

Here θ is the technical efficiency of oth firm and λ is an Nx1 vector of weights. The efficiency score ranges from 0 to 1. All the efficient firms lie on the efficiency frontier and have a score of 1. The inefficient firms fall within the frontier with scores less than 1.

3.1.1 Smoothed Homogeneous Bootstrapped DEA Based Procedure

One issue with traditional DEA measure is complete absence of statistical properties, rendering examination of its significance impossible and leading to biases. The point estimates of efficiency scores produced thus carry no measure of uncertainty associated with them. This is one of the main reasons of relative apathy of decision makers in using DEA (Wijesiri et al., 2015). To overcome this problem, we employ Simar and Wilson (2008) bias-corrected DEA approach with bootstrap (Efron, 1992). Bootstrap is a popular statistical technique in which a large number of new samples are generated from the sample at hand, and the test statistics are computed for each new sample. Then the distribution of test statistic is used to create confidence intervals.

3.2 Second-Stage Truncated Regression

The default method for conducting second-stage analysis in DEA is censored (Tobit) regression. However, this approach has a number of problems. It has been shown that since input and output variables are correlated, the independent variables turn out to be correlated with the error term in Tobit (Simar & Wilson, 2007). In addition, DEA estimates of efficiency suffers from serial correlation and therefore produces biased estimates (Wijesiri et al., 2015). Therefore, we apply a bootstrapped truncated regression in the second stage.

In this approach, we regress the bias-corrected efficiency scores ibid on the explanatory variables as follows:

$$\bar{\bar{\theta}}_i = \alpha + \beta z_i + e_i \tag{2}$$

$I = 1,2,3 \ldots\ldots\ldots\ldots\ldots N$

Here, α is a constant, β is the slope, z_i is a vector of regressands and e_i is a random error term. The estimation procedure employed is Systematically Trimmed Least Square (STLS) of Powel (1986). As discussed by Wijesiri et al. (2015), the details of bootstrapped truncated procedure are available in Simar and Wilson (2007).

3.3 Data

Availability of data on microfinance firms is erratic at best. One of the reliable sources for global MFI data is the MIX Market database. However, since the data reporting on MIX is voluntary, only a few MFIs do so. For the year 2018, we find that a total of 79 MFIs reported their performance data. However, there are a number of omissions. We tried to fill the missing data by hand by visiting websites of individual MFIs. In spite of this, complete data on all the variables for 2018 was available for only 27 firms. We also used MFI directory published by Small Industries Development Bank of India to get data on year of establishment and Type.

3.4 Input and Output Variables

For financial firms, the selection of input and output variables can be done either by production approach or by intermediation approach. Both have their merits. The number of inputs-output variables to be selected is also an important consideration. A rule of thumb followed in literature is that sample size should be at least three times total number of variables (input + output).

One of the commonly used input variables in DEA literature on financial firms is Total Assets (Barth et al., 2013; Haslem & Scheraga, 2003; Wijesiri et al., 2015). Number of loan officers is an important variable affecting the MFIs (Agier & Szafarz, 2010). They collect field data, meet with the applicants and provide personal recommendations to the credit committee that takes the final decisions (loan approval/denial, and loan size). We include number of loan officers as an input variable in the manner of a number of other studies (Qayyum & Ahmad, 2006; Wijesiri et al., 2015). The third input variable we chose is Cost Per Borrower which is also used in a number of studies (Qayyum & Ahmad, 2006; Segun & Anjugam, 2013; Wijesiri et al., 2015).

Our choice of output variables for Financial and Social models are Financial Revenue and Number of Female Borrowers, respectively. In many societies, women still get discriminated against. Financial empowerment of women will also enable them to make financial choices for other consumption-based needs of their households, thus resulting in overall business growth for microfinance players (PwC & SIDBI, 2019). Therefore, Number of Female Borrowers is a proxy for social outreach of MFI

Table 2 Variable definition

Variable	*Specification*	*Definition*
TA	Input	Total Assets
NLO	Input	The number of credit officers
CPB	Input	Operating Expenses/Average Active Borrowers
FR	Output-Financial Model	Total Revenue
FEMBOR	Output-Social Model	Number of Active Female Borrowers

Table 3 Descriptive statistics

Variable	*Mean*	*Std.Dev.*
TA (INR Million)	700.62	1146.35
NLO	641.00	942.00
CPB (INR'000)	1.65	0.51
FR (INR Million)	1221.89	1878.07
FEMBOR	335400	533211
CAR	0.30	0.27
Return on Assets (RoA%)	0.03	0.04
Age (In Years)	16.85	8.83
Type (% of NBFC-MFI)	67.00	--

(*INR* Indian National Rupee)

in terms of quality and quantity (Kar, 2012; Wijiseri et al., 2015; Yaron et al., 1998).

Our input and output variables are defined in Tables 2 and 3 gives the descriptive statistics.

3.5 Selection of Determinants of Efficiency

We select four explanatory variables viz. Age, Type (Legal Type), Return on Assets (RoA) and Capital to Asset Ratio (CAR). The specification of second-stage model is:

$$\bar{\bar{\theta}} = a + b_1 AGE_i + b_2 TYPE_i + b_3 EQAST_i + b_4 RoA_i + e_i \quad (5)$$

MFIs with longer experience (Age) are more likely to have a stable management through technology progress and market power (Kai, 2009). However, empirical studies have given mixed results on whether older MFIs are more efficient (e.g., Hermes et al., 2011; Paxton, 2007 give contradictory results). However, following Wijiseri et al. (2015), we include Age as one of the variables. A majority of MFIs in India are Non-Banking Finance Company (NBFC) MFIs. The other structures popular are section 25 Companies, Trusts and Societies. We use the dummy explanatory variable Type in our regression. It takes a value of 1 if the MFI is an NBFC and 0 otherwise.

Only recently MFIs in India have started accessing equity markets. They usually depend on debt heavily for funding requirements. Therefore, following Hermes et al. (2011) and Wijiseri et al. (2015) we include Capital to Asset Ratio (CAR) as the next explanatory variable. This ratio is also a proxy for the risk of the MFI. However, the effect of CAR has on efficiency is mixed. Some studies report a positive association and explain that higher capital means lower risk and therefore higher efficiency. On the other hand, studies reporting a negative association are closer to the inferences of agency cost theory. The last variable we use is RoA as it is an indicator of Financial Sustainability (Hartarska, 2005; Mersland & Strom, 2008).

4 Empirical Results

4.1 *First-Stage Results: Efficiency Measures*

We find that in the base-DEA model 8 firms are financially efficient (Table 4). Out of this 5 are NBFC-MFIs and 3 have non-NBFCs. However, none of the firms are found financially efficient in the bias-corrected DEA measure (Table 4 Left Panel). In the social model, 10 firms are socially efficient, out of which 6 are NBFC-MFIs and 4 are otherwise. Again, none of the firms if found socially efficient by bias-corrected DEA measure. In Figs. 1 and 2, base-DEA and bias-corrected DEA efficiency scores of financial and social models, respectively, are plotted along with 95% confidence interval estimates. Whereas bias-corrected estimates are always inside the confidence interval, the base-DEA efficiency scores are outside it in most cases. Therefore, it is difficult to place confidence in the estimates of efficiency in base-DEA approach both in financial and social models. This highlights the pitfalls of relying solely on base DEA for efficiency measurement.

Interestingly, 7 out of 8 firms which are financially efficient are socially efficient too. This points toward financial and social efficiency going hand in hand. This is further corroborated by Fig. 3 where bias-corrected

Table 4 Efficiency scores under the CRS assumption: DEA with bootstrap

Financial model						*Social model*				
MEI	*T*	*T*	*BIAS*	*LB*	*UB*	*T*	*T*	*BIAS*	*LB*	*UB*
1	0.9418	0.8131	0.1287	0.7432	0.9077	1.000	0.670	0.330	0.436	0.935
2	0.8810	0.7714	0.1095	0.7166	0.8659	0.812	0.652	0.160	0.570	0.793
3	0.8346	0.7174	0.1172	0.6511	0.8025	0.548	0.420	0.127	0.345	0.523
4	0.7266	0.6202	0.1064	0.5583	0.7396	0.769	0.555	0.214	0.415	0.822
5	1.0000	0.7259	0.2741	0.5126	1.1807	1.000	0.290	0.710	-0.320	2.447
6	1.0000	0.7214	0.2786	0.5096	1.1825	1.000	0.250	0.750	-0.394	2.683
7	0.7085	0.5872	0.1213	0.5096	0.7431	0.208	0.124	0.083	0.062	0.268
8	0.7801	0.6795	0.1005	0.6279	0.7469	0.497	0.379	0.118	0.310	0.467
9	0.9359	0.7745	0.1615	0.6702	0.9783	0.680	0.455	0.225	0.293	0.788
10	0.7001	0.6117	0.0884	0.5648	0.6719	0.421	0.310	0.112	0.240	0.408
11	1.0000	0.8170	0.1830	0.6973	0.9571	1.000	0.626	0.374	0.355	0.927
12	0.9675	0.8460	0.1215	0.7831	0.9293	0.971	0.725	0.246	0.577	0.924
13	0.5333	0.4532	0.0801	0.4059	0.5413	0.349	0.232	0.116	0.148	0.402
14	0.7325	0.6450	0.0874	0.6033	0.6997	0.534	0.408	0.125	0.337	0.504
15	1.0000	0.7286	0.2714	0.5165	1.1869	1.000	0.314	0.686	-0.277	1.702
16	0.8706	0.7240	0.1465	0.6318	0.8890	0.936	0.636	0.299	0.426	1.062
17	1.0000	0.7145	0.2855	0.4924	1.1573	1.000	0.456	0.544	0.004	1.672
18	0.8219	0.7205	0.1014	0.6690	0.7951	0.726	0.569	0.157	0.485	0.688
19	0.6238	0.5471	0.0767	0.5086	0.6011	0.643	0.502	0.141	0.421	0.601
20	1.0000	0.7502	0.2498	0.5637	1.0806	1.000	0.565	0.435	0.233	1.240
21	0.9159	0.8027	0.1132	0.7479	0.8781	1.000	0.724	0.276	0.556	0.921
22	0.7397	0.6422	0.0975	0.5909	0.7187	0.685	0.516	0.168	0.415	0.663
23	1.0000	0.8372	0.1628	0.7376	0.9500	0.727	0.542	0.184	0.433	0.699
24	1.0000	0.8566	0.1434	0.7757	0.9402	1.000	0.728	0.272	0.563	0.909
25	0.6018	0.5331	0.0687	0.5010	0.5778	0.312	0.243	0.069	0.203	0.301
26	0.7509	0.6590	0.0919	0.6127	0.7164	0.927	0.719	0.208	0.598	0.875
27	0.7767	0.6352	0.1415	0.5414	0.8282	1.000	0.593	0.407	0.292	1.343

financial and social efficiency scores are plotted against each other. A clear pattern can be discerned that as financial efficiency increases, social efficiency also increases.

4.2 *Second-Stage Results: Factors Determining Variations in Efficiency*

In the second-stage analysis, we attempt to find out the determinants of financial and social efficiencies. In the financial model, we find that both

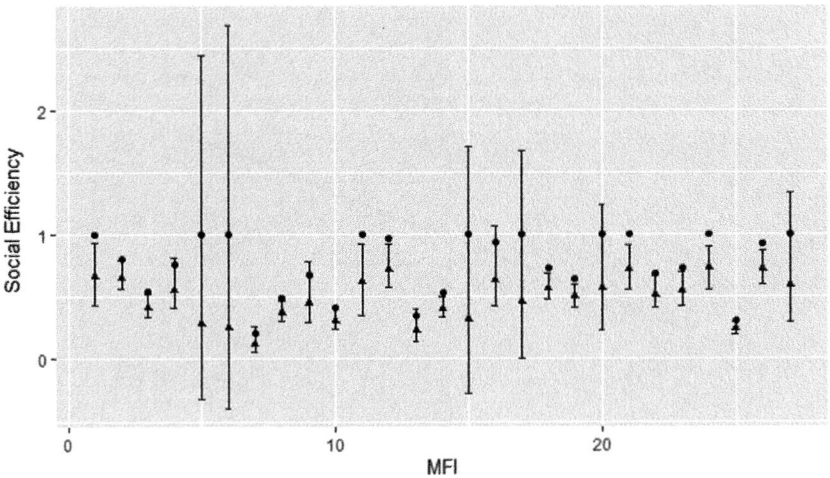

Fig. 1 The graph of $\bar{\theta}$ (.), $\bar{\bar{\theta}}$ (▲) and 95% CI for the social model

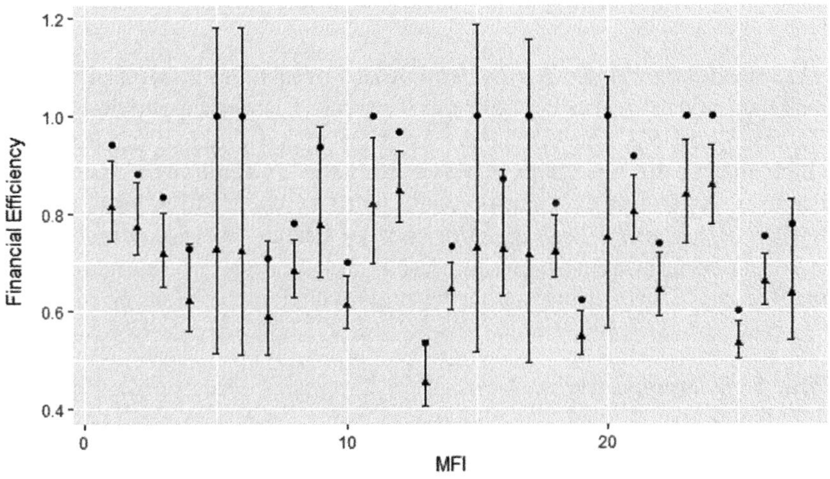

Fig. 2 The graph of $\bar{\theta}$ (.), $\bar{\bar{\theta}}$ (▲) and 95% CI for the financial model

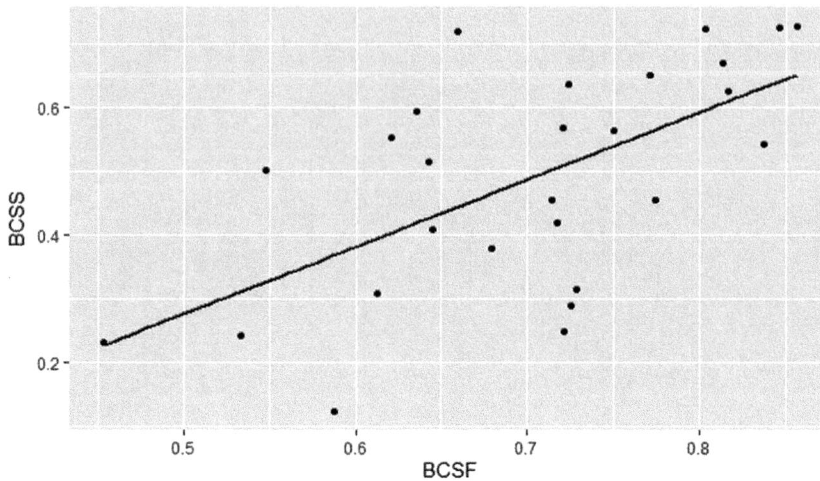

Fig. 3 Scatter plot of the bias-corrected financial efficiency score (BCSF) versus the bias-corrected social efficiency score (BCSS)

CAR (Capital to Asset Ratios) and RoA (Return on Assets) are statistically significant in both Tobit and Truncated Bootstrapped Regression (Tables 5 and 6). The Capital to Asset Ratio has a negative coefficient, which means the financial efficiency decreases as Capital to Asset Ratio increases. A possible explanation could be that if an MFI has lesser capital, it will employ more leverage. Presence of higher leverage would mean there is a commitment to pay interest as well as replay the principal. It is possible that a firm using higher leverage will then be more circumspect

Table 5 Regression results (Tobit)

Variable	*Financial model*	*Social model*
(Intercept)	0.7431***	0.5685***
Age	– 0.0014	0.0023
Type	0.0431	– 0.0104
CAR	– 0.2653***	– 0.3756***
RoA	1.0089*	0.0088

*, ** and *** significant at the 0.1,0.01 and 0.001 level respectively (2-tailed)

Table 6 Regression results (bootstrap truncated)

Variable	*Financial model*	*Social model*
(Intercept)	0.7431***	0.5699***
Age	– 0.0014	0.0022
Type	0.0431	– 0.0108
CAR	– 0.2653***	– 0.376*
RoA	1.0089*	0.0019

*, ** and *** significant at the 0.1,0.01 and 0.001 level respectively (2-tailed)

and disciplined in utilization of funds, leading to higher efficiency. The positive coefficient of RoA has obvious explanation.

However, Age and Type are not statistically different from zero in both the models. Therefore, we do not get any insights into how age affects efficiency or whether organization structure has a bearing on it. However, Age does have a negative sign which has been identified in the literature as mission drift.

In social model, only the CAR variable is significant with a negative sign in both regression approaches. The presence of leverage perhaps keeps the MFIs focused on achievement of its social goals too.

5 Conclusion

We examine the efficiency and its determinants for 27 MFIs in India. We estimate a social as well as a financial model given the duality of objectives of MFIs. We perform a new two-stage double bootstrapped DEA approach to uncover robust inferences about performance of MFIs. In the first stage, we estimate efficiency scores of MFIs on both financial and social parameters with a bootstrapped DEA approach. In the second stage, these efficiency scores are regressed on variables affecting efficiency by using a bootstrapped truncated regression. The use of this procedure is intended to overcome problem of bias and serial correlation. The results of this paper are therefore more robust and offer better insights into efficiency of MFIs in India.

We find that the base-DEA efficiencies of firms disappear in the bias-corrected DEA run. On financial parameter, 8 firms are efficient in base-DEA model but none in the bias-corrected one. Similarly, 10 firms are socially efficient in base DEA model but none in the bias-corrected one. However, we find evidence in India, the financial and social efficiency go hand in hand. Therefore, an important policy imperative that emerges from this paper is that in order for the MFIs to achieve their social objectives, it is important to see that they remain financially afloat and well-managed.

We further find that it is that the Capital Structure of MFIs is the most important determinant of efficiency of MFIs in India on both financial and social dimension. In addition the profitability too plays an important role, although the evidence is weaker. However, out of the five types of MFIs working in India, it is difficult to say which type is more efficient as a class. Another important finding of this study is that the age of MFIs does not appear to be affecting the efficiency significantly. This is an interesting insight as generally older MFIs are considered to be performing better with learning curve.

These findings have relevance for policymakers, MFI firms and donors. Policymakers can streamline the recent constraints on accessing funds by MFIs in as social and financial performance move together and leverage is playing an important role in efficiency. The MFI firms could benefit by this study by examining their efficiencies and focusing on financial or operational for improvement. The donors can use the results for decisions on funding.

The study has the limitation of using only one-year data. Perhaps a time-series analysis of productivity may uncover deeper insights. In addition, the number of firms for which we could get data is rather small at 27. A larger dataset could have resulted in more meaningful inferences. Future research may be done accordingly and by considering newer variables.

References

Agier, I., & Szafarz, A. (2010). *Credit officers and loan granting in microfinance: Brazilian evidence*. Available at SSRN 1729234.

Barth, J. R., Lin, C., Ma, Y., Seade, J., & Song, F. M. (2013). Do bank regulation, supervision and monitoring enhance or impede bank efficiency? *Journal of Banking & Finance, 37*(8), 2879–2892.

Bassem, B. S. (2008). Efficiency of microfinance institutions in the Mediterranean: An application of DEA. *Transition Studies Review, 15*(2), 343–354.

Abdelkader, I. B., Hathroubi, S., Jemaa, B., & Mekki, M. (2012). *Microfinance institutions' efficiency in the MENA region: A bootstrap-DEA approach*.

Charnes, A., Cooper, W. W., & Rhodes, E. (1978). Measuring the efficiency of decision making units. *European Journal of Operational Research, 2*(6), 429–444.

Efron, B. (1992). Bootstrap methods: Another look at the jackknife. In *Breakthroughs in statistics* (pp. 569–593). Springer.

Gutiérrez-Nieto, B., Serrano-Cinca, C., & Mar Molinero, C. (2009). Social efficiency in microfinance institutions. *Journal of the Operational Research Society, 60*(1), 104–119.

Gutierrez-Nieto, B., Serrano-Cinca, C., & Molinero, C. M. (2007). Microfinance institutions and efficiency. *Omega, 35*(2), 131–142.

Haq, M., Skully, M., & Pathan, S. (2010). Efficiency of microfinance institutions: A data envelopment analysis. *Asia-Pacific Financial Markets, 17*(1), 63–97.

Hartarska, V. (2005). Governance and performance of microfinance institutions in Central and Eastern Europe and the newly independent states. *World Development, 33*(10), 1627–1643.

Haslem, J. A., & Scheraga, C. A. (2003). Data envelopment analysis of Morningstar's large-cap mutual funds. *The Journal of Investing, 12*(4), 41–48.

Hermes, N., Lensink, R., & Meesters, A. (2011). Outreach and efficiency of microfinance institutions. *World Development, 39*(6), 938–948.

Kai, H. (2009). Competition and wide outreach of Microfinance Institutions" . *Economics Bulletin, 29*(4), 2628–2639.

Kar, A. K. (2012). Does capital and financing structure have any relevance to the performance of microfinance institutions? *International Review of Applied Economics, 26*(3), 329–348.

Kleiber, C., & Zeileis, A. (2008). *Applied econometrics with R*. Springer Science & Business Media.

Mersland, R., & Strøm, R. Ø. (2008). Performance and trade? offs in microfinance organisations-does ownership matter? *Journal of International Development: THe Journal of the Development Studies Association, 20*(5), 598–612.

Nghiem, H., Coelli, T., & Rao, P. (2006). The efficiency of microfinance in Vietnam: Evidence from NGO schemes in the north and the central regions. *International Journal of Environmental, Cultural, Economic and Social Sustainability, 2*(5), 71–78.

Paxton, J. (2007). Technical efficiency in a semi? formal financial sector: The case of Mexico. *Oxford Bulletin of Economics and Statistics, 69*(1), 57–74.

Powell, J. L. (1986). Symmetrically trimmed least squares estimation for Tobit models. *Econometrica: Journal of the Econometric Society*, 1435–1460.

PwC & SIDBI. (2019). *Vision of microfinance in India*. PwC.

Qayyum, A., & Ahmad, M. (2006). *Efficiency and sustainability of micro finance*. MPRA Paper,v11674, University Library of Munich, Germany

Segun, K. R. S., & Anjugam, M. (2013). Measuring the efficiency of Sub-Saharan Africa's microfinance institutions and its drivers. *Annals of Public and Cooperative Economics, 84*(4), 399–422.

Servin, R., Lensink, R., & Van den Berg, M. (2012). Ownership and technical efficiency of microfinance institutions: Empirical evidence from Latin America. *Journal of Banking & Finance, 36*(7), 2136–2144.

Simar, L., & Wilson, P. W. (1998). Sensitivity analysis of efficiency scores: How to bootstrap in nonparametric frontier models. *Management Science, 44*(1), 49–61.

Simar, L., & Wilson, P. W. (2000). A general methodology for bootstrapping in non-parametric frontier models. *Journal of Applied Statistics, 27*(6), 779–802.

Simar, L., & Wilson, P. W. (2007). Estimation and inference in two-stage, semi-parametric models of production processes. *Journal of Econometrics, 136*(1), 31–64.

Tahir, I. M., & Tahrim, S. N. C. (2015). Efficiency and productivity analysis of microfinance institutions in Cambodia: A DEA approach. *International Review of Business Research Papers, 11*(1), 25–42.

Wijesiri, M., Viganò, L., & Meoli, M. (2015). Efficiency of microfinance institutions in Sri Lanka: A two-stage double bootstrap DEA approach. *Economic Modelling, 47*, 74–83.

Yaron, J., Benjamin, M. P., & Piprek, G. L. (1997). *Rural finance: Issues, design, and best practices* (Vol. 14). World Bank.

Yaron, J., Benjamin, M., & Charitonenko, S. (1998). Promoting efficient rural financial intermediation. *The World Bank Research Observer, 13*(2), 147–170.

Zeller, M., & Meyer, R. L. (Eds.). (2002). *The triangle of microfinance: Financial sustainability, outreach, and impact*. Intl Food Policy Res Inst.

Impact of Microcredit on Livelihood Status of Women in Rural India

Tarak Nath Sahu, Srimoyee Datta, and Sudarshan Maity

1 Introduction

Financial inclusion attracts the interest of policy makers for it is on the whole effect on growth and betterment of the individual as well as social front. It refers to the non-existence of price and non-price obstacles for utilising financial services. However, explanation to such definition holds a considerable extent of divergence so far as literary evidence insisted upon by several authors and practitioners in different contextual flavour are concerned. Issues concerning financial reforms have been prioritised in the constructive plans of our nation from the very beginning. But certain impositions restrict general financial organisations to penetrate population excluded from the realm of formal financial system. Consequently,

T. N. Sahu
Department of Commerce, Vidyasagar University, Midnapore, West Bengal, India

S. Datta (✉)
Department of Management Studies, Bengal Institute of Science & Technology, Purulia, West Bengal, India

S. Maity
The Institute of Cost Accountants of India, Kolkata, India

Ananda S. and D. Singh (eds.), *Financial Inclusion in Emerging Markets*,
https://doi.org/10.1007/978-981-16-2652-4_9

the need for convenient financial service provider was felt out to resurrect the situation leading to sustainable growth.

The notion of microfinance came into limelight after the glorious possession of the "Nobel Prize" by Md. Yunus in 2006. MFIs are constantly operating towards creating positive outcomes like employability, inculcating savings habit, etc. for economic recuperation of the intended clientele base worldwide (Odoom et al., 2019). Microfinance is a long-lived development tool for low-income households with high repayment rate. It offers win–win situation for both demand and supply end. The endowment of credit and credit plus services, position itself as the solution to the problems associated with poverty and associated issues (Memon et al., 2020). Beyond poverty alleviation it also supports the enhancement of private sector segment in building up entrepreneurship and micro-organisation set up. Basically, the inimitability of MFIs lies in its duality for-profit and social well-being nature. As MFIs takes position as an alternative with more operational elasticity paralleled to the conventional financial institutions (banks), it can grab the attention of people who are identical as financially excluded, economically backward and more specifically women with its collateral free financial services (RBI Bulletin, 2006).

Commonly, the intention of microfinance curriculums does converge considering rectification of the market malfunctions. Microcredit, micro-pension (safeguarding the worker from informal sector after a certain age) and micro-insurance (providing security to population belonging from the low-income stratum) stands among the prominent offerings of MFIs. The target of microfinance institutions, both on the way to employment generation and struggle counter to poverty to advance the economic eminence of women lives, is well applauded. The journey with microcredit helps in attitude formation towards socio-economic upliftment, freedom of movement and economic freedom. These changes in economic condition inculcate towards empowerment in economic terms in due course. The term empowerment is a full of thought and meanings. Females still have the hindrances in exercising their rights. So, they should be empowered with the power of education, security, health, skill, decision-making authority, capital, better living of standard and respect. Microfinance with its offering helps to increase the potential of empowerment level among them.

Considering the phenomena, the study is an endeavour which exemplifies the true impression of microcredit considering employability generation, economic improvement and empowerment of the female borrowers with empirical validation from the selected backward districts of West Bengal.

2 Literature Review and Hypotheses Development

2.1 Review of Literature

To impart financial inclusion's benefits, numerous financial institutions like banks along with different digital services work together (Bansal, 2014; Gomathy, 2015; Kumbhar, 2011). But due to different setbacks and formalities, certain regions are not able to incur itself in the financial inclusion map of our nation till date. Beyond banking sector offerings and technological advancements, there is another financial institution that also able to mark its footprint quite well in the domain of financial inclusion.

This section unearths the assessment of MFIs impact considering employment generation and economic exhilaration. Available literatures validate that such institutions have an imperative role towards financial inclusion (Datta & Sahu, 2017; Datta & Sahu, 2021; Shankar, 2013), predominantly in the setting of rural backdrop with zero or low exposure of conventional financial institutions (Rajasekaran, 2018). Microfinance as an establishment of extending services be it in the form of savings, credit, pension and insurance amenities has anchored the economy with some positive outcomes like employability, income generation, lessening in poverty level and female empowerment (Hussain et al., 2019; Khandekar, 2003; Lakwo, 2006; Loice & Razia, 2013; Park & Mercado, 2015; Pathak & Gyakali, 2010; Taiwo, 2012; Wahab et al., 2018). To cut down poverty and income disparity, financial inclusion accompanied by microfinance activities has a key position to play (Khandker, 2003; Milana & Astha, 2020; Park & Mercado, 2015).

In line with that, "microcredit has a constructive effect on the economic grade of the borrowers' individual and household front", according to Adhikari and Shrestha (2013) and Datta and Sahu (2018), and it can be more successful if it is sustained with viable economic activities (Akhtar & Cheng, 2020; Dev, 2006). Not only that, in Nigeria involvement in microcredit programmes enhances employment opportunities in households and at community level including a diverse set of dimensions affecting the borrower lifestyle from building up savings practice, employability and income generation, increase in the figure of microenterprises within the entrepreneurs belong to MSMEs (Taiwo, 2012).

The above literatures support that MFIs do have supportive influences among the borrowers and in the society as well (Shankar, 2013). It helps to reduce poverty (Christabell & Raj, 2012; Park & Mercado, 2015; Taiwo, 2012; Wahab et al., 2018) and act as a way in the direction of economic exhilaration (Adhikari & Shrestha, 2013; Pathak & Gyakali, 2010). Beyond that it also assists to bring down an additional crucial concern, i.e. women empowerment (Lakwo, 2006; Loice & Razia, 2013). Women empowerment in today's time has been regarded as one of the most imperative outcomes of MFI's borrowing. Empowerment being qualitative in nature is one of the sensitive criteria to track down the sustainable progress of society (Datta & Sahu, 2018). It drives towards gender equality (Duflo, 2012), ensure mobility and socio-economic freedom (Akram et al., 2015). A series of constructive programme have been targeted for the advancement and progression of the feminine sector of the society (Singh, 2013) which contribute towards empowerment and realisation of own rights and powers for betterment of economy (Rajak, 2008). But it has been observed that empowerment is the outcome of multiple variables, microcredit access only enhances the possibilities of empowerment and self-dependence (Cheston & Kuhn, 2002). MFIs can provide short-term working capital to engage themselves in the income engendering and asset building activities (Blumberg, 2005). This phenomenon boosts up the awareness about well-being and helps in practices the rights which previously were denied of (Hunt & Kasynathan, 2002).

The above-mentioned literatures support the notion that microcredit has a far-reaching bearing on the general lifestyle practices along with employability and economic upliftment. But majority of the literatures consider employability as an individual effort but in setting up microenterprise the encouragement of supporting individuals as groups are needed to be analysed in the literatures. Moreover, economic changes in most literatures are restricted into income and consumption patterns. Therefore, the study is an attempt to understand and scrutinise the influence of services extended by microfinance institutions in relation to employment generation along with economic upliftment and empowerment of the borrowers for the selected underdeveloped districts of West Bengal.

2.2 Objective and Hypotheses

The study tries to reveal the microcredit role towards generation of employment and economic transformation along with empowerment of the female borrowers in the selected underdeveloped districts of West Bengal with the following three explicit objectives.

- To ascertain the effect of microcredit on employment generation.
- To analyse the role of microcredit concerning income generation and changes of consumption pattern of the rural women borrowers.
- To observe the changes in economic empowerment level among the beneficiaries.

Based on the previous discussion and research objectives, the following hypotheses are formulated:

H_1: There is no impact of microcredit on the rural female beneficiaries in terms of employment.
H_2: There is no significant difference in income generation and changes in consumption pattern due to the utilisation of credit into different avenues.
H_3: There is no difference in economic empowerment level of the respondents.

3 Research Methodology

3.1 Sample Design

This study has been purposeful on the position of microcredit offered by the MFIs, who are operational in selected districts of West Bengal, India. The selected districts have been chosen as they represent rural India with dominancy of rural region, majority of domicile lives below poverty line, filled with remote location and less financial literacy. The selected districts are Bankura, Purulia, Jhargram, Paschim Medinipur and Birbhum (Jangal Mahal area, to be precise) which further subdivided into different subdivisions and MFIs are active in these regions for the previous five years (2013–2018), for supporting economic upliftment, generation of employment and empowerment of the borrowers. The target population of this study is the microfinance borrowers (one time or repetitive) of the selected district. The estimated population was 64 million who were registered as borrowers under different MFIs in West Bengal (*The Economic Times*, 2019).

In order to choose the correct sample size, Cochran's formula has been used here as the population size is comparatively large. Assume there is a large population but the variability in the proportion that will adopt the practice is unknown to us; therefore, assume p = 0.5 (maximum variability). Furthermore, assume we desire a 95% confidence level and +5 precision. Then the calculation for the required sample size is as follows:

$$\text{Here, } p = 0.5; \quad q = (1 - p) = (1 - 0.5) = 0.5; \quad Z = 1.96; \quad e = 0.05$$
$$(z^2)(p)(q) = (1.96 * 1.96)(0.5 * 0.5)$$
$$\text{Then } n_0 = (1.96 * 1.96)(0.5 * 0.5)/0.05 * 0.05 = 384$$

As here the population size is infinite (more than 10,000) so the sample size in this study is 384 but we have used 481borrowers for analysing the impact of microcredit on the livelihood for more robustness of result of this study.

In this study, total 481 borrowers having 37 samples from each subdivision have been considered for analysis. While selecting the respondents (one time or repetitive MFI borrower), the study only counted on those borrowers who completed minimum one year of post-loan stage or continuing the loan repayment cycle throughout the survey. For carrying out this study, the required data have been collected for a period ranging from April 2019 to September 2019.

3.2 Statistical and Econometric Tests Used

To explore the stated objectives of employment generation and credit utilisation both open and questionnaire with close end has been applied in this study. To measure questionnaire efficacy, proper reliability test has been applied on 50 samples pilot study. Zikmund and Babin (2012) say, "The pilot was intended to verify the clarity of words, sentence sequence and their relevance". The score of Cronbach alpha is 0.713. Alpha score above 0.60 is considered as good in social sciences (Shelby, 2011). So, in this study the designed questionnaires are reliable considering the entire questionnaire.

For the purpose of analysing the outcome of microcredit on employment generation, "multiple regression analysis" has been followed. Here three elements, i.e. categories of microenterprise, volume of credit and duration, have been mentioned as dependent variable, and employability has been reflected as dependent variable. In consideration of composed primary data, microenterprises set-up has been alienated into six different comprehensive classes (animal husbandry, agriculture based, business, cottage industries, transport and service-related microenterprises). On the basis of the average incremental annual income, all the classifications have been allotted values extending from 1 to 6. The variable duration of the microcredit entails the duration among the day of taking credit from any of the MFIs and the day of survey has materialised. Volume of borrowings entails for the advance one individual procure from the MFIs. In this study, employability is the dependent variable that has been computed with the numeral of total manpower tied up in any microenterprise set-up, regular time for work and numeral of days' work per week and transforms the total number into monthly basis. Further, to apprehend credit utilisation pattern of the borrowers, the economic upliftment and changes in economic empowerment status samples *t*-test has been applied.

Here, the empowerment has been judged through economic dimension. The details are:

- Economic Empowerment—the economic empowerment has been measured by financial contribution which has three specific areas—children education, health and family overheads or expenditures. As per the additional contribution in the above-mentioned fields in the post-loan phase, the weightage of 3, 2 or 1 or in case of absence 0 have been awarded accordingly.

4 Analysis and Findings

4.1 *Impact of Microcredit on Employability*

This section of the study assesses the impact of microcredit on employability by considering employability as dependent variable. The results of regression analysis (Table 1) indicate that the coefficients of duration of credit and the volume of credit are significant at 5% level, contending that

Table 1 Results of multiple regression analysis considering employability as dependent variable

Independent variable	*Coefficient*	t-*values*	p-*values*	*VIF*
Category of microenterprise	1.53	0.01	0.78	1.32
Duration of credit	10.14	1.37	0.03	1.03
Volume of credit	0.07	6.48	0.00	1.16
Constant	2047.37	2.89	0.003	
Value of R= 0.54, R^2= 0.29		**F-value** 18.33	**0.000**	

Source Calculated by researcher

the duration of credit and the volume of credit has a significant positive impact on the employment generation through microenterprises.

The other variable, category of microenterprise has no significant impact as $p = 0.78$ (>0.05). The insignificant result may be due to the fact that whatever the types of micro-set-up the borrowers have with efficient management of resources is able to generate employability within time with right amount of capital and manpower.

The Regression equation is:

$$Employability = 2047.37 + 1.53 \times Category + 10.14 \times Duration + 0.07 \times Volume + \varepsilon$$

4.2 Credit Utilisation and Economic Upliftment of the Borrowers

In this study, there are two categories of credit utility pattern which are productive and unproductive. Productive credit utilisation includes—income-generating purposes and education. The other one as unproductive credit handling includes, utilisation of loan amount for family health purposes, social obligations and festivals, redemption of old debt, family consumption and other miscellaneous purposes (Fig. 1).

Figure 2 depicts that 78% and 22% of respondents utilise the credit for productive and unproductive purposes, respectively. Further, as presented in Fig. 2, 93% of the total productive sample respondents (78%) utilise credit for income generation and rest 7% for education purposes.

Among the six microenterprises, animal husbandry utilises maximum credit amount (65%) followed by small business with 13%, agriculture-based small enterprises with 12%, cottage industry with 5%, service-related

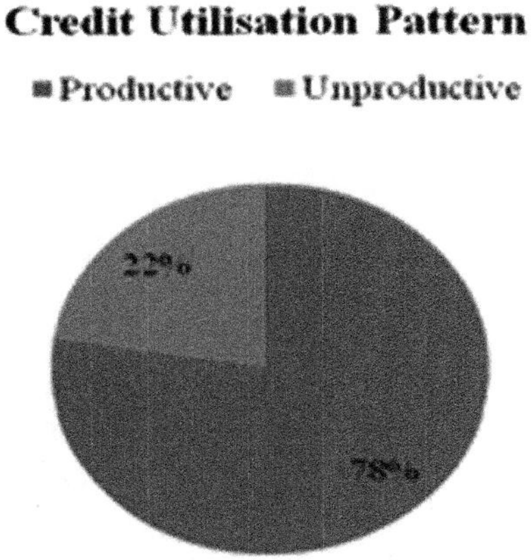

Fig. 1 Credit utilisation pattern of the respondents (*Source* Prepared by researchers)

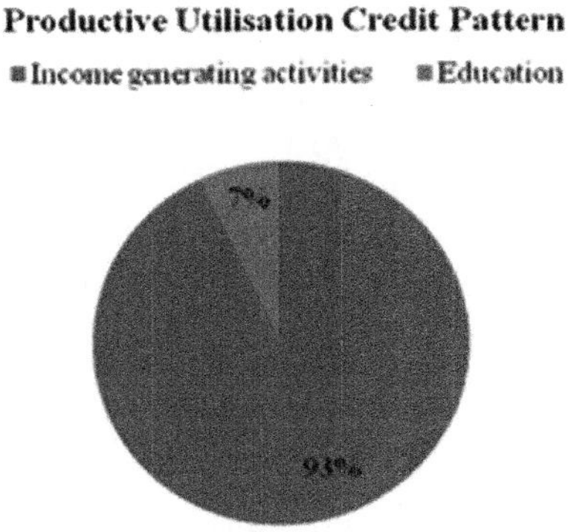

Fig. 2 Productive utilisation credit pattern (*Source* Prepared by researchers)

small enterprises with 3% and transportation-based small enterprises with 2% (Fig. 3).

Here, among the six microenterprises, animal husbandry sector generates maximum average annual income compare to the other five and further, small business enterprises earn lowest average income (Fig. 4).

Bearing the second objective of scrutinising the usage of credit by the beneficiaries for income generation, the study has considered the two phase data of 481 respondents. To firmly decide the existence of any significant difference in the mean income level, we incline to rely on the parametric test (i.e. dependent samples t-test). Performing such analysis however requires satisfying at least the condition of normality, which

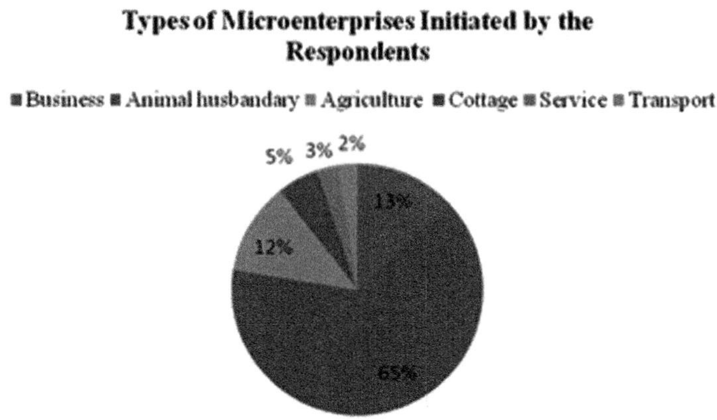

Fig. 3 Types of microenterprise initiated by the respondents (*Source* Prepared by researchers)

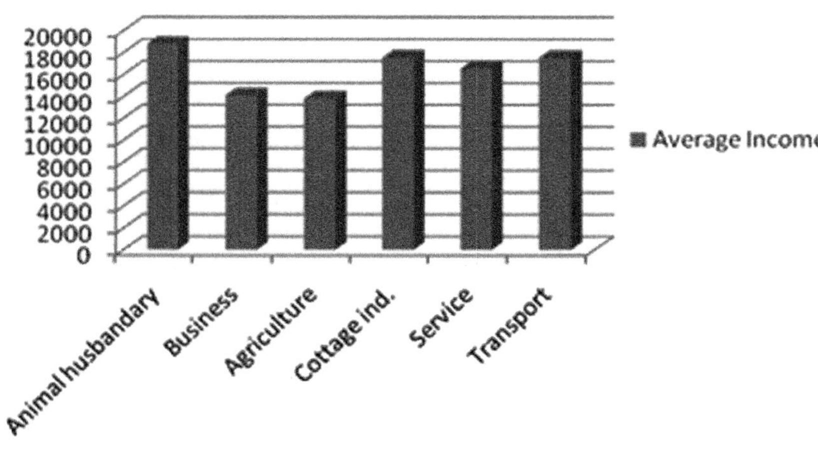

Fig. 4 Average level of income of the different categories of microenterprise (*Source* Prepared by researchers)

seems to be duly satisfied with z-values for both the skewness and kurtosis (range within of ± 1.96) (Posten, 1984) along with a non-significant value for the Shapiro–Wilk test (Shapiro & Wilk, 1965).

Table 2 Paired samples t-test (income level of the respondents)

	Mean	*Variance*	t-*value*
Post-loan phase	7053.73	3.33E+08	12.275
Pre-loan phase	5126.52	2.43E+08	(0.000)

Source Calculated by researchers

The result shows that the calculated value of t in Table 2 is significant with the mean income for post-loan phase standing higher than that of the pre-loan phase confirming that the microcredits provided by the different MFIs in the backward districts of West Bengal have a significant impact on the monetary uplift of the women borrowers considered in the study.

The significant changes in income level of pre-post-phase encouraged us in addition to explore their consumption pattern in pre-post-loan period. Accordingly based on pre- and post-loan phase consumption expenditures, parametric test (t-test) has been further applied to look after whether mean consumption expenditure be different for the two groups significantly.

As the differences between the pre- and post-consumption expenditures take form approximately close to a normal distribution with z-values for both the skewness and kurtosis lying within a range of ± 1.96 and having a non-significant value of Shapiro–Wilk test, we apply the dependent samples t-test to explore whether the mean consumption expenditure significantly be different from pre-loan segment to post-loan segment.

The result shows that significant difference exists between the pre-post-credit periods so far as consumption expenditure levels of the selected sample are concerned. Observation from Table 3 reveals that the mean value of consumption level in post-loan phase being higher than that of the mean value of consumption level in pre-loan phase, contending us to

Table 3 Paired samples t-test (consumption level of the respondents)

	Mean	*Variance*	t-*value*
Post-loan phase	62,391.02	4.25E+08	13.148
Pre-loan phase	43,796.54	1.84E+08	(0.000)

Source Calculated by researchers

Table 4 *F*-test and *t*-test for economic empowerment

	Mean	*Variance*	F-*value*	t-*value*
Pre-loan phase	0.183	0.734	0.616	41.024
Post-loan phase	2.077	0.428	(0.053)	(0.000)

Source Calculated by researcher

believe that microcredit not only executes a stimulating role for employability and to enrich the income status of the borrowers. As a matter of fact, statistics in this regard do confirms that MFIs contributes simultaneously towards healthy life, superior nutrition level and also help in shaping a superior lifestyle in a sustainable means.

4.3 Observation of Economic Empowerment Comparing the Pre- and Post-credit Phase

Out of the total respondents, 68% belongs to 25–35 years of age and 76% are illiterate. Further, according to the respondents' profile of the selected respondents, 73% sample are married, 68% are housewives, 68% belongs to SC category, 62% practices Hinduism, 57% composed of nuclear family and all reside in the rural area.

To check the economic empowerment of the borrowers, researchers have run both *F* test and *t*-test. The results presented in Table 4 indicate the presence of unequal variance (*F* test) and existence of mean difference (*t*-test). Further, mean value of post-loan phase indicates an increasing trend towards economic empowerment.

5 Conclusion and Recommendations

The primary intention of MFIs is to poverty elimination, inclusion of the excluded into the mainstream and gradually wind-up related issues associated to it. To succeed, microcredit helps by providing collateral free loan as a motivation to start up new venture, generate employability, creation of a better lifestyle and in ultimate elevating the economic grade of the borrowers along with their household. In the present study, animal husbandry comes out as preferred microenterprises with maximum average income compare to the other enterprises. This may be due to the geographical features and unsuitability of agricultural accomplishments in the selected region. However, demand schedule from the daily chores of life reveals a tiny percentage of the samples compelling to consume the credit for unproductive purposes which somehow distract the focus of MFIs. This issue needs some formative policies to overcome such matters with utmost care and hassles.

Further, duration and volume of credit have positive significant bearing on employability. The reason may be with the collateral free credit amount and management of other resources compelling borrowers to create employability and enhance economic upliftment gradually. Further, maximum beneficiaries are in their second loan cycle that supports to influence the employability and better economic conditions for their household.

In line with most of the earlier studies (Khan et al., 2020; Omar et al., 2012; Salia & Mbwambo, 2014) the current study also confirms that generation of microcredit positively affect the extent of employment along with the magnitude of economic grade of the borrowers. This is possible as the MFIs active in the selected backward zones offer flexible, hassle and indemnity free credit, execute group lending model and safeguard the issues of superior rural penetration. However, a considerable amount of literature (Chowdhury et al., 2005; Dahal & Fiala, 2020; Li, 2010) declines any notable influence particularly due to short time span, provision of credit to the incorrect segment, awareness lacking, and borrowers with high liability of debt, etc.

In order to have a more economically viable condition for the borrowers and society as well, active participation is sought from both the government and non-government institutions, especially MFIs. Different initiatives like introduction of NBFCs, extension of MFIs role and responsibilities, associated services, customer care, restricting policies to safeguard the borrowers, awareness campaign, etc., are expected to help in the process of rehabilitation of the economy concerned.

Along with economic upliftment and livelihood transformation, empowerment has been taken place which co-exists with this entire phenomenon. In this backdrop, being economically empowered changes the attitude of female creditors towards saving behaviour, asset management, monitory contribution pattern, money management, etc. It also helps to shape the perspective of lifestyle management in the long run.

References

Akhter, J., & Cheng, K. (2020). Sustainable empowerment initiatives among rural women through microcredit borrowings in Bangladesh. *Sustainability*. https://doi.org/10.3390/su12062275

Adhikari, D. B., & Shrestha, J. (2013). Economic impact of microfinance in Nepal: A case study of the Manamaiju Village Development Committee, Kathmandu. *Economic Journal of Development Issues, 15 & 16* (1–2), 36–49.

Akram, S., Shaheen, I., & Kiyyani, S. M. (2015). Socio-economic empowerment of women through micro enterprises: A case study of AJK. *European Scientific Journal, 11*(22), 197–211.

Bansal, S. (2014). Perspective of technology in achieving financial inclusion in rural India. *Procedia Economics and Finance*. https://doi.org/10.1016/S2212-5671(14)00213-5

Blumberg, R. L. (2005, August). Women's economic empowerment as the magic potion of development. In *100th Annual Meeting of the American Sociological Association, August*, Philadelphia.

Cheston, S., & Kuhn, L. (2002). *Empowering women through microfinance* (Draft). UNIFEM.

Chowdhury, M. J. A., Ghosh, D., & Wright, R. E. (2005). The impact of microcredit on poverty: Evidence from Bangladesh. *Progress in Development Studies, 5*(4), 298–309.

Christabell, P., & Raj, V. (2012). Financial inclusion in rural India. *IOSR Journal of Humanities and Social Science, 2*(5), 21–25.

Dahal, M., & Fiala, N. (2020). Retrieved from https://doi.org/10.1016/j.worlddev.2019.104773

Datta, S., & Sahu, T. N. (2017). An empirical study on the impact of microfinance on women empowerment: Evidence from West Bengal. *Indian Journal of Commerce and Management Studies, 8*(3), 53–62.

Datta, S., & Sahu, T. N. (2018). Role of microfinance institutions on the empowerment of female borrowers: Evidence from West Bengal. *JIMS8M: The Journal of Indian Management & Strategy, 23*(1), 32–38.

Datta, S., & Sahu, T. N. (2021). Impact of Microcredit on Employment Generation and Empowerment of Rural Women in India. *International Journal of Rural Management, 17*(1), 140–157.

Dev, S. M. (2006). Financial inclusion: Issues and challenges. *Economic and Political Weekly, 41*(41), 4310–4313.

Duflo, E. (2012). Women empowerment and economic development. *Journal of Economic Literature, 50*(4), 1051–1079.

Gomathy, M. (2015). An overview of financial inclusion and rural development in India. *IOSR Journal of Business and Management (IOSRJBM), 17*(8), 06–11.

Hunt, J., & Kasynathan, N. (2002). Reflections on microfinance and women's empowerment. *Development Bulletin, 57*, 71–75.

Hussain, J., Mahmood, S., & Scott, J. (2019). Gender, microcredit and poverty alleviation in a developing country: The case of women entrepreneurs in Pakistan. *Journal of International Development, 31*(3), 247–270.

Khan, A. A., Khan, S. U., Fahad, S., Ali, M. A., Khan, A., & Luo, J. (2020). Microfinance and poverty reduction: New evidence from Pakisthan. https://doi.org/10.1002/ijfe.2038

Khandker, S. R. (2003). *Microfinance and poverty: Evidence using panel data from Bangladesh* (Working paper 2945, World Bank Policy Research).

Kumbhar, V. M. (2011). Alternative banking channels and customers' satisfaction: An empirical study of public and private sector banks. *International Journal of Business and Management Tomorrow., 1*(1), 28–45.

Lakwo, A. (2006). *Microfinance, rural livelihoods, and women's empowerment in Uganda* (Ph.D. thesis). African Studies Centre, Uganda.

Li, X. (2010). *An empirical analysis of microcredit on China rural household* (Ph.D. thesis). Lincoln University.

Loice, M., & Razia, C. (2013). Microfinance interventions and empowerment of women entrepreneurs rural constituencies in Kenya. *Research Journal of Finance and Accounting, 4*(9), 84–95.

Memon, A., Akram, W., & Abbas, G. (2020). Women participation in achieving sustainability of microfinance institutions (MFIs). *Journal of Sustainable Finance & Investment*. https://doi.org/10.1080/20430795.2020.1790959

Milana, C., & Ashta, A. (2020). Microfinance and financial inclusion: Challenges and opportunities. *Strategic Change, 29*(3), 257–266.

Odoom, D., Fosu, K. O., Ankomah, K., & Amofa, M. B. (2019). Investigating the challenges faced by microfinance institutions in Ghana: Evidence from Takoradi. *Journal of Research on Humanities and Social Sciences, 9*(10), 91–104.

Omar, M. Z., Noor, C. S. M., & Dahalan, N. (2012). The economic performance of the Amanah Ikhtiar Malaysia rural microcredit programme: A case study in Kedah. *World Journal of Social Sciences, 2*(5), 286–302.

Park, C. Y., & Mercado, R. V. (2015). *Financial inclusion, poverty and income inequality in developing Asia* (Working paper. 426, ADB working paper series).

Pathak, H. P., & Gyakali, M. (2010). 'Role of microfinance in employment generation: A case study of microfinance program of Paschimanchal Grameen Bikash Bank'. *Journal of Nepalese Business Studies, 7*(1), 31–8.

Posten, H. O. (1984). Robustness of the two-sample t-test. In *Robustness of statistical methods and nonparametric statistics* (pp. 92–99). Springer, Dordrecht.

Rajak, D. (2008). Uplift and empower: The market, morality and corporate responsibility on South Africa's platinum belt. *In Hidden hands of market: Ethnographies of fair trade, ethical consumption, and corporate social responsibility* (pp. 297–324). Emerald Group Publishing Limited.

Rajasekaran, N. (2018). Including the excluded: The scenario of financial inclusion in India. *IOSR Journal of Business and Management, 20*(2), 64–69.

RBI Bulletin, 2006. Retrieved from https://rbidocs.rbi.org.in/rdocs/Bulletin/PDFs/68236.pdf.

Salia, P. J., & Mbwambo, J. S. (2014). Does microcredit make any difference on borrowers' businesses? Evidences from a survey of women owned microenterprises in Tanzania. *International Journal of Social Sciences and Entrepreneurship, 1*(9), 431–444.

Shankar, S. (2013). Financial inclusion in India: Do microfinance institutions address access barriers. *ACRN Journal of Entrepreneurship Perspectives, 2*(1), 60–74.

Shapiro, S. S., & Wilk, M. B. (1965). An analysis of variance test for normality (complete samples). *Biometrika, 52*(3/4), 591–611.

Shelby, L. B. (2011). Beyond Cronbach's alpha: Considering confirmatory factor analysis and segmentation. *Human Biases of Wildlife, 16*(2), 142–148.

Shyam, A. (2019). East India leads with 40% microfinance business. *The Economic Times*. http://www.google.com/amp/s/m.economictimes.com/markets/stocks/news/east-india-leads-with-40-microfinance-business/amp_articleshow/70238386.cms.

Singh, Y. (2013). Effect of self-help group in economic empowerment of rural women in Himachal Pradesh. *Journal of Indian Research, 1*(3), 54–61.

Taiwo, J. N. (2012). *The impact of microfinance on welfare and poverty alleviation in Southwest Nigeria* (Ph.D. thesis). Department of Banking and Finance, Covenant University.

Wahab, H., Bunyau, W., & Rezaul Islam, M. (2018). Microcredit for rural poverty alleviation and social well-being: A study of Sabah. *Malaysia*. https://doi.org/10.1111/aswp.12133

Zikmund, W. G., & Babin, B. J. (2012). *Marketing research* (10th ed.). South-Western/Cengage Learning.

Determinants of Trust, Security, Privacy and Risk Factors in Embracing Online Banking

M. Krishna Murthy and S. Varalakshmi

1 Introduction

In the past years, the banks have introduced various services like opening different types savings bank accounts to the customers, issuing various cards namely debit cards and credit cards, providing various bank loans and creating opportunities for the customers to invest their money safely with different schemes. Online banking is nerve center of a nation which helps to achieve the objectives of a country. Banks provide E-banking services to the customer through telephone lines and computer channels (Kalakota & Whinston, 1996). The banking industry has completely transformed into online mode of providing various hi-tech services to its customers. (Ghaziri, 1998). Customers receive various online banking

M. Krishna Murthy (✉)
Higher College of Technology, University of Technology and Applied Sciences, Muscat, Sultanate of Oman
e-mail: krishna.murthy@hct.edu.om

S. Varalakshmi
Department of Business and Accounting, Muscat College, Muscat, Sultanate of Oman
e-mail: drsv2012@gmail.com

Ananda S. and D. Singh (eds.), *Financial Inclusion in Emerging Markets*,
https://doi.org/10.1007/978-981-16-2652-4_10

services with the same set of staff by sitting in one corner which is high speed and latest in nature.

In the past, banks used to provide various traditional services of providing loans, checking accounts, managing savings accounts, issuing debit and credit cards to its customers (Chai et al., 2015). It is the need of the hour that technology is fundamental requirement for everyone in financial sector. In recent years, banks have shifted traditional paradigm into online form. Technological enlargement has taken to the center position in providing financial services (Lumb, 2019). Globalization and technological advancement urged every banking institution to provide competitive services that stipulate economic growth (Goudarzi, 2013). Most of the studies have been carried out to find the perception of the customers related to trust and privacy factors but the studies must adopt the internet banking services. Hi-tech banking services in the financial industry have been changing from time to time with upgradation. Technological development in the banking industry replaced human activities into machine activities with fast mode.

2 Theoretical Background and Hypothesis Development

Every commercial bank started providing hi-tech e-services ensuring accuracy, reliability and efficiency for the customers. Theory of Reasoned Action developed by (Fishbein & Ajzen, 1975) supported with evidence that intention is the instant outcome of human behavior. Ajzen (1991) redefined the earlier theory and introduced one more important variable of behavior control. It is important to create trust on the technology that urges the customers to accept the adoption of online banking services (Akhlaq & Shah, 2011). Higher the percentage of customer's satisfaction adoption of technology is higher. Technology acceptance model stresses two important factors of ease of usage and usefulness. The aim of the TAM is to predict the acceptance of the customers and to diagnose the issues relating to technological adoption (Davis, 1986). Understanding of TAM help to determine the resistance level of the customers and to provide required suggestions to understand the adoption level. TAM 2 and TAM 3 models were redefined by (Venkatesh & Davis, 2000) and (Venkatesh & Bala, 2008) in continuation of TAM and have come up with different important determinants in the behavioral attitude of customers in taking a decision on technological updates.

Lee (2009) highlighted the determinants influencing the adoption of online banking services in addition to TPB and TAM considered additional variables consist of social aspects, performance aspects, security concerns, time factors and financial risks to understand and to integrate the model established. Technological acceptance model was base, and many studies were carried out determining the important factors influencing the use of information and adoption of information technologies. Later the authors have come across with a very important theory called UTAUT (Unified theory of acceptance and use of technology) that is considered as one of the most forceful and acceptable (Venkatesh et al., 2016). UTAUT and UTAUT 2 have been used by many scholars to find the determinants in adopting online banking services (Afshan & Sharif, 2016; Hui Ling et al., 2015; Lazuras & Ketikidis, 2016; Williams et al., 2015). It is concluded that the UTAUT factors namely performance expectancy, effort efficacy, facilitating conditions and behavior intentions have found most significant determinants in adopting online banking services (Rahi et al., 2019). Taking UTAUT model as base this study has been carried by considering very important determinants of trust, security, privacy and risk in adoption of online banking services by establishing a conceptual model. A study on investigation of determinants of acceptance factors of online banking services in extension of UTAUT model revealed that experience of the users of banking customers also impacting factor in adoption of online banking services (Tarhini et al., 2016). This proposed model would help to identify the important determinants that influence the customer behavior in adopting online banking services in Sultanate of Oman.

2.1 Determinants of Trust

Trust is trustworthiness of the service provider of online services (Alsajjan & Dennis, 2010). Trust is not one component as it is complicated that consists of various dimensions (McKnight & Chervany, 2014). Trust is very important factor that influence the customer loyalty on the service provider (Hernandez-Ortega, 2011). According to Kim et al. (2009), trust is one of the important aspects of traits which is believed with the honest and consist of reliability on a particular activity. Trust is essential in a customer's decision to go for online purchase to proceed for a transaction on seller's integrity and honesty (Zhu et al., 2011). This is a key variable in online transactions as it is not easy to believe a seller with a sense of uncertainty (Afshan & Sharif, 2016; Akhlaq & Ahmed, 2013). Trust has been registered as one of the essential factors that determine the success of adoption of online banking services (Benbasat et al., 2016; Yousefi & Nasirpour, 2015). Low trust factor of the customers influenced the low degree of adoption of subsequent online banking services (Kumar et al., 2017).

H1: Trust factors of banking services have a positive influence on adoption of online banking services.

2.2 *Determinants of Security*

Website security is primary factor for the customers to enter and try their transactions in online (Al Sharafi et al., 2018; Flavian et al., 2006; Kim et al., 2008). According to Crabbe et al., (2009), the internet banking using wired network and other online channels are dangerous to security attacks. Wireless technologies provided by the banks are more secured, reliable when compared to traditional wired technologies (Lafraxo et al., 2019). Security of the banking technologies urge the customers to enter online transactions (Kim et al., 2008). While carrying out the financial transactions through various sources of online basis, customers expect the bank website ensure safety and security which was antecedent factor to adopt online banking services (Enrique et al., 2015). According to Myung et al., (2011) and Mukti (2000), security is the essential factor in the e-commerce development as the customers are scared and perceived high risk on online transactions. Hijacking and online frauds hinder customers to proceed online banking services and reflects negative publicity and hurt customer belief. They added that open networks are vulnerable and challenging the security factors and trustworthiness of the services provider (Ganesan & Vivekanandan, 2009). Banks serve services to the customers which are high-quality services with less expensive. Most of the customers use the E-banking channels to buy and sell goods and services which are less expensive with more security.

H2: Security factors of banking services have a positive influence on adoption of online banking services.

2.3 Determinants of Privacy

New generation banking services to the customers are slowly improving due to the privacy factor which has been a major barrier. Banks should ensure privacy and confidentiality of the data used in carrying out the various banking services that urge the customers to shift entirely to the technological paradigm (Pavlou, 2001). The level of customer's confidence and dissatisfaction is due to unsecured infrastructure in online banking transactions (Brack, 2000). It is the right of the customers to control their personal data on internet and personal information (Gerrard & Cunningham, 2003; Gerrard et al., 2006; Roberts, 2009). Essential factor for the failure of e-commerce technology-based transactions is privacy. Customers sacred to use their sensitive personal information in online channels (Walker et al., 2002). These transactions happen between various parties with the help of online that gives easy access to the customers to sell, buy, pay, receive and exchange of information easily, quickly with more security without risk (Poole, 2003).

H3: Privacy factors of banking services have a positive influence on adoption of online banking services.

2.4 Determinants of Risk

Most of the studies proved the risk in using online banking services is one of the primary obstacles for the customers to proceed online transaction and subsequent growth in e-commerce technologies (Bhatnagar et al., 2000; Featherman, 2001; Jarvenpaa & Tractinsky, 1999; Kolsaker et al., 2004; Liao & Cheung, 2001; Park et al., 2004; Pavlou, 2003; Ruyter et al., 2001). Risk is uncertainty linked with the magnitude of negative perception of the customers (Bauer, 1960). Customer's perception and their tolerance level on approaching buying strategies determine the degree of risk (Chan & Lu, 2004). Risk is key element and deciding factor among many variables on accepting the online banking tasks for the customers (Juwaheer et al., 2009). Major concern in online banking transactions is high risk of security as it involves financial information and determined as big challenge and barrier for the customers (Stafford, 2001).

H4: Risk factors of banking services have a positive influence on adoption of online banking services.

3 Methodology

3.1 Data Collection

A survey has been conducted to find the determinants of trust, security, privacy and risk factors in adoption of online banking services around Muscat City. Convenient Sampling method has been chosen to find the perception of the respondents form different age work group, different educational qualification and different income levels. Questionnaire consists of demographical variables of the customers and the variables relating to the trust, security, privacy and risk to adopt the online banking services. A pilot study was conducted by considering 10% (31 samples) of the original samples size of the study consist of various factors of demographical details and various determinants of trust, security, privacy and risk factors as pre-testing analyses to verify the reliability and validity of the questions included in the research instrument, to ensure the scale development of the questions and to ensure internal consistency. A total of 350 structured questionnaires were distributed to get the perception of the customers on the adoption of online banking services and 311 completed questionnaires were retrieved.

3.2 Scale Measurement

The study has used 5-point Likert scale as method of measurement and Cronbach's Alpha test was conducted on the samples estimated for pre-testing to modify the research instrument and to find the trustworthy and internal consistency of different variables considered in the study (Lehman et al., 2013). Cronbach's Alpha is stronger the relationship when the values are higher. The value of Alpha is equal or more than the standard value of 0.6 is treated as reliable and the value is less than 0.6 is treated as unreliable. The values are above 0.9 and above are treated as excellent and show having best internal consistency of the variables in the instrument.

4 Data Analysis

The study has adopted descriptive methodology to review and highlight the theoretical background and related conceptual factors relating to online banking technologies and analytical methodology to analyze the relationship between dependent and independent variables. SPSS latest software version 22 is used in the study (Chai et al., 2015). PLS-SEM v 3.0 has been used to evaluate the conceptual model and helps as the base of covariance based on structural equation modeling (SEM) to test the speculated hypothesis on the determinants of trust, security, privacy and risk factors in adoption of online banking services. Partial Least Square Structural Equation Modelling (PLS-SEM) is a common technique of estimating causal connection in path models that consist of latest constructs that measure and analyze indirectly by other various indicators (Ringle et al., 2010). SEM is set of multivariate statistical technique that helps to analyze the relationship between the one or more independent variables with one or more dependent variables (Tabachnick & Fidell, 1996). SEM ensure the in the research to analyze the multiple relationship between dependent and independent variables with the help of one of the most multivariate techniques in social sciences (Hair et al., 2011). In general, PLS-SEM is a component-based approach which is similar kind of principal components factor analysis. SEM ensures the estimation of the linear relationship between the dependent and independent variables, and it has the ability to test the several relationships with the help of single model without analyzing the relationship individually (Gefen, 2000).

4.1 Construct Reliability and Validity

The aim of the outer estimation model in the study analyzes the reliability, internal consistency and validity of the variables considered with the help of convergent and discriminant validity assessment (Hair et al., 2012). Cronbach's Alpha and composite reliability methods were used for evaluating the internal consistency in the construct reliability. Moreover, composite reliability is assumed to be better estimation and assessment than the Cronbach's Alpha assessment to estimate the internal consistency which ensures standardized loadings of the observed variables (Fornell & Larcker, 1981). From Table 1, it is found that the composite reliability values and Cronbach's values are above 0.70, the scales considered in the study are reasonably reliable as the values of the latent variables are

Table 1 Reliability and validity

Main constructs	*Items*	*Loadings*	*Cronbach's Alpha*	*CR*	*AVE*
Adoption of online banking services	Adoption1	0.794	0.814	0.867	0.568
	Adoption2	0.691			
	Adoption3	0.720			
	Adoption4	0.793			
	Adoption5	0.764			
Privacy	Privacy1	0.617	0.802	0.855	0.544
	Privacy2	0.655			
	Privacy3	0.765			
	Privacy4	0.822			
	Privacy5	0.806			
Risk	Risk1	0.773	0.756	0.846	0.582
	Risk2	0.826			
	Risk3	0.804			
	Risk4	0.633			
Security	Security1	0.722	0.767	0.850	0.588
	Security2	0.690			
	Security3	0.867			
	Security4	0.779			
Trust	Trust1	0.781	0.806	0.865	0.563
	Trust2	0.672			
	Trust3	0.775			
	Trust4	0.781			
	Trust5	0.736			

Source Developed by author using data obtained using Smart PLS v 3.0

more than the threshold level of 0.70. It is also found the average variance extracted from the average variance extracted table are more than 50% of the variance are considered in the model which are above 0.5 thus convergent validity was established and confirmed in the model. The above analysis established the validity of convergent and good internal consistency in the estimation mode (Barclay et al., 1995).

4.2 Fornell–Larcker Criterion Test

The Fornell and Larcker technique and its cross-loadings were considered to estimate the discriminant validity (Fornell & Larcker, 1981). The recommended standard of Fornell and Larcker techniques is that it should not get the same variances as any other variables which are more than

Table 2 Fornell-Larcker criterion test

	Adoption of online banking	*Privacy*	*Risk*	*Security*	*Trust*
Adoption of online banking	**0.753**				
Privacy	0.399	**0.738**			
Risk	0.595	0.424	**0.763**		
Security	0.521	0.595	0.338	**0.767**	
Trust	0.619	0.512	0.408	0.807	**0.750**

Source Developed by author using data obtained using Smart PLS v 3.0

average variance extracted. Table 2 shows that the squared correlation values are compared with the correlations from other latent variables. It is ensured that the correlation values are smaller values while compared to the squared root of the average variance extracted diagonally which ensures the satisfaction of the discriminant validity. The values ensured that the variables observed in the model in each construct show the given latent variable authenticating the discriminant validity of the model.

4.3 Cross-Loadings

Table 3 indicates the cross-loading of all the variables were more than the variables of inter-correlation of the latent variables of the other observed values in the study. Thus, it is ensured the cross-loadings estimation and analysis standard has supported with the acceptable validation for the discriminant validity of the estimation model in the study. Therefore, the conceptual model recommended is acceptable with adequate reliability, required convergent validity and discriminant validity and the verification of the research model.

From Table 4, it is verified the significance of path co-efficients using *t*-values under the non-parametric bootstrap techniques with the help of Smart PLS software. Bootstrap is a method of analyzing and evaluating the shape of the sampling distribution, spread of sampling distribution and bias of the sampling distribution of a particular statistic. Bootstrapping consider the large pre-specified samples of 5000 as the original samples (Chin, 1998).

Table 3 Cross-loading of variables

	Adoption of online banking	*Privacy*	*Risk*	*Security*	*Trust*
Adoption1	**0.794**	0.212	0.427	0.169	0.242
Adoption2	**0.691**	0.288	0.520	0.551	0.628
Adoption3	**0.720**	0.381	0.445	0.348	0.535
Adoption4	**0.793**	0.158	0.323	0.211	0.313
Adoption5	**0.764**	0.378	0.433	0.502	0.421
Privacy1	0.213	**0.617**	0.170	0.552	0.423
Privacy2	0.114	**0.655**	0.201	0.321	0.274
Privacy3	0.195	**0.765**	0.270	0.335	0.312
Privacy4	0.337	**0.822**	0.429	0.462	0.407
Privacy5	0.422	**0.806**	0.370	0.482	0.423
Risk1	0.477	0.345	**0.773**	0.226	0.231
Risk2	0.410	0.413	**0.826**	0.222	0.295
Risk3	0.494	0.390	**0.804**	0.349	0.436
Risk4	0.419	0.131	**0.633**	0.217	0.268
Security1	0.304	0.498	0.129	**0.722**	0.545
Security2	0.412	0.403	0.209	**0.690**	0.622
Security3	0.497	0.506	0.372	**0.867**	0.703
Security4	0.338	0.425	0.279	**0.779**	0.577
Trust1	0.524	0.267	0.342	0.467	**0.781**
Trust2	0.348	0.190	−0.025	0.612	**0.672**
Trust3	0.508	0.367	0.335	0.653	**0.775**
Trust4	0.501	0.507	0.339	0.627	**0.781**
Trust5	0.404	0.588	0.478	0.716	**0.736**

Source Developed by author using data obtained using Smart PLS v 3.0

4.4 *Path Co-efficients*

H1 made that trust factors of banking services have a positive influence on adoption of online banking services. Table 4 shows (mean value 0.410, standard deviation 0.064, *t*-statistics 6.452 and *p* values are 0.000) which are less than 5% level of significance proved that the trust factors of the respondents have positive and significant impact on selection of online banking services. H2 made that security factors of banking services have a positive influence on adoption of online banking services (mean value 0.065, standard deviation 0.061, *t*-statistics 1.049 and *p* values are 0.294) which are more than 5% level of significance proved that there is no influence of security factors of the respondents in adoption of online banking services. H3 made that privacy factors of banking services have a positive influence on adoption of online banking services (mean value −0.026,

Table 4 Path co-efficients

	Original sample (O)	*Sample mean (M)*	*Standard deviation (STDEV)*	t *statistics* (|*O/STDEV*|)	p *values*
Privacy → adoption of online banking Services	−0.026	−0.023	0.042	0.632	**0.528**
Risk → adoption of online banking Services	0.417	0.417	0.043	9.665	**0.000**
Security → adoption of online banking services	0.064	0.065	0.061	1.049	**0.294**
Trust → adoption of online banking services	0.410	0.410	0.064	6.452	**0.000**

Source Developed by author using data obtained using Smart PLS v 3.0

standard deviation 0.042, t-statistics 0.632 and p values are 0.528) which are more than 5% level of significance proved that there is no influence of privacy factors of the respondents in adoption of online banking services. H4 made that Risk factors of banking services have a positive influence on adoption of online banking services (mean value 0.417, standard deviation 0.043, t-statistics 9.665 and p values are 0.000) which are less than 5% level of significance proved that the risk factors of the respondents have positive and significant impact on selection of online banking services.

4.5 Collinearity Variance Inflation Factors

Full collinearity variance inflation factors (VIFs) could be carried out as a common technique bias test than the traditional test on exploratory factor analysis. When the latest variables have threshold is perfect word we can use that the resultant variable should be less than 3.3 could be

Table 5 Collinearity variance inflation factor

Privacy3	2.022
Privacy4	1.776
Privacy5	1.521
Risk1	1.740
Risk2	2.007
Risk3	1.745
Risk4	1.482
Security1	2.174
Security2	1.501
Security3	1.967
Security4	1.934
Trust1	1.657
Trust2	1.463
Trust3	1.828
Trust4	1.807
Trust5	1.744

Source Developed by author using data obtained using Smart PLS v 3.0

considered as the indication that the model created on the study is free from common techniques of bias (Kock, 2015).

It is important to understand that there exist no collinearity issues in the model before estimating the structural model. Table 5 shows that collinearity variance inflation factors of each construct in the study of PLS are less than the threshold value of 3.3, and therefore, it ensures that there are no inner collinearity issues in the model.

4.6 Evaluation of Structural Relationships

Structural relationship can be verified and analyzed by considering the explained variance on endogenous latent variables with the help of calculating R2. The results of the structural relationship model are depicted in Fig. 1 (Cohen et al., 2003). R2 estimates the overall effect on the size of the model created in the study. Similar to the regression that the model explains 0.525% of the variance in the adoption of online banking services is explained by the model and in other words the model is satisfactory which is greater than the cut off value and the greater the co-efficient more significance level of effect on endogenous latent variables. Risk factors have highest co-efficient value of 0.417 and trust factors with the co-efficient value of 0.410 have maximum effect in adoption of the online

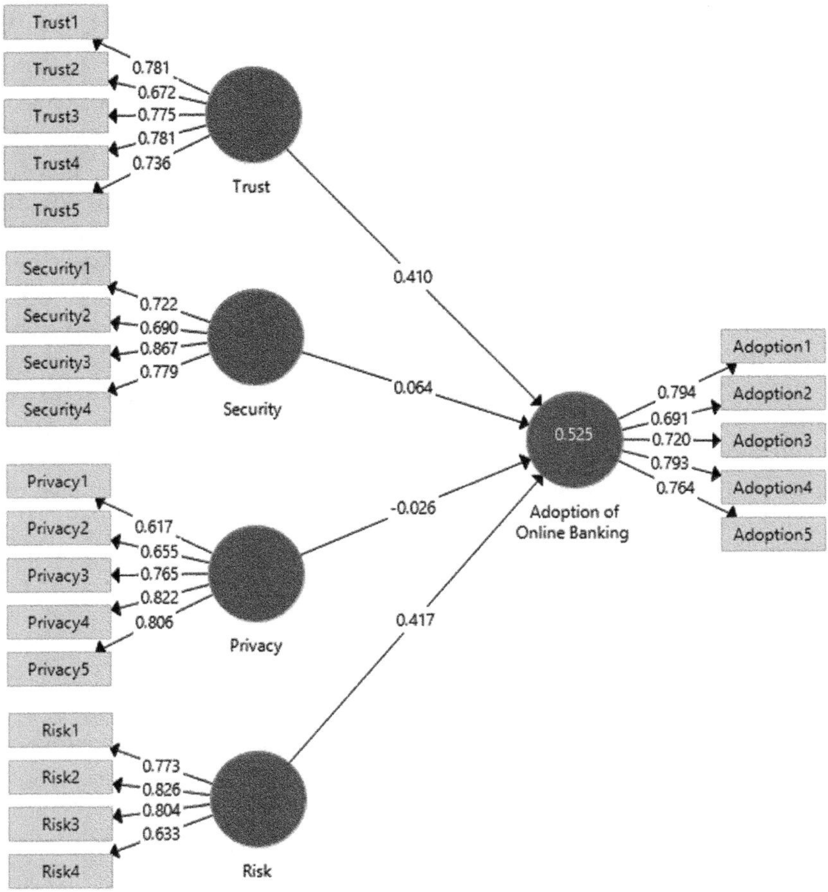

Fig. 1 Graphical representation of the model (*Source* Developed by author using data obtained using Smart PLS v 3.0)

banking services. Security factors with the co-efficient values of 0.064 and privacy factors −0.026 show the weak and negative effect in adoption of online banking services.

5 Conclusion

This study has investigated in detail the adoption of online banking services at Muscat, Sultanate of Oman. Theories like TAM, TAM2, TAM3, UTAUT and UTAUT 2 have been explored in developing the framework. Literatures were reviewed on very important determinants of trust, security, privacy and risk factors in embracing online banking services using partial least square technique to structural equation modeling. The study concluded that customer's trust factors and risk factors while using online banking services have significant positive relationship in adoption of online banking services and at the same time privacy factors and security factors have insignificant relationship with co-efficient values of −0.026 and 0.064 with weak and negative impact in adoption of online banking services. Structural relationship verified and analyzed by considering of explained variance on endogenous latent variables and model explained that 0.525% of the variance in embracing of online banking is explained by the model. Moreover, the novelty and model of this study can be conducted on the customers of banking industry throughout the country to understand the determinants of banking in adoption of online banking services.

References

Afshan, S., & Sharif, A. (2016). Acceptance of mobile banking framework in Pakistan. *Telematics and Informatics, 33*(2), 370–387.

Ajzen, I. (1991). The theory of planned behavior. *Organizational Behaviour and Human Decision Process, Scientific Research, 50*(2), 179–211.

Akhlaq, A., & Ahmed, E. (2013). The effect of motivation on trust in the acceptance of internet banking in a low income country. *International Journal of Bank Marketing, 32*(2), 15–125.

Akhlaq, M. A., & Shah, A. (2011). Internet banking in Pakistan: Finding complexities. *Journal of Internet Banking and Commerce, 16*(1), 1–14.

Alsajjan, B., & Dennis, C. (2010). Internet banking acceptance model: Cross market examination. *Journal of Business Research, Advances in Internet Consumer Behaviour and Marketing Strategy, 63*(9), 959–963.

Al Sharafi, M., Arshah, R. A., Herzallah, F. A. T., & Abu Shanab, E. A. (2018). The impact of customer trust and perception of security and privacy on the acceptance of online banking services. *Structural Equation Modeling Approach, 4*(1), 1–14.

Barclay, D., Thompson, R., & Dan Higgins, C. (1995). The partial least square approach to causal modeling: Personal computer adoption and use an illustration. *Technology Studies, 14*(2), 189–217.

Bauer, R. (1960). Consumer behavior as risk taking, in dynamic marketing for a changing world. *American Marketing Association, 1*(1), 389–398.

Benbasat, M. S., Gefen, D., Leimeister, J. M., & Pavlou, P. A. (2016). Trust: An MIS. *Quarterly Research, 34*(2), 361–371.

Bhatnagar, A., Misra, S., & Rao, H. R. (2000). On risk, convenience and internet shopping behavior. *Communication of the ACM, 43*(1), 98–105.

Brack, K. (2000). E procurement: The next frontier. *Industrial Distribution, 89*(1), 65–70.

Chai, B.-H., Tan, P. S., & Goh, T. S. (2015). Banking Services that influence the bank performance. *Social and Behavioral Sciences, 224*(1), 401–407.

Chan, S., & Lu, M. T. (2004). Understanding internet banking adoption and use behavior: A Hong Kong perspective. *Journal of Global Information Management, 12*(3), 21–43.

Chen, F. F. (2007). Sensitivity of goodness of fit indexes to lack of measurement invariance. *Structural Equation Model, 14*(3), 464–504.

Chin, W. W. (1998). The partial least squares approach for structural equation modeling. In G. A. Marcoulides (Ed.), *Modern methods for business research*. Lawrence Erlbaum Associates Publishers (vol. 1, issue no. 1, pp. 295–336).

Cohen, J., Cohen, P., West, S. G., & Aiken, L. S. (2003). *Applied multiple regression/correlation analysis for the behavioral sciences* (3rd ed., pp. 147–151). Lawrence Erlbaum associates publishers.

Crabbe, M., Standing, C., Standing, S., & Karjaluoto, H. (2009). An adoption model for mobile banking in Ghana. *International Journal of Journal of Mobile Communications, 7*(5), 515–543.

Davis, F. D. (1986). A technology acceptance model for empirically testing new end-user information system: Theory and results. *Sloan School of Management, Massachusetts Institute of Technology, 13*(3), 319–340.

Enrique, B. D., Elena, C. T., & Tomas Escobar, R. (2015). Influence of trust and perceived value on the intention to purchase travel online: Integrating the effects of assurance on trust antecedents. *Tourism Management, 47*(1), 286–302.

Fishbein, M., & Ajzen, I. (1975). Belief, attitude, intention and behavior: An introduction to theory and research. *Addison Wesley, 27*(1), 41–57.

Featherman, M. (2001). Is perceived risk germane to technology acceptance research? *AMCIS Proceedings, Boston, MA, 1*(1), 1–5.

Flavian, C., Guinaliu, M., & Gurrea, R. (2006). The role played by perceived usability, satisfaction and consumer trust on website loyalty. *Information & Management, 43*(1), 1–14.

Fornell, C., & Lrcker, D. F. (1981). Evaluating structural equation models with unobservable variables and measurement error. *Journal of Marketing Research, 18*(1), 39–50.

Fornell, C., & Larcker, D. F. (1981). *Structural equation models with unobservable variables and measurement error: Algebra and statistics*, (vol. 18, issue no. 3, pp. 1–5).

Ganesan, R., & Vivekanandan, K. (2009). A secured hybrid architecture model for internet banking. *Journal of Internet Banking and Commerce, 8*(12), 415–418.

Gefen, D. (2000). Structural equation modeling and regression: Guidelines for research practice. *Structural Equation Model, 18*(2), 7–34.

Gerrard, P., & Cunningham, J. B. (2003). The diffusion of internet banking among Singapore consumers. *International Journal of Bank Marketing, 21*(1), 16–28.

Gerrard, P., Cunningham, J. B., & Devlin, J. F. (2006). Why consumers are not using internet banking: A qualitative study. *Journal of Services Marketing, 20*(3), 161.

Ghaziri, H. (1998). Information technology in the banking sector: Opportunities, threats strategies. *IT Banking, 98*(2), 175–212.

Goudarzi, S. (2013). Impact of trust on internet banking adoption: A literature review. *Australian Journal of Basic and applied Sciences, 7*(7), 334–347.

Hair, J. F., Ringle, C. M., & Sarstedt, M. (2011). PLS-SEM: Indeed a silver bullet. *Journal of Marketing Theory and Practice, 19*(2), 139–152.

Hair, J. F., Sarstedt, M., Ringle, C. M., & Mena, J. A. (2012). An assessment of the use of partial least squares structural equation modeling in in marketing research. *Journal of Academic Marketing Sciences, 40*(1), 414–433.

Hernandez-Ortega, B. (2011). The role of post use trust in the acceptance of a technology: Drivers and consequences. *Technovations, 31*(10), 523–538.

Hui Ling, C., Islam, M. A., Abdul Manaf, A. H., & Wan Mustafa, W. M. (2015). Users satisfaction towards online banking in Malaysia. *International Business Management, 9*(1), 15–27.

Jarvenpaa, S., & Tractinsky, N. (1999). Consumer trust in an internet store: A cross-cultural validation. *Journal of Computer Mediated Communication, 5*(2), 1–35.

Juwaheer, T., Pudaruth, S., & Lee, M.c. (2009). Factors influencing the adoption of internet banking: An integration of TAM and TPB with perceived risk and perceived benefit. *Electronic Commerce Research and Application, 8*(3), 130–141.

Kalakota, R., & Whinston, A. B. (1996). *Frontiers of electronic commerce*. Addison-Wesley Publishing Company, 96(41134), 1–5.

Kim, D. J., Steinfield, C., & Lai, Y. (2008). Revising the role of web assurance seals in business to consumer electronic commerce. *Decision Support Systems, 44*(4), 1000–1015.

Kim, K., Prabhakar, B., & Park, S. (2009). Trust, perceived risk, and trusting behavior in internet banking. *Asia Pacific Journal of Information Systems, 19*(3), 3–1.

Kock, N. (2015). Common method bias in PLS-SEM: A full collinearity assessment approach. *International Journal of e-Collaboration, 11*(4), 1–10.

Kolsaker, A., Lee-Kelley, L., & Choy, P. C. (2004). The reluctant hong kong consumer: Purchasing travel online. *International Journal of Consumer Studies, 28*(3), 295–304.

Kumar, M., Sareen, S., & Barquissau, E. (2017). Relationship between types of trust and level of adoption of internet banking. *Problems and Prospective in Management, 10*(1), 82–92.

Lafraxo, Y., Hadri, F., Amhal, H., & Rossafi, A. (2019). The effect of trust, perceived risk and security on the adoption of mobile banking in Morocco. *20th International Conference on Enterprise Information Systems, 2*(1), 497–502.

Lazuras, Kurila, J. L., & Ketikidis, P. H. (2016). Message framing and acceptance of branchless banking technology. *Electronic Commerce Research and Applications, 17*(1),12–18.

Lee, M. C. (2009). Factors influencing the adoption of internet banking: An integration of TAM and TPB with perceived risk and perceived benefit. *Electronic Commerce Research and Applications, 8*(3), 130–141.

Lehman, A., O'Rourke, N., Hatcher, L., & Stepanski, E. (2013). JMP for basic Univariate and Multivariate statistics: Methods for researchers and social scientists. *SAS Institute, 2*(2), 412–417.

Liao, Z., & Cheung, M. T. (2001). Internet-based e-shopping and consumer attitudes an empirical study. *Information & Management, 38*(5), 299–306.

Lumb, R. (2019). Bridging the technology gap in financial boardrooms. *Accenture Strategy, 1*(1), 1–10.

McKnight, H. D., & Chervany, N. L. (2014). What trust means in e-commerce customer relationships: An interdisciplinary conceptual typology. *International Journal of Electronic Commerce, 6*(2), 35–59.

Mukti, N. (2000). Barriers to putting businesses on the internet in Malaysia. *The Electronic Journal of Information Systems in Developing Countries, 2*(6), 1–4.

Myung, J. K., Namho C., & Choong, K. L. (2011). The effect of perceived trust on electronic commerce: Shopping online for tourism products and services in South Korea. *Tourism Management, 32*(1), 256–265.

Park, J., Lee, D., & Ahn, J. (2004). Risk-focused e-commerce adoption model: A cross-country study. *Journal of Global Information Management, 7*(1), 6–30.

Pavlou, P. (2001). *Integrating trust in electronic commerce with the technology acceptance model: Model development and validation*. Conference Proceedings, Americas Conference on Information Systems. https://citeseerx.ist.psu.edu/viewdoc/download?doi=10.1.1.859.567&rep=rep1&type=pdf.

Pavlou, P. A. (2003). Consumer acceptance of electronic commerce: Integrating trust and risk with the technology acceptance model. *International Journal of Electronic Commerce, 7*(3), 101–134.

Poole, W. (2003). Housing in the macroeconomy. *Federal Reserve Bank of St. Louis Review, 85*(3), 1–8.

Rahi, S., Mansour, M. M. O., Alghizzawai, M., & Alnaser, F. M. (2019). Integration of UTAUT model in internet banking adoption context. *Journal of Research in Interactive Marketing, 13*(3), 411–435.

Ringle, C. M., Sarstedt, M., & Mooi, E. A. (2010). Response based segmentation using finite mixture partial least squares theoretical foundations and an application to American Customer satisfaction Index Data. *Data Mining Annals of Information System, 8*(1), 19–49.

Roberts, B. (2009). Stakeholder power in e-business adoption with a game theory perspective. *Journal of Theoretical Applied Electronic Commerce Research, 4*(1), 12–22.

Ruyter, Ko de., Wetzels, M., & Kleijnen, M. (2001). Customer adoption of e-service: An experimental study. *International Journal of Service Industry Management, 12*(2), 184–207.

Stafford, B. (2001). Risk management and internet banking: What every banker needs to know community Banker. *Research Gate Publications, 51*(5), 935–965.

Tabachnick, B., & Fidell, L. (1996). *Using multivariate statistics* (3rd ed., pp. 1–11). Harper Collins College Publications.

Tarhini, A., El Masri, M., Ali, M., & Serrano, A. (2016). Extending the UTAUT model to understand the customer acceptance and use of internet banking in Lebanon: A structural equation modeling approach. *Emerald Insight, 29*(4), 830–834.

Venkatesh, V., & Bala, H. (2008). Technology acceptance model 3 and a research agenda on interventions. *Journal of the Decision Sciences Institute, 39*(2), 273–315.

Venkatesh, V., & Davis, F. D. (2000). A theoretical extension of the technology acceptance model: Four longitudinal field studies. *Research Gate Publications, 46*(2), 186–204.

Venkatesh, V., James, Y., Thong, L., & Xin, X. (2016). Unified theory of acceptance and use of technology: A synthesis and the road ahead. *Journal of the Association for the Information System, 17*(5), 328–376.

Walker, R. H., Hecker, R., Francis, H., & Craig Lees, M. (2002). An empirical investigation of Malaysia, technology enabled service delivery: An investigation of reasons affecting customer adoption and rejection. *International Journal of Service Industry Management, 13*(1), 91–106.

Williams, Michael-D., Rana, Nripendra-P., & Dwivedi, Y.-K. (2015). The unified theory of acceptance and use of technology (UTAUT): A literature review. *Journal of Enterprise Information Management, 28*(3), 433–488.

Zhu, D. S., Chih Lee, Z., & O'Neal, G. S. (2011). Mr. Risk, Please trust me: Trust antecedents that increase online consumer purchase intention. *Journal of Internet Banking and Commerce, 16*(3), 1–23.

Government Policies and Regulations

Microfinance Sector and the Supportive Role of Regulator in its Transformation: A Case Study from India

Jesu Raju Thomas and Jyothi Kumar

1 Introduction

Microfinance business model's social relevance and ability to establish a sustainable financial institution resulted in emphasizing the act of balancing the social return and financial returns. The twin nature of financial return and social return resulted in capital flow to the sector. Microfinance institution's primary customers are from bottom of pyramid mass population. Generally, Bottom of pyramid population is excluded from the formal banking system. Government agencies also monitor and introduce policy directions periodically to protect the interest of all the stakeholders of microfinance sector and link the bottom of pyramid mass population to formal banking system.

Microfinance institutions achieve the financial sustainability through providing different financial products and services, namely credit and savings, insurance, money transfer, ATM and bank linkage. The development objective of microfinance institutions is achieved through financial

---

J. R. Thomas (✉) · J. Kumar
CHRIST (Deemed to be University), Bengaluru, India

J. Kumar
e-mail: jyothi.s@christuniversity.in

Ananda S. and D. Singh (eds.), *Financial Inclusion in Emerging Markets*,
https://doi.org/10.1007/978-981-16-2652-4_11

inclusion of marginalized, promoting financial literacy program, poverty reduction, creating employment, social justice and economic empowerment.

In many countries, microfinance has been used as a tool for formal banking system since the early 1970s, but it became prevalent after the Nobel Peace Prize awarded to Professor Muhammad Yunus and Grameen Bank of Bangladesh (Faruk Ahmeti & February, 2014). At the same period, i.e., in the early 1970s, India also witnessed microfinance services when Self-Employed Women's Association (SEWA) formed Shri Mahila Sahakari Bank that provides financial services to economically weaker working in the unorganized sector in urban areas (Devaraja, 2011).

Grameen Bank of Bangladesh played a very important role in developing and promoting Grameen model in the microfinance sector all over the world. Non-Governmental Organizations in India with different legal status such as mutual benefits trust and societies which are engaged in various social development initiatives started to implement microfinance program in their target areas. National Bank for Agriculture and Rural Development (NABARD) is an apex Development Finance Institution in India also started to promote microfinance through in a different model, namely Self-Help Group Model and bank linkage program. Financial institutions and banks used to provide microcredit through Non-Governmental Organizations. Non-Governmental Organizations are witnessed the financial sustainability and social development through microfinance initiatives. Non-Governmental Organizations are not for-profit organization and not able to appeal investors and lenders to scale-up their outreach and operation area. Constraint in the legal structure pushed the NGOs to adopt the for-profit legal entity of Non-Banking Finance Company (NBFC) which allowed the institution to raising capital, having diversified ownership, and attaining legality (Satagopan & Ravindran, 2012).

Till the Notification of Reserve Bank of India dated December 2, 2011, for-profit microfinance institutions are registered as Non-Banking Finance Company. By studying the importance of microfinance in reaching the unbanked and to protect the interest of microfinance clients, a special regulatory framework for Non-banking Finance Company-Microfinance institution (NBFC-MFI) was introduced by Reserve Bank of India on December 2, 2011 as per Y H Malegam committee recommendation, thereafter all the exiting for-profit microfinance institutions and new for-profit microfinance institutions are obligate registered as Non-Banking Company-Microfinance Institutions (Reserve Bank of India, 2015).

1.1 Mission Drift of Microfinance Institutions

Microfinance business model with an objective to provide the financial services to the marginalized became successful program in all the developing countries. Along with the success stories of microfinance, paradox of mission drift of microfinance institutions became a global phenomenon which was noticed in South Asia, East Asia, Africa Eastern Europe and Latin America.

To understand whether microfinance institutions deserting the purpose of microfinance that to help the poor in reducing the poverty level or alleviate poverty in attaining the institutional sustainability. Mr. Afsheen Abrar and Attiya Y. Javid two researchers tried to study how microfinance institution's social mission and sustainability could be managed to prevent mission drift. For this study, they have collected the data from 382 microfinance institutions. These 382 microfinance institutions were in 70 countries in South Asia, East Asia, Africa Eastern Europe and Latin America. They hypothesized that profitability of microfinance institutions positively depends on size of average microfinance loan. The study findings gave indication that average loan size has increased and this gave indication that there was mission drift of poverty reduction in microfinance institutions because the average loan size symbolizes the depth of outreach consideration. These outcomes are similar to the results of Mersland and Strom. They also found that in Africa and the American region, to make higher profits, older microfinance institutions have given larger loan amounts to clients (Abrar & Javaid, 2014).

Banco Compartamos, a Mexico-based microfinance institution was started in 1990 as a Non-Governmental Organization that was transformed as for-profit company in the year 2000. Banco Compartamos received grants from different development organization namely USAID and ACCION. USAID has given $2 million, ACCION has given grant for technical assistance and to buy the share of new for-profit company of $ 2million and $8 million, respectively. Apart from this, ACCION has also given $1 million subordinate to the finance company. Banco Compartamos received banking license in 2006, after receiving full banking license in the year 2007, they listed for Initial Public Offer that was oversubscribed 13 times. Investors have paid roughly around $6 million for the shares of Compartamos in year 1998–2000 that was increased to book value of $126 million by the end of 2006. The increase of book value is due to higher profit by way of charging higher interest to their borrowers. Interest yield was 86.3% plus value-added tax of 15%, all together interest paid by the customers were about 100% (Rosenberg, 2007).

Likewise, in India also Swayam Krishi Sangam (SKS), the first microfinance institution in the country that launched Initial Public Offer was in the news for its commercialization assertion of forceful loan collection practices on those clients who were unable to pay the high interest rates and committed suicides. The promoter of SKS microfinance, Mr. Vikram Akula accepted that 17 suicides out of the total 30 suicides happened because of the higher interest rate (Alok & Joseph, 2012). Going further, Mr. Vikram also acknowledged that Noble Lauriat Yunus was right when he quoted "Bringing private equity into social enterprise was much harder than anticipated." Mr. Vikram told in social enterprise conference at Harvard University that "he had focused on scaling SKS's model and had not fully anticipated the potential downside of accessing the public market for social enterprise," (Thirani, 2012).

Mission drift trends were observed in the three publicly traded microfinance institutions in different countries, namely SKS of India, Banco Compartamos of Mexico and Equity Bank of Kenya. In the study, it is noticed that in the three microfinance institutions, there was increase in portfolio and number of clients heading up to the IPO and substantial increase after IPO. The portfolio and number of clients of these microfinance institutions were high compared to the competitor's microfinance institutions in the respective countries of these three microfinance institutions. Operation expenses to portfolio of these three microfinance institutions were reduced in the year before and after IPO. Two important variables of the study were average loan size per borrower and percentage of women served. SKS used to sever only women, i.e., 100% women borrowers before and after IPO so there was no mission drift when it comes to reaching women members but average loan per borrower decreased after IPO issue from $121 to $77. The average loan size per borrower was increased before IPO, i.e., in the year 2010 but after IPO in 2011 the average loan size per borrower reduced, compared to the competitors so there may be mission drift after the IPO in August 2010 by providing smaller average loans. After the IPO of Banco Compartamos, number of women borrowers were reduced and average loan per borrower was increased which was the sign of mission drift after IPO.

The results of Equity Bank were different compared to SKS and Compartamos. After IPO of Equity Bank, average size of the loan did not change significantly, and women borrowers were significantly increased. There was no change in the situation before and after IPO in the case of Equity Bank. Above all, Equity Bank has reduced the interest rate than its competitors. The researcher concluded that there is some indication of mission drift in the limited samples of publicly traded microfinance institutions but these evidences are not enough to conclude that IPO of microfinance institutions will result in mission drift (Segill & Ascioglu, 2013).

2 Commercialization of Microfinance in India

Microfinance syndicates the two important aspects of its business, i.e., culture of development and capitalism for providing credit to the unbanked to improve living conditions, labor productivity, manage risk and enable consumptions and generate social capital (World Economic Forum, 2014). Commercialization of microfinance has affected the development culture of microfinance that resulted in neglecting the interest of the borrowers, aggressive growth and irresponsible collection practices. SKS's Initial Public Offer success transformed microfinance to high profit-making business from social business. Microfinance institutions used to charge exorbitant interest rate to achieve sustainability that welcomed the disparagement from politicians in the countries like India, Sri Lanka, Bangladesh and Cambodia (Fernando, 2008).

SKS microfinance's IPO oversubscribed 13 times (Singh, 2013). After the successful Initial Public Offer of SKS microfinance in August 2010, the Government of Andhra Pradesh came up with an ordinance to regulate the microfinance industry on 10th October 2010 in the entire state of Andhra Pradesh that distorted the entire microfinance industry of Andhra Pradesh. Political sentiments toward the microfinance sector seriously affected the microfinance institutions and sector of India who were working in other states. The ordinance is issued by the Panchayat Raj and Rural Development (RD-I) Department titled "Andhra Pradesh Microfinance institutions (Regulation of money lending) ordinance 2010." The ordinance covered Self-Help Groups, microfinance institutions, Society under mission for eliminating poverty under municipal areas and Society for elimination of rural poverty. Government of Andhra Pradesh created

Self-Help Groups to promote financial inclusion mission of Government, the microfinance institutions started to capture the Self-Help groups formed by the government and started to lend microcredit to the same group with higher interest rates compared to the interest rates of Government promoted bank linkage program. To protect the poor from exploiting and stop lending to the Self-Help Group by microfinance institutions and individuals State Government of Andhra Pradesh introduced the Andhra Pradesh microfinance ordinance (Government of Andhra Pradesh, 2010).

Microfinance institutions stakeholders, industry associates and industry experts come together to explain the role of microfinance in reaching the marginalized and misconceptions about the microfinance sector. Microfinance institutions collectively come together with various social performance management initiatives to protect the interest of the microfinance clients like adopting the code of conduct, multiple borrowers tracking and establishing a credit bureau. The Reserve Bank of India also introduced regulation on microfinance business operation of Non-banking finance company like interest cap, transparency in financial products and fair collection practices. Indian microfinance sector experienced high growth rate, until Andhra Pradesh microfinance crisis in the year 2010. After Andhra Pradesh microfinance ordinance, microfinance sector of India experienced uncertainty during the year 2010 and 2011. "During this period annual growth of portfolio and borrowers of 24 larger MFIs of India has reduced. The portfolio growth has reduced from 76% to 7.2% in the year 2010–2011. The borrower's growth has reduced from 43% to 7.5% in the year 2010–2011. During the financial year 2011–2012, there was no growth in borrowers and portfolio. Borrowers and portfolio grown negatively i.e. −27.3% and −18.3% compared to 2010–2011 as shown in the table 1."

Table 1 Indian Microfinance sector-borrowers and portfolio growth

Year	*2006–2007*	*2007–2008*	*2008–2009*	*2009–2010*	*2010–2011*	*2011–2012*
Borrowers	35%	66%	59%	43%	7.5%	−27.3%
Portfolio	45%	132%	125%	76%	7.2%	−18.3%

Source Prepared by the authors based on Effect of Social Performance on sustainability of Microfinance Institutions Thesis (2018) (Thomas & Kumar, 2018)

3 Reserve Bank of India's Supportive Regulations for the Growth of Microfinance Sector

Indian microfinance industry faced setback after introducing Andhra Pradesh microfinance ordinance. By understanding the need of microfinance sector to achieve the financial inclusion objectives, RBI has formed the Melegam committee to study the Indian microfinance sector in October 2010. After evaluating the Melegam committee report, RBI recognized the broad framework of the committee report and according to the recommendation, a special category of non-banking finance company was introduced who are engaged in microfinance business called Non-Banking Finance Company-Microfinance Institution. Following are the direction of RBI toward Non-Banking Finance Company-Microfinance institutions Direction 2011.

To be a NBFC-MFI following conditions needs to be fulfilled:

a. Minimum net owned fund. Minimum owned fund INR 5 Crore, for North-East region INR 2 crore
b. Qualifying assets norms: Qualifying assets norms means financial institution needs to fulfill the following criteria
i. Loans disbursed by the NBFC-MFI to borrowers whose family annual income is not more than INR. 100,000 in rural areas and 160,000 in urban or semi-urban areas.
ii. Disbursed loan amount does not exceed INR 60,000 when it comes to first loan cycle and INR 100,000 in subsequent loans.
iii. Total indebtedness of the borrowers should not exceed INR 100,000.
iv. If loan amount exceeds INR 15,000, tenure of the loan should not be less than 24 months.
v. Loan should be provided without any collateral security.
vi. Fifty percent of aggregate of total loans should be given for income generating activity
vii. Loan repayment schedules, e.g., weekly, fortnightly or monthly should be fixed based on the choice of the clients.
c. Other NBFC or NBFC which does not qualify NBFC-MFI cannot extend loans to microfinance sector not more than 10% of its total assets (Reserve Bank of India, 2015)

Prudential norms: Capital adequacy ratio for NBFC-MFI is 15% considering tier-I and tier-II capital. Tier-II capital should not exceed 100% of Tier-I capital at any point of time.
Asset classification norms: if interest and principle are overdue for a period of more than 90 days, they are considered as non-performance assets. Standard assets are those assets having no default of principle and interest rate.
Provision norms: Aggregate loan provision should not be less than the higher of 1 percent of the outstanding loan portfolio, 50% aggregate loan provision installments that are overdue over 90 days and less than 180 days, 100% aggregate loan provision installments that are overdue for over 180 days or more.
Pricing norms: Margin cap of 12% for the MFIs whose outstanding portfolio is less than INR 100 Crore and 10% for the MFIs whose outstanding portfolio is more than INR 100 Crore. Pricing norms is cost of funds plus margin or the average base rate of the five largest commercial banks multiplied by 2.75, whichever is lower. Processing charges should not be more than 1%.
Fair practice in lending norms: there should be only three components of charges that are interest rate, processing fee and insurance premium. There should not be any penalty charges for delay in payment and security deposit or margin money. MFIs should provide a loan agreement along with a loan card with vernacular language specifying the effective rate of interest, terms and conditions, borrower identification proof and acknowledgment of repayments. Effective rate of interest should be displayed in the website of the MFIs and in offices.
Lending norms: NBFC-MFI can lend to an individual borrower, member of Self-Help Groups (SHG) or Joint Liability Group (JLG). The borrower cannot be a member of more than one SHG or JLG. Loan sanctions and disbursements of loans should be done at a central place where more than one individual should be involved.
Fair practice code: The RBI has come up with fair practice code norms on loan application and processing, loan appraisal and terms and conditions, disbursement of loans including changes in terms and conditions, non-coercive method of recovery and disclosure in loan agreement and loan card (Thomas & Kumar, 2018).

Table 2 RBI revised the norms of qualifying assets criteria of NBFC-MFI

S.No	*Qualifying assets Criteria*	*Former criteria*	*Revised criteria*
1	Household income limit: increased	Rural: INR 100,000 Urban: INR 160,000	Rural: INR 125,000 Urban: INR 200,000
2	Total indebtedness of the borrower: increased	INR 100,000	INR 125,000
3	Limit on disbursement of loans: increased	First loan cycle: INR 60,000 Subsequent loan cycle: INR 100,000	First loan cycle: INR 75,000 Subsequent loan cycle: INR 125,000

Source Prepared by the authors based on Reserve Bank of India publication (2019) (Reserve Bank of India, 2019)

RBI revised the norms of qualifying assets criteria of NBFC-MFI through a notification dated November 08, 2019, considering the important role played by the NBFC-MFIs in delivering the credit to the bottom of the pyramid of the society to perform the designated role in a growing economy. Following are the amendments in qualifying assets criteria Table 2.

3.1 *Regulator Influence in Shaping the Microfinance Sector*

Timely intervention of Reserve Bank of India shaped the microfinance sector outlook which played a very important role in financial inclusion mission. RBI guidelines helped Indian microfinance sector to grow. It also protected the interest of microfinance borrowers and created a sustainable business environment where capital is attracted, and clients are benefited. Reserve Bank of India calculated the average effective interest rates of microfinance institutions by analyzing the financials of March 31, 2010 in which they found that larger microfinance institutions interest rate was 36.79% and smaller microfinance institutions average interest rate was 28.79% (Reserve Bank of India, 2011). After implementing the pricing norms of RBI by all the Non-Banking Finance Company-Microfinance Institutions (NBFC-MFIs), the interest rate of large NBFC-MFIs reduced to 23%, small and medium Non-Banking Finance Company-Microfinance Institutions reduced to 25.15% and 25%, respectively (MFIN, 2019). There is reduction of average interest rate of

13.79% in larger Non-Banking Finance Company-Microfinance Institutions and 3.64% in smaller Non-Banking Finance Company-Microfinance Institutions compared to the average interest rate of larger and smaller Microfinance Institutions in the year 2011. RBI directions on minimum net-owned fund and qualifying assets created a specialized financial institution in India to serve the needs of bottom of the pyramid of population, who were highly depended on informal sector for credit. To target the marginalized, Reserve Bank of India allowed microfinance institution to extend credit only to the borrowers whose household income is not more than INR 125,000 in rural area and INR 200,000 in urban areas. To prevent the overindebtedness of borrowers, RBI directions limited the total indebtedness of the borrower to 125,000 and not more than two NBFC-MFIs can lend to the same borrowers. Reserve Bank of India also given clear directions on prudential norms, assets classification norms, provision norms, lending norms, fair practices norms and pricing norms which strengthen the microfinance institutions and protected the borrowers and created a win-win situation for the microfinance institution and the clients of microfinance institutions.

4 Microfinance Sector Growth in India—Microfinance Crisis to Growth

After intervention of RBI, microfinance sector has grown drastically in the past years. After Andhra Pradesh microfinance crisis, there was negative growth in microfinance sector in the Financial Year 2011–2012. Quick proactive response from Reserve Bank of India toward microfinance crisis streamlined the business environment of microfinance which resulted in portfolio and client's growth (Fig. 1 and Fig. 2) and helping in achieving the financial inclusion mission.

Earlier 90% of total microfinance business of the country was controlled by Non-Banking Finance Company-Microfinance Institutions (NBFC-MFIs) but as microfinance became popular and provided good business opportunities, it is adopted by different types of financial institutions like Banks, NBFCs, Small Finance Bank and non-profit microfinance institutions. Different types of lenders captured the market share of microfinance as shown in the Fig. 3. Different types of lenders and their microfinance portfolio market share.

Earlier around 90% market share was with Non-Banking Finance Company-Microfinance Institutions but now it reduced to 38.17%, one

Fig. 1 Portfolio growth (*Source* *Prepared by the authors based on mfin Micrometer report [2016] [MFIN, 2016]; **Prepared by the authors based on Microfinance Plus report [2019] [Equifax Credit Information Services Private Limited & Small Industries Development Bank of India, 2019])

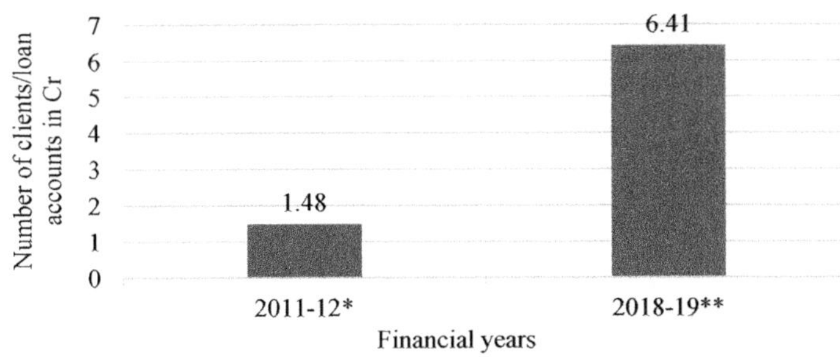

Fig. 2 Clients growth (*Source* *Prepared by the authors based on mfin Micrometer report [2016] [MFIN, 2016]; **Prepared by the authors based on Microfinance Plus report [2019] [Equifax Credit Information Services Private Limited & Small Industries Development Bank of India, 2019])

of the major reasons for reduction in market share of Non-Banking Finance Company-Microfinance Institutions was eight Non-Banking Finance Company-Microfinance Institutions received small finance bank license from Reserve Bank of India and one Non-Banking Finance Company-Microfinance Institutions (NBFC-MFI) received universal banking license. The portfolio of 9 Non-Banking Finance Company-Microfinance Institutions moved to Small Finance Banks and Banks. Apart from that also banks are built their microfinance portfolio. This clear indication of need and business opportunity in microfinance sector

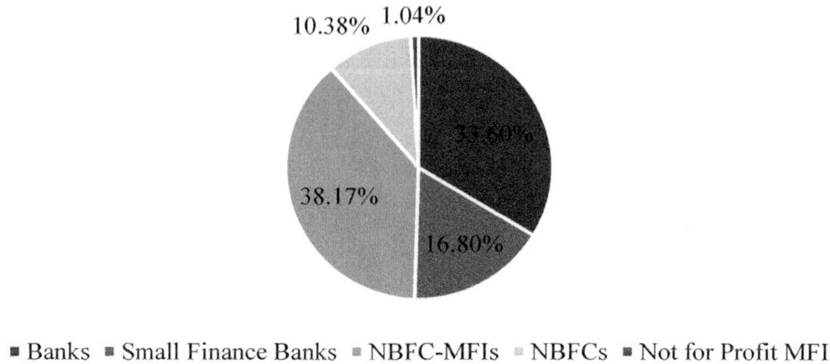

Fig. 3 Different types of lenders and their microfinance portfolio market share in percentage (*Source* Prepared by the authors based on Microfinance Plus report [2019] Equifax Credit Information Services Private Limited & Small Industries Development Bank of India, 2019)

of India. This would have not happened without proactive policies implemented by the RBI for microfinance sector and institutions.

4.1 Transformation of Microfinance Institutions

The concept of transformation to origin is based on the two goals of exponentially outreaching the number of members with access to microfinance and reducing the dependency of donors. These two goals encouraged the industry to look toward the greater integration with formal financial sector. So, Non-Governmental Organizations (NGOs) started the transformation into regulated entities and privately owned. Interestingly, it was noticed almost two decades ago that transformation is one of the elements of commercialization and integration to the formal financial sector. Transformation also became necessary to reach the target segments of microfinance in terms of business operation and outreach with financial viability and profitability. Competition and successful business model from transformed microfinance institutions have triggered banks to reach lower income section of the society and microenterprises (Campion & Victoria, 2001).

Indian microfinance industry also experienced the transformation of microfinance institutions to commercially viable formal financial institution. It also underwent commercialization trend. Reserve Bank of India's intervention through its microfinance sector evaluation and directions established a conducive environment to achieve the financial inclusion objective, institutional sustainability and institutional transformation, considering financial inclusion is the key driver of economic growth. In India, also like in other developing countries, microfinance model initially adopted by the Non-Governmental Organization later is transformed to Non-banking finance companies, after Reserve Bank of India's intervention to create a responsible microfinance sector as it associated with the marginalized, a special category of Non-Banking Finance Company (NBFC), namely NBFC-MFI was formed. All the for-profit microfinance institutions are fetched under the jurisdiction of Non-Banking Finance Company-Microfinance Institutions (NBFC-MFI).

During 2014, out of 903.1 Million adults, only 53% of adults own a transaction account for financial access which was increased to 80% during the year 2017. When it comes to adults that are banked and borrowed from formally, during 2014, only 5% of the adult banked and borrowed formally, i.e., out of 903.1 million adults only 45.1 million adults. During 2017, adult banked and borrowed formally increased to 8%, i.e., out of 903.1 million adults, 72.2 million adults banked and borrowed formally (The World Bank, 2020). During Financial Year 2013–2014, there were 16.5 million microfinance clients that was increased to 64.1 million microfinance clients as on September 2019. This helps to understand the important role of formal microfinance institutions to reach marginalized.

"The Government of India and Reserve Bank of India came up with banking reforms Fig. 4 shows the banking reforms by the regulators, from 1969 to 1980, 20 nationalized banks were formed. From1993 to 2014, 14 news banks were formed. In the year 2014, the RBI has given universal banking license to IDFC and Bandhan. Bandhan had microfinance as their major business. In the year 2015, RBI has given 21 banking licenses as shown in the diagram 2 Banking reforms, out of which 11 are payments banks license and 10 are small bank license. Under small banking licenses out of 10, eight were having microfinance as major business. Since 2014, 9 NBFCs having microfinance as a major business got banking license, which shows the importance of microfinance institution's social face in financial inclusion" (Thomas & Kumar, 2018).

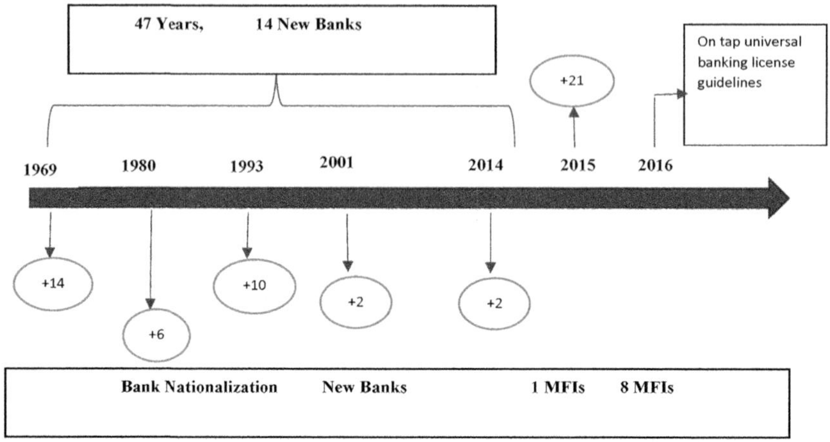

Fig. 4 Banking reforms (*Source* Prepared by the authors based on Indian Banking - In a Time For Change - Nandan Nilekani report [2016] [Nilekani, 2016])

5 Conclusion

Microfinance model emerged as tool for the development of marginalized who are excluded from formal banking system. During the year 2001, around 7000 Non-Governmental Organizations (NGOs) were proving microfinance services to the poor throughout the world (Campion & Victoria, 2001). International development institution like United Nation also recognized the microfinance as a tool for eradicating poverty by announcing the year 2005 as international year of microcredit. Followed by international year of microcredit, in 2006, Nobel peace prize was awarded to Grameen Bank and the founder of Grameen Bank Prof. Muhammad Yunus. International recognition and business opportunity in microfinance drawn the attention of social and commercial investors. Commercialization of microfinance institutions created a paradox environment between development and exploitation of poor. Development professionals criticized the commercialization of microfinance. Reserve Bank of India has come up with stringent guidelines to protect the interest of the clients. Larger microfinance in India used to charge 36.79% and smaller microfinance institutions used to charge 28.79% before implementation of Reserve Bank of India directions, after implementation of

Reserve Bank India's pricing policy direction larger NBFC-MFIs reduced to 23%, small and medium NBFC-MFIs interest rated reduced to 25.15% and 25%, respectively. Reserve Bank of India directions helped in scaling up the microfinance industry. During the Financial Year 2011–2012, i.e., immediately after the Andhra Pradesh Microfinance Crisis period, microfinance portfolio was 13,799 crores which was increased to 178,547 crore portfolios as on September 2019. In the last seven years, microfinance portfolio has grown 1293%. Likewise, during the Financial Year 2011–2012, total number of microfinance clients was 1.48 crores which was increased to 6.41 crore clients as on September 2019. In the last seven years, there was 433% growth in clients. Formalizing microfinance sector attracted different types of lenders, earlier 90% of market share was with Non-Banking Finance Company-Microfinance Institutions (NBFC-MFIs). Now different types of lenders like banks, small finance banks, NBFC-MFIs, NBFC and not-for-profit having microfinance portfolio market share. Reserve Bank of India's intervention played very important role in mainstreaming the microfinance sector and creating formal financial institutions. Indian microfinance experience counters the argument of free market principle when it comes to interest cap and regulations. Regulation in microfinance sector helped in reducing the interest rates of microfinance borrowers, and it compels the microfinance institutions to enhance their efficiency which helps establish a win-win situation for all the stakeholders, especially borrowers who are marginalized and microfinance institutions for long-term sustainability.

References

Abrar, A., & Javaid, A. Y. (2014). Commercialization and mission drift — A cross country evidence on transformation of microfinance industry. *International Journal of Trade, Economics and Finance*, 122–125. https://doi.org/10.7763/IJTEF.2014.V5.353.

Ahmeti, F. (2014, February). Microfinance as a tool for economic development in transitional countries: Experience from Kosovo. *European Scientific Journal, 10*(4), 269–287. ISSN: 1857 7431.

Alok, A., & Joseph, N. (2012). Regulating the growing commercialisation of microfinance institutions in India. *NUJS Law review, 5*, 62–91. http://nujslawreview.org/wp-content/uploads/2016/12/aditya-alok-and-nihal-joseph.pdf.

Campion, A., & Victoria, W. (2001). *NGO Transformation*. Development Alternatives Inc.

Devaraja T. S. (2011, May). *Society Interdisciplinary Business Research*. http://sibresearch.org/uploads/2/7/9/9/2799227/microfinance-_devaraja.pdf.

Equifax Credit Information Services Private Limited & Small Industries Development Bank of India. (2019, June). Microfinance Pulse.

Fernando, N. A. (2008). *Managing microfinance risks some observations and suggestions*. Asian Development Bank. https://www.microfinancegateway.org/sites/default/files/mfg-en-paper-managing-microfinance-risks-some-observations-and-suggestions-jul-2008.pdf.

Government of Andhra Pradesh. (2010, October 19). The Andhra Pradesh Micro Finance Institutions (Regulation of Money Lending). Boston University, http://www.bu.edu/bucflp/files/2012/01/Andhra-Pradesh-Micro-Finance-Institutions-Ordinance.pdf.

MFIN. (2016, March 31). micrometer issue 17.

MFIN. (2019). *Micromiter issue 31*. MFIN.

Nilekani, N. (2016, August 09). *In slide share*. http://www.slideshare.net/ProductNation/indian-banking-in-a-time-for-change-nandan-nilekani-64679460?utm_source=slideshow02&utm_medium=ssemail&utm_campaign=share_slideshow_loggedout.

Reserve Bank of India. (2011, January 19). *Reserve Bank of India*. https://www.rbi.org.in/scripts/PublicationReportDetails.aspx?ID=608.

Reserve Bank of India. (2015a, July 1). *Reserve Bank of India*. https://rbidocs.rbi.org.in/rdocs/notification/PDFs/20BF010715FSCFC4543A097A94AA3B1B9133EBE9C602B.PDF.

Reserve Bank of India. (2015b, April 08). *Reserve Bank of India*. https://www.rbi.org.in/Scripts/BS_NBFCNotificationView.aspx?Id=9651.

Reserve Bank of India. (2019). *Qualifying Assets Criteria - Review of Limits*. Reserve Bank of India .

Rosenberg, R. (2007). *CGAP reflections on the Compartamos intial public offering: A case study on microfinance interest rates and profits*. Consultative Group to Assist the Poor. http://documents.worldbank.org/curated/en/168341468136793588/CGAP-reflections-on-the-Compartamos-initial-public-offering-a-case-study-on-microfinance-interest-rates-and-profits.

Satagopan, H., & Ravindran, G. (2012, July). Transformation of MFIs is a long term process requiring a fundamental change in management practices and culture. *International Journal of Marketing, Financial Services & Management Research, 1*(7), 160–179. ISSN: 2277 3622.

Segill, S., & Ascioglu, A. (2013, April). *Initial public offerings in the microfinance industry: Does a mission drift occur?* Bryant University, http://digitalcommons.bryant.edu/cgi/viewcontent.cgi?article=1026&context=honors_finance.

Singh. (2013). A study of success of first IPO of SKS Microfinance. *Global Journal of Management and Business Studies*, 163–170.

The World Bank. (2020, January 11). *Universal Financial Access 2020*. The world Bank, https://ufa.worldbank.org/en/country-progress/india.

Thirani. (2012, February 27). *The New York Times*. The New York Times, https://india.blogs.nytimes.com/2012/02/27/yunus-was-right-sks-microfinance-founder-says/.

Thomas, J. R., & Kumar, J. (2018, May). Effect of social performance on sustainability of microfinance institutions. Christ Deemed to be University.

Key Drivers of Financial Inclusion

Transforming Financial Sector Through Financial Literacy and Fintech Revolution

Priya Makhija, Elizabeth Chacko, and Mudita Sinha

1 Introduction

Financial literacy generally refers to the individual's capacity to acquire, understand and gauge the information required for decision-making toward a secure financial future. Adequate level of financial literacy is required for the financial stability of an individual and his family. Feeble management of money may influence the spending pattern and make the family more vulnerable to a financial crisis. Knowledge of financial literacy has become important today to reduce the chances of being deceived in investment decision-making (Braunstein & Welch, 2002). Increase in the financialized world has created the need for improvement in financial literacy as everyone has complex financial decisions to make due to rapid

P. Makhija (✉) · E. Chacko
Center for Management Studies, Jain University, Bangalore, India
e-mail: priya_m@cms.ac.in

E. Chacko
e-mail: elizabeth_c@cms.ac.in

M. Sinha
Christ (Deemed to be University), Bangalore, India
e-mail: mudita.sinha@christuniversity.in

Ananda S. and D. Singh (eds.), *Financial Inclusion in Emerging Markets*,
https://doi.org/10.1007/978-981-16-2652-4_12

development in the financial products and services (Bannier & Schwarz, 2018).

Almost all the countries are facing the low rates issue of financial literacy (Rai et al., 2019) (The importance in the Rai et al., 2019). In a research by (Huston, 2010), it was proposed that application of financial knowledge must be included in financial literacy and post reviewing 71 studies four main components of financial knowledge: basic money concepts, saving or investment, borrowing and protection. Organization for Economic Cooperation and Development (OECD) defines financial literacy as a blend of behavior, awareness, skill, attitude and knowledge which are essential for a fruitful financial decision heading toward a safe future. Three key aspects of financial literacy which are important as per OECD are financial awareness, financial conduct and financial attitude (Atkinson & Messy, 2012; OCDE, 2013; OECD, 2014; OECD INFE, 2011). In India, Financial literacy is still taken a back seat, unlike other developed nations because of which Indian citizens lack financial knowledge resulting in poor investments and financial decisions. People invest in short-term plans and physical assets to accomplish personal goals, which does not add to the economic development of the country. According to a global survey, 76% of Indian adults still don't have knowledge about financial concepts and are regrettably financially illiterate even today (Patel & Rajendran, 2018; Power To Me, 2019). Consumers who do not have idea of compounding interest end up paying more on transaction fees, run up large debts and interest rates on loans (Lusardi & Scheresberg, 2013; Lusardi & Tufano, 2015) due to which their borrowing will be more and saving will be less (Stango & Zinman, 2009). The potential benefits of financial literacy are assorted which assists people with powerful financial skills toward an improved job planning and better savings for old age (Behrman et. al., 2012; Lusardi & Mitchell, 2014). Well-informed and financially literate investors diversify the risk by investing the funds across a number of ventures (Abreu & Mendes, 2010). It is believed in India that anyone who is 'literate' or 'rich' is also 'financially literate' which is certainly not true, it is also believed that financial literacy is more essential for adults which again is completely an incorrect notion toward financial literacy. Financial industry is amalgamated in daily lives of people worldwide and there has been a major transformation in it over the years due to several factors such as political, geographical, regimes and legislation. According to authors (Berger, 2016; Shim & Shin, 2016, these changes in the banks have taken place with the rise of fin-tech which is in the development stage, which is a big significant challenge for both academia and managers in the financial sector (Dapp, 2014; DeYoung, 2005; Gábossy, 2016; Iwata, 2017; Schueffel, 2016). FinTech defines a company that uses software and digital technology to provide financial services (Fintech Weekly, 2016) and, organizations that combine creative business models and technologies to allow, develop and disrupt financial services (EY, 2016).Traditional players in banking and financial services face a major transformation with the growth in digital finance, which has led fin-tech startups and IT companies to enter the financial industry (Gomber et al., 2017). The way individuals make multiple transactions and control their cash has changed with a variety of fintech platforms and applications being launched in the market. The increasing number of startups can be measured by the increasing number of the fin-tech market. As per report (The Free Press, 2019) with the largest number of financial technology (fintech) startups, India has hit the second place worldwide, United States leads the list and reserves the first place. Out of 2,000 fin-tech startups in India, Bengaluru and Mumbai have around 42 percent of them followed by New Delhi, Gurgaon and Hyderabad. Payment firms, lending, insurance and personal finance management startups form the major component of the fin-tech startups. Some significant names that have made an impact include Paytm, LendingKart, MobiKwik, PhonePe, Policy Bazaar, PayU, Kissht, Shubh Loans and Faircent. As per NASSCOM, Indian financial technology market is likely to hit 2.4 billion US dollars by 2020. Artificial intelligence (AI), blockchain, cryptography, biometrics, identity management, cyber protection and robotic process automation (RPA) are major technologies involved in the fin-tech field. As per Global Fintech Market Report Increasing popularity of the AI-oriented fin-tech market is expected to develop at a Compound annual growth rate (CAGR) of 21.72% during 2018–2023 (Research & Markets, 2019).

1.1 *Financial Literacy among Youth*

Every human being learns a lot of skills during their lifetime and everyone attempts to develop certain abilities that will enhance their lifestyle in future. Financial literacy is one among such abilities that will provide a promising future (Kumar & Bansal, 2020). Financial literacy is an essential component of the well-being of the person as well as the financial stability of a country. Proper understanding of financial concepts enhances financial knowledge, behavior and attitude, equipping everyone with a secure future.

For youth of today, knowledge of personal finance and financial literacy are important as they are more exposed to upcoming financial decision-making than their parents (Aprea et al., 2016). Young adults generally depend on the financial support of their parents to learn from their parents on the path to financial independence by observing and imitating their attitudes and behavior (Gutter et al., 2010; Shim et al., 2010). Financial activity practiced during the young age is likely to extend into adult life as most young people consciously practice and develop the skills that they need to be financially stable at this stage of life (Shim et al., 2010).

There is a noticeably low financial literacy rate among youth of India in comparison to other developed countries, which is a major worry. Family financial conduct contributes majorly to the financial literacy of youth which implies that actively seeking financial information plays a role in the financial literacy of young people (Pahlevan Sharif & Naghavi, 2020). Demographic and socioeconomic characteristics such as age, gender, income, marital status and academic attainment have been reported to influence level of financial knowledge among young individuals and there is a significant relationship between financial awareness, financial knowledge and financial literacy (Garg & Singh, 2017, 2018). (Huang et al., 2013) considered financial knowledge as an individual's understanding of financial aspects and it has been reported in several studies that youth of India are not very well informed on financial knowledge. The element of financial literacy which was demonstrated by the lack of fundamental numeracy, lack in ability to comprehend the basic money-related standards and low competency in assessing the influence of inflation on rate of return (Agarwalla et al., 2015).

Financial behaviors and preferences are considered critical elements of financial literacy which was very low for India in the survey conducted by Organization for Economic Co-operation and Development (OECD) for 13 countries (OCDE, 2013). Almost half of the working young respondents disclosed positive attitude toward financial planning but were least interested in investing for their own future. It was found in the survey that the young citizens of India were repaying the home loan. According to (Lusardi et al., 2016), millennials know very little about their student loans and most of them don't even estimate the EMI amounts that will be associated with the amount of loans they opt for. Financial education can update the financial literacy level of the students in schools and can enhance the capability for taking better financial decisions. School-based financial literacy and financial education programs might improve the financial knowledge and attitudes of adolescents toward financial importance, however, the retention can be for a shorter period. However, the financial literacy programs in colleges and secondary schools will be effective for reducing the gender gap. Financial education must start in schools as early as possible and must be repeated in colleges and secondary schools. Financial education must be mandatory in school curriculum for continuous learning (Amagir et al., 2018).

1.2 Financial Literacy Among Women

Women play an important role in the development of the economy but women are more illiterate than men. Not only in India, but almost in all other countries, women are 5% less financially literate than men (Singh & Kumar, 2017). The global literacy rate of all the males and females who are 15 years and above is 86.3 percent where male literacy rate is 90 percent and female literacy rate is 82.7 percent (World Population Review, 2020). Considering female literacy rate from the ages 15–24 as per UNESCO Institute for Statistics 2018 San Marino has 100 percent literacy rate followed by Italy and Singapore with 99.95 and 99.94 percent and India with 90.17 percent (UNESCO, 2019). As per the latest national statistical office survey issued by Household Social Consumption: Education in India overall literacy rate in India among persons aged seven years and above is 77.7 percent with male literacy rate as 84.7 percent and female literacy rate as 70.3 percent (IE, 2020). It is observed that with the engagement of digital financial services there is an improvise in women's resilience to economic, financial and health status (Demirguc-Kunt et al., 2018). As per the report compared to 2014, there are million opportunities for women across the globe and more than 240 million women have financial institutions or mobile money service (United Nations, 2018). As per Global Findex database, in India accounts at financial institutions were held by 83 percent of males aged above 15 years of age compared to women with 77 percent (Draboo, 2020). The income and education level of the respondents doesn't play a significant role in the financial literacy level of people as it can be seen that people who are Senior Secondary and Graduate are much more financially literate and due to digital financial growth they know where they want to invest their savings (OECD, 2018). Age is a major factor in determining financial literacy. Educated people manage their money in a better way for budgeting, savings, and in selecting investments with higher returns and financial illiteracy will create problems in taking financial decisions. The results displayed that the Occupation and type of organization will also have a positive effect on the barriers of financial literacy for working women. Whereas marital status has no association with the barriers affecting financial literacy; this implies that marital status has no significant effect on barriers of financial literacy. These results indicate that working women need to be informed about financial literacy (Manchanda & Sukhija, 2019). It is further observed that Lack of Knowledge and confidence are the main reasons which restrict women to do investment but women always prefer to be risk averse investors who look only for safe returns (Sharma & Kota, 2019).

2 Review of Literature

Financial literacy among youngster needs to be more emphasized as the saving and spending behavior can help them to have financial sustainability. As per (Jariwala, 2015) study financial education is strongly associated with the satisfaction among people. As it makes them more secure and study financial market for proper investment decisions (Xiao & Porto, 2017). Since last two decades, it has been observed that prominence for financial literacy has facilitated professional financial advises which helped in quality well-being and proper planning of financial decisions (Stolper & Walter, 2017). As per few reviews on the usage of credit cards or plastic money when compared to the expense had low-cost borrowing. So, it was suggested by scholars that the literacy to the youth benefits globally for a better environment. (Mouna & Jarboui, 2015) study in Tunisia, states that financial literacy helps in diversifying portfolio. Awareness regarding factors leading to financial decisions is less among small investors. Furthermore, (Taylor, 2011) study shows that people having money management skill can take better financial decisions. Also, the study compared between the individual and households with dependents, where households having dependent are capable of managing finances.. Patterns of living are also considered while studying financial literacy. (Kuntze et al., 2019) suggest that financial teaching provided to young people must not be traditional but should also include use of web tools, which can help them to understand and adapt. The web teaching tools such as applications or videos can bring out personal growth and financial stability among the youth. As per the study conducted by (Kuntze et al., 2019) where the comparison was between teaching through courses and innovative ways of learning, it was analyzed that more inclination was for innovative tools used by youth in learning financial aspects and in making better decisions on the same. As per (Kojo Oseifuah, 2010) study the financial literacy in African entrepreneurs is above average about 69% of the youth are able to save and 83% of the respondent says that documentation and records are maintained. The financial term's knowledge is there among them the only lag is having less awareness regarding the stock markets. It was concluded that the response of one district in South Africa, cannot be interpreted as for the whole country. It was also found through research that African–American female students were having less literacy on application of financial tools. While studying emerging countries like India it was found that savings are considered more, still the portfolio investment compared to other countries is less because traditional ways of savings and investments. Stock market participation needs to be influenced more among investors, so that people have awareness on risk aversion. Various factors taken into consideration by (Sivaramakrishnan et al., 2017) includes, 'hassle factor, risk aversion, risk avoidance, perception of regulator and financial well-being'. As per the study proposed by (Riitsalu & Murakas, 2019) on subjective financial literacy has higher significant relation with the individual savings. The income level also has relation with the financially strong. As per the study by (Candiya Bongomin et al., 2017) proposed that knowledge, skill, behavior and attitude in financial literacy, it was resulted educating is not only for improving the financial well-being but, also more needed to be converting the negative attitude into positive attitude toward financial security among youth. (Abubakar, 2015) states that there was a gender gap as female were less aware of the financial market. It also tried to link between financial literacy and entrepreneurship, as more knowledge shared and implied by youth and adults will improve the proper access of finance. They also suggested the need of activities concerned with literacy and entrepreneurship programs. But in contrary, as per the study of (Mindra & Moya, 2017), review of (Ahmad & Arif, 2015), said that women in developing countries have comparative higher rate in financial literacy and growing in women entrepreneurship at all incomes levels. They also proposed that government and all financial institutions must share the responsibility of designing policies for better financial literacy to be given to citizens for the overall economic and social development. As per the study conducted for Indian financial market, it was said that still 80 percent of the financial decisions are dominated by the males and similar to Africa financial institution need to give right education regarding financial market to individuals for changing their behavior toward financial inclusion for decision-making (Baker et al., 2019). The financial sector has also welcomed Artificial Intelligence in their services too. According to (Bachinskiy, 2019) article on the growth of AI is studied in various service sector. In financial sector AI has been a great help in the credit rating, and personalized banking where individuals can get on spot suggestions and can map their expenses and plan out well for their expenses and have financial well-being. AI provides data quality assurance and reduces the cybercrimes and KYC done by all banks through proper verification of digital ID (*Artificial Intelligence and Machine Learning in Financial Services Market Developments and Financial Stability Implications*, 2017). According to (Murugesan, 2019), AI-Artificial Intelligence created a crystal picture of fin-tech companies in enhancing financial literacy and financial inclusion. As stated above financial literacy must have usability through AI as globally technology has taken charge on all sectors. Nowadays people use smart phones, through which we can educate and use financial services not only for spending but to track the spending and control for improving saving and better financially sound future. (Bapat, 2020) states that there is a significant relation between financial literacy, financial locus of control and financially responsible attitude. Financial literacy is not only required for deciding various investment avenues but also to improve the well-being of the households (Amari et al., 2020). As per (Anand et al., 2020) observed during pandemic, it was the time when people were affected physically, mentally and financially. During this time, financial literacy program was advised to provide help in investing and savings which can reduce stress and upkeep the health. According to (Pearson, 2020) report, it says that finance rules the world since long time but now it's time technology rules. So financial institution needs to be well equipped with finance through technology. So to have the right pool of talent more financial literacy courses must be provided and informed to the youth about the scope of these education.

To sum up, financial literacy is encouraged in many parts of the world toward youth. Literacy and practicality or practicing the knowledge still have a wider gap. In all the research, the study was conducted relating financial literacy and investment pattern, financial literacy and gender studies, or financial knowledge related with living standards. There are studies conducted showcasing the urban and the rural state of financial knowledge. But still there are various areas yet to be researched like creating new competencies defining job roles, ways to improve the acceptability of fintech among people. Policies need to be more aligned and clearer for the youth to improve the learning and acceptability for better financial decisions and foreseeing. Usage of technology for social media needs to be promoted for financing services also and youth need to have clear understanding to know about the unethical financial applications. Overall research has been conducted regarding financial literacy but not having a direct focusing on youth and their spending and saving behavior is still.

3 Analysis

The international study shows that financial insensitivity is pervasive in all well-developed financial markets such as Germany, the Netherlands, Sweden, Japan, Italy, New Zealand and the United States. Due to lack of finance knowledge and money management skills, a substantial portion of the youngsters have been detected as 'economically marginalized'.

In the recent past, companies have managed to play a crucial role in the management of finance on behalf of people and this has led to shifts in society support structures around the world. These efforts have enhanced the accountability of groups of people to manage their own affairs and secure their future. Given the continuous growth in the range and complexity of managers and investors, it is essential that people have a fuller insight of payment methods in order to find the appropriate investment paths society in general (Datta, 2019).

A survey conducted by National Financial Capability, evaluated that the monetary management proficiency and practices of US adults aged 18 and over are only 22%, however, 18–24 years old were considered as financially stable, according to the lead author Gaurav

Sinha, a graduate in the social work from the University of Illinois (Sinha et al., 2018).
In India, RBI is seeing an increase in lending, and as per Reed and Cochrane two-third of the respondents who graduated from US College showed that borrowing was becoming more and more common, due to lending for academic achievement and debt on credit cards.
A survey conducted by Financial Services giant Visa was analyzed among 28 countries Indian figures appeared to be one of the least economically trained with professionals aged between 25 and 45 years are employees having more number of private loans (home, vehicle and education loans). It is said that intelligent investments make intelligent citizens and intelligent citizens in return make a clever world financially independent in crisis times (Datta, 2019).

4 Suggestions

Poor money management can get worsened if there is no financial education which will impact Socioeconomic status, financial literacy, financial well-being and personal well-being which are an essential component for the growth of any economy.

Government and financial providers have made the agreement to provide a financial support and guidance. But the major growth has come only in Urban areas, for example, industry body, Association of Mutual Funds of India, have been running a successful campaign to raise awareness about the benefits of investing in mutual funds to create long-term wealth which has made India growth in mutual fund market double than the rest of the world (Iyer, 2019). However, even in rural segments, government programs have been started for rural housing. As per an article published in the world economic forum, the rural housing which was 4,00,000 before has been raised to 70 million new houses have been built in the last five years (Iyer, 2019). Though there is a massive growth, but government can still work on Cash Comprehensive Social Security Assistance, Old Age Allowance, Old Age Living Allowance and Disability Allowance.

Financial technology (Fin-tech) has brought many benefits including improving financial inclusion in some areas. It can provide easy access to economical credit, appropriate remittance and worldwide shopping for financial consumers. Cashless society has changed youth consent and attitude toward money, leading to lose money management practices among younger generations but fin-tech may provide financial exclusion. Machine-learning applications can enable banks to create financial worth for their customers, employees, shareholders and society in new ways. With the use of artificial intelligence, a lot of frauds which are happening can be found easily but addressing the risk of machine learning and addressing this issue systematically will be a major constraint for the banks.

Financial well-being can be achieved only through financial education but change in people's attitude and behavior toward the adoption of fin-tech is also very important which can be done by bringing awareness in the policy areas. Today youth have adopted the concept of 'live for today and let tomorrow take care of itself'. attitude (Financial Literacy Monitor, Investor Education Centre, 2018), but with the help of money management skills, young people can achieve their life goals. Money Management can be done by having control over excessive spending and by cultivating a habit of savings. With financial education and wealth management plans, individuals can be more self-reliant.

Preparing financially for future personal goals, youth and school children have to be more focused in today's scenario as they are the future of any country. Youth must be trained on how they can play for their short, medium and long-term finances or requirements of finance. The financial planning, developing saving habit's concept should be embedded into career and life planning education.

People have to be trained or educated toward the habit of making the most efficient use of income or from limited resources. In today's world as online education has taken over, several courses can be a part of education or training where students or people can learn concepts virtually to have a better understanding. Whether its Youth or School children or working professionals should have a habit of 'saving to buy rather than "borrowings to buy" to manage minimum debt'.

5 Conclusion

Financial literacy can be achieved through financial education, but it is observed that women and youth are yet to get the insight on the savings and investment pattern. From overall population, majority of the youth are the Tech-savvy, however, they are not aware about the application and usage of fin-tech, which will be the major source of managing finance in the future. It is must that the government and financial institutions take initiative to propagate and promote financial learning through financial technology. Most of the research have focused either on financial literacy rate among genders or on the usage of financial technology but the focus on how fin-tech can bring the change among the attitude and behavioral pattern of women and youth toward the knowledge of financial aspects and investment pattern is yet to be analyzed.

References

Abreu, M., & Mendes, V. (2010). Financial literacy and portfolio diversification. *Quantitative Finance, 10*(5), 515–528. https://doi.org/10.1080/14697680902878105.

Abubakar, H. A. (2015). Entrepreneurship development and financial literacy in Africa. *World Journal of Entrepreneurship, Management and Sustainable Development, 11*(4), 281–294. https://doi.org/10.1108/wjemsd-04-2015-0020.

Agarwalla, S. K., Barua, S. K., Jacob, J., & Varma, J. R. (2015). Financial literacy among working young in Urban India. *World Development, 67*(2013), 101–109. https://doi.org/10.1016/j.worlddev.2014.10.004.

Ahmad, S. Z., & Arif, A. M. M. (2015). Strengthening access to finance for women-owned SMEs in developing countries. *Equality, Diversity and Inclusion: An International Journal, 34*(7), 634–639. https://doi.org/10.1108/edi-11-2012-0104.

Amagir, A., Groot, W., Maassen van den Brink, H., & Wilschut, A. (2018). A review of financial-literacy education programs for children and adolescents. *Citizenship, Social and Economics Education, 17*(1), 56–80. https://doi.org/10.1177/2047173417719555.

Amari, M., Salhi, B., & Jarboui, A. (2020). Evaluating the effects of sociodemographic characteristics and financial education on saving behavior. *International Journal of Sociology and Social Policy*. https://doi.org/10.1108/IJSSP-03-2020-0048.

Anand, S., Mishra, K., Verma, V., & Taruna, T. (2020). Financial literacy as a mediator of personal financial health during COVID-19: A structural equation modelling approach. *Emerald Open Research, 2*, 59. https://doi.org/10.35241/emeraldopenres.13735.1.

Aprea, C., Wuttke, E., Breuer, K., Koh, N. K., Davies, P., Greimel-Fuhrmann, B., & Lopus, J. S. (2016). International handbook of financial literacy. *Springer*. https://doi.org/10.1007/978-981-10-0360-8.

Artificial intelligence and machine learning in financial services Market developments and financial stability implications. (2017). *November*.

Atkinson, A., & Messy, F.-A. (2012). Measuring Financial Literacy: Results of the Oecd Infe Pilot Study. *Oecd, 15*, 1–73.

Bachinskiy, A. (2019, February 21). *The Growing Impact of AI in Financial Services: Six Examples | by Arthur Bachinskiy | Towards Data Science*. Towards Data Science. https://towardsdatascience.com/the-growing-impact-of-ai-in-financial-services-six-examples-da386c0301b2.

Baker, H. K., Kumar, S., Goyal, N., & Gaur, V. (2019). How financial literacy and demographic variables relate to behavioral biases. *Managerial Finance, 45*(1), 124–146. https://doi.org/10.1108/MF-01-2018-0003.

Bannier, C. E., & Schwarz, M. (2018). Gender- and education-related effects of financial literacy and confidence on financial wealth. *Journal of Economic Psychology, 67*, 66–86. https://doi.org/10.1016/j.joep.2018.05.005.

Bapat, D. (2020). Antecedents to responsible financial management behavior among young adults: Moderating role of financial risk tolerance. *International Journal of Bank Marketing, 38*(5), 1177–1194. https://doi.org/10.1108/IJBM-10-2019-0356.

Behrman, J. R., Mitchell, O. S., Soo, C. K., & Bravo, D. (2012). How financial literacy affects household wealth accumulation. *The American Economic Review, 102*(3), 300–304.

Berger, A. N. (2016). The economic effects of technological progress: Evidence from the banking industry. *Journal of Money, Credit and Banking, 35*(2), 141–176.

Braunstein, S., & Welch, C. (2002). Financial literacy: An overview of practice, research, and policy. *Federal Reserve Bulletin, 88*(11), 445–457.

Candiya Bongomin, G. O., Munene, J. C., Ntayi, J. M., & Malinga, C. A. (2017). Financial literacy in emerging economies: Do all components matter for financial inclusion of poor households in rural Uganda? *Managerial Finance, 43*(12), 1310–1331. https://doi.org/10.1108/MF-04-2017-0117

Dapp, T. (2014). Fintech – The digital (r)evolution. *Deutsche Bank Research*.

Datta, A. (2019, July). *Importance Of Financial Literacy Among Growing Youngsters - BW people*. BW People.

Demirguc-Kunt, A., Klapper, L., Singer, D., Ansar, S., & Hess, J. (2018). The Global Findex Database 2017: Measuring Financial Inclusion and the Fintech

Revolution. In *The Global Findex Database 2017: Measuring Financial Inclusion and the Fintech Revolution*. World Bank. https://doi.org/10.1596/978-1-4648-1259-0.

DeYoung, R. (2005). The performance of internet - Based business models: Evidence from the banking industry. *Chicago Journals, 78*(3), 893–948.

Draboo, S. (2020, April). *Financial Inclusion and Digital India: A Critical Assessment | Economic and Political Weekly*. EPW Engage.

EY. (2016). The upside of disruption. In *Ernst & Young* (Vol. 111, Issue 32).

Fintech Weekly. (2016). *Fintech DEfinition.*

Gábossy, Á. (2016). New directions in crowdfunding. *Public Finance Quarterly, 61*(4), 533–544.

Garg, N., & Singh, S. (2017). A study on socio-demographic factors affecting financial literacy with specific reference to Ph. D. Scholars. *Asian Journal of Research in Banking and Finance, 7*(5), 117. https://doi.org/10.5958/2249-7323.2017.00032.3.

Garg, N., & Singh, S. (2018). Financial literacy among youth. In *International Journal of Social Economics* (Vol. 45, Issue 1, pp. 173–186). Emerald Group Publishing Ltd. https://doi.org/10.1108/IJSE-11-2016-0303.

Gomber, P., Koch, J. A., & Siering, M. (2017). Digital Finance and FinTech: Current research and future research directions. *Journal of Business Economics, 87*(5), 537–580. https://doi.org/10.1007/s11573-017-0852-x.

Gutter, M. S., Garrison, S., & Copur, Z. (2010). Social learning opportunities and the financial behaviors of college students. *Family and Consumer Sciences Research Journal, 38*(4), 387–404. https://doi.org/10.1111/j.1552-3934.2010.00034.x.

Huang, J., Nam, Y., & Sherraden, M. S. (2013). Financial knowledge and child development account policy: A test of financial capability. *The Journal of Consumer Affairs, 47*(1), 1–26.

Huston, S. J. (2010). Measuring financial literacy. *Journal of Consumer Affairs, 44*(2), 296–316. https://doi.org/10.1111/j.1745-6606.2010.01170.x.

IE. (2020, September). *Report on Literacy Rate*. Drishti.

Iwata, D. (2017). A new relationship between financing and technology in the FinTech era. *NEC Technical Journal, 11*(2), 12–15.

Iyer, R. (2019, January). *Financial inclusion in India is soaring. Here's what must happen next | World Economic Forum*. Weforum.Org.

Jariwala, H. V. (2015). Analysis of financial literacy level of retail individual investors of gujarat state and its effect on investment decision. *Journal of Business and Finance Librarianship, 20*(July 2014), 133–158. https://doi.org/10.1080/08963568.2015.977727.

Kojo, E. (2010). Financial literacy and youth entrepreneurship in South Africa. *African Journal of Economic and Management Studies, 1*(2), 164–182. https://doi.org/10.1108/20400701011073473.

Kumar, S., & Bansal, M. (2020). Financial Literacy-the essential skill to enhance well being of the students (A review of earlier studies). In H. Karadal, M. Nureddin, A. T. Erdem, D. CHowdhury, & M. Hasanoglu (Eds.), *5. International EMI Entrepreneurship and Social Sciences Congress Proceedings E-Book* (Issue September, p. 249).

Kuntze, R., Wu, C. (Ken), Wooldridge, B. R., & Whang, Y. O. (2019). Improving financial literacy in college of business students: Modernizing delivery tools. *International Journal of Bank Marketing, 37*(4), 976–990. https://doi.org/10.1108/IJBM-03-2018-0080.

Lusardi, A., De, C., Scheresberg, B., & Oggero, N. (2016). *Student Loan Debt in the US: An Analysis of the 2015 NFCS Data.*

Lusardi, A., & Mitchell, O. S. (2014). The economic importance of financial literacy: Theory and evidence. *Journal of Economic Literature, 52*(1), 5–44. https://doi.org/10.1257/jel.52.1.5.

Lusardi, A., & Scheresberg, C. de B. (2013). Financial Literacy and High-Cost Borrowing in the United States. *NBER Working Papers.*

Lusardi, A., & Tufano, P. (2015). Debt literacy, financial experiences, and overindebtedness. In *Journal of Pension Economics and Finance* (Vol. 14, Issue 4). https://doi.org/10.1017/S1474747215000232.

Manchanda, P., & Sukhija, S. (2019). A study on barriers affecting financial literacy of working women in Punjab. *Journal of Emerging Technologies and Innovative Research, 3085*(01), 666–671.

Mindra, R., & Moya, M. (2017). Financial self-efficacy: A mediator in advancing financial inclusion. *Equality, Diversity and Inclusion, 36*(2), 128–149. https://doi.org/10.1108/EDI-05-2016-0040.

Mouna, A., & Jarboui, A. (2015). Financial literacy and portfolio diversification: An observation from the Tunisian stock market. *Marketing Intelligence and Planning, 33*(6), 808–822. https://doi.org/10.1108/IJBM-03-2015-0032.

Murugesan, R. (2019). AI in Financial Sector – A Driver to Financial Literacy. *Shanlax International Journal of Commerce, 7*(3), 66–70. https://doi.org/10.34293/commerce.v7i3.477.

OCDE. (2013). *Education at a Glance 2013: OECD Indicators.* OECD Publishing. http://doi.org/10.1787/eag-2013-en.

OECD. (2014). Education at a Glance 2014 - OECD Indicators. In *Oecd* (Issue September). OECD Publishing. http://doi.org/10.1787/eag-2014-en.

OECD. (2018). Education at a Glance 2018: OECD Indicators. *OECD Publishing.* https://doi.org/10.1787/eag-2018-25-en.

OECD INFE. (2011). Measuring Financial Literacy : Questionnaire and Guidance Notes for Conducting an Internationally Comparable Survey of Financial Literacy. *OECD*, 31.

Pahlevan Sharif, S., & Naghavi, N. (2020). Family financial socialization, financial information seeking behavior and financial literacy among youth. *Asia-Pacific*

Journal of Business Administration, 12(2), 163–181. https://doi.org/10.1108/APJBA-09-2019-0196.

Patel, H., & Rajendran, M. (2018, December). *76% Indians Lack Financial Knowledge*. Outlook Money.

Pearson, S. (2020, May). *This Why Financial Education is Key in the Fintech Revolution By Simon Pearson - Hedge Think*. HedgeThink.

Power To Me. (2019, February). *Why is financial literacy important in India?* Your story.

Rai, K., Dua, S., & Yadav, M. (2019). Association of financial attitude, financial behaviour and financial knowledge towards financial literacy: A structural equation modeling approach. *FIIB Business Review, 8*(1), 51–60. https://doi.org/10.1177/2319714519826651.

Research and Markets. (2019, July). *Global Fintech Market (2018–2023) - Market Set to Reach USD 305.7 billion by 2023*. Global Newswire.

Riitsalu, L., & Murakas, R. (2019). Subjective financial knowledge, prudent behaviour and income: The predictors of financial well-being in Estonia. *International Journal of Bank Marketing, 37*(4), 934–950. https://doi.org/10.1108/IJBM-03-2018-0071.

Schueffel, P. (2016). Taming the beast: A scientific definition of Fintech. *Journal of Innovation Management, 4*(4), 32–54.

Sharma, M., & Kota, H. B. (2019). The role of working women in investment decision making in the family in India. *Australasian Accounting, Business and Finance Journal, 13*(3), 91–110. https://doi.org/10.14453/aabfj.v13i3.6.

Shim, S., Barber, B. L., Card, N. A., Xiao, J. J., & Serido, J. (2010). Financial socialization of first-year college students: The roles of parents, work, and education. *Journal of Youth and Adolescence, 39*(12), 1457–1470. https://doi.org/10.1007/s10964-009-9432-x.

Shim, Y., & Shin, D. H. (2016). Analyzing China's fintech industry from the perspective of actor-network theory. *Telecommunications Policy, 40*(2–3), 168–181. https://doi.org/10.1016/j.telpol.2015.11.005.

Singh, C., & Kumar, R. (2017). Financial Literacy among Women - Indian Scenario. *Universal Journal of Accounting and Finance, 5*(2), 46–53. https://doi.org/10.13189/ujaf.2017.050202.

Sinha, G., Tan, K., & Zhan, M. (2018, August 27). Millennials lack money management skills: A study. *News Mobile Lifestyle Bureau*. Retrieved July 19 2021, from News Mobile Lifestyle Bureau website: https://newsmobile.in/articles/2018/08/27/millennials-lack-knowledge-of-money-management-skills-a-study/.

Sivaramakrishnan, S., Srivastava, M., & Rastogi, A. (2017). Attitudinal factors, financial literacy, and stock market participation. *International Journal of Bank Marketing, 35*(5), 818–841. https://doi.org/10.1108/IJBM-01-2016-0012.

Stango, V., & Zinman, J. (2009). American finance association exponential growth bias and household finance. *The Journal of Finance, 64*(6), 2807–2849. https://doi.org/10.1111/j.1540-6261.2009.01518.x.
Stolper, O. A., & Walter, A. (2017). Financial literacy, financial advice, and financial behavior. *Journal of Business Economics, 87*(5), 581–643. https://doi.org/10.1007/s11573-017-0853-9.
Taylor, M. (2011). Measuring financial capability and its determinants using survey data. *Social Indicators Research, 102*(2), 297–314. https://doi.org/10.1007/s11205-010-9681-9.
The Free Press. (2019). *Globally India ranks 2nd in Fintech startups: Report.*
UNESCO. (2019). *Countries ranked by Literacy rate, youth female (% of females ages 15–24).* Index Mundi.
United Nations. (2018). *Igniting Sdg Progress Through Digital.* 45.
World Population Review. (2020). *Literacy Rate by Country 2020.*
Xiao, J. J., & Porto, N. (2017). Financial education and financial satisfaction: Financial literacy, behavior, and capability as mediators. *International Journal of Bank Marketing, 35*(5), 805–817. https://doi.org/10.1108/IJBM-01-2016-0009.

Impact of Financial Factors on Social and Financial Sustainability in Banking Sector: A Mediating Role of Financial Literacy

Sarfaraz Javed and Uvesh Husain

1 Introduction

In the current competitive business world, financial literacy is not only compulsory for financial professionals but also for general peoples because we are all financial consumer in the current era; thus, we need to be financial literate nearby every nation encountering a lack of financial education among the inhabitants. The monetary fortune of an individual and dependents too, monetary learning is obligatory. The term financial literacy is used for one's set of skills to utilize their financial resources in a way considering how to make, manage, invest and expand money effectively (Saeidi et al., 2015). Association of financial literacy is checked with factors like financial attitude, financial behaviour and financial knowledge.

Today India likewise other countries are also facing a lack of financial literacy and the prior studies show the rate of lack of financial literacy is much higher in women than the men due to certain different reasons and in women, rate of financial literacy is higher in educated and working

S. Javed (✉) · U. Husain
Economics and Business Studies Department, Mazoon College, Muscat, Oman

U. Husain
e-mail: owais.husain@mazcol.edu.om

Ananda S. and D. Singh (eds.), *Financial Inclusion in Emerging Markets*,
https://doi.org/10.1007/978-981-16-2652-4_13

ladies than the uneducated and non-working ladies (Rai et al., 2019). Reasons are some common, and some are different based on different scenarios. Ladies with early age fertility problems in wedded relations are identified to suffer more likely from the monetary crisis (Okello Candiya Bongomin et al., 2017). Women are feeble in financial literacy because they are not encouraged to take adequate financial decisions i.e. expenses, budgets and investments, and wealth creation and savings are the foundations of a sound financial plan. Financial literacy should be part of the educational institute's curriculums because gaining financial literacy at an early age benefits more than the financial literacy gained at the old age.

Moreover, in working single women, women take debt and invest money less due to fear of risk, as they are to look after the whole family on their own. For improving the financial education, bank managers of commercial banks were authorized to take essential steps to improve skills, knowledge and ability of financial institutions (Rutskiy et al., 2020). The three essential determinants; financial attitude, financial behaviour and financial knowledge reveal a relationship with financial literacy among the job-oriented ladies of India, and monetary literacy is the critical path to social sustainability and financial sustainability (Grewatsch & Kleindienst, 2017). Only a financial literate woman can have social sustainability and financial sustainability, as she knows all the pros and cons of investment (Malik et al., 2020). Without fear, because of financial literacy, she takes wise decisions regarding wealth, when and how to invest money to get maximum benefit without any loss. She takes massive debts for investment as she knows that ultimately she is going to get positive feedback; hence she succeeds in her such wise decisions. She also knows the value of credit cards and debit cards; she utilizes it in some productive ways (Batty et al., 2015). She takes responsible decisions regarding saving money or investing money in productive ways.

That is why this study was going to fill this gap by taking the data from both genders to assess the impact of financial factors on sustainability. As per the report of WEF (Fig. 1) 400 million of the world's unbanked live in India, out of which 37% are women and 55% are men. Therefore, it is necessary to research by taking data from both genders to fulfil this gap and open a new avenue.

When a person is financially literate, then, he or she can prove to be an excellent asset for the firm. A financially literate person is capable of planning, saving, borrowing, investing and spending wisely. All of these aspects have a key link with the success of an organization (Chu et al.,

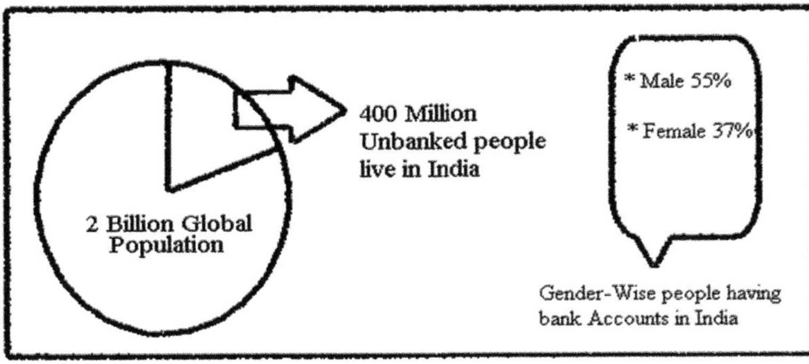

Fig. 1 World economic forum report (*Source* World Bank Report)

2017). Even though financial attitude, behaviour and knowledge are highly important for the success of organizations, however, Indian banks are not giving much importance to these aspects (Khan & Javed, 2017). It is important for the management of Indian banks to focus on improving financial knowledge and literacy of employees and to build positive attitude and behaviour among employees so that they can bring positivity to the social and financial sustainability (Clark et al., 2017). Previously, there has been no study conducted on analysing the key impact of financial attitude, behaviour and knowledge on social and financial sustainability in Indian banks, along with studying the mediating role played by financial literacy. Hence, the current study has been carried out to fill this gap by investigating the impact of financial attitude, behaviour and knowledge on social and financial sustainability.

The findings of this study are useful for the management of Indian banks as they will get to know about key factors which need to be focused properly in order to enhance their financial and social sustainability performance (Jamal et al., 2015). Moreover, they can also get to know about the importance of financial literacy for enhancing financial performance. In addition to this, this study also has some academic implications. As no study has been conducted previously for testing the relationship between financial attitude, behaviour & knowledge and financial performance in Indian banks, so this study has added value to the literature. This paper-based on five sections first contains the introduction. Second contains the literature review in which, we analysed the need for monetary education, determinant of learning finance terms and the influence of specific factors that explain financial practical understanding. Sustainability is consisting of two aspects that cover that position of social sustainability and financial literacy(Alhroob et al., 2017). The research methodology describes the method that is used for analysing explained and explanatory variables. The data analysis gives the relationship and level of influence of the variables. The conclusion covers the outcome of the study and provides recommendations based on the outcome of the study.

2 Literature Review & Hypothesis Development

In behavioural science, people are known as irrational, having limited access to information and focus on enjoying utility derived through short-term decisions. The financial well-being of a person can get affected through financial decisions, made by them with provided level of financial literacy. Financial behaviour is key in order to succeed and survive in the modern dynamic nature of the world. Investor behaviour differentiates and changes due to the difference in approach to make financial decisions. Analysed the behaviour theory and identify the need for financial behavioural theory. The author identifies that its monetary knowledge is vital for investment decisions influenced by factors like human emotions, investment perspectives and investment decisions. The investment decision is influenced by the psychological and emotional factors of humans. Davies (2015) analyses the position of the firm and its ability to generate finance and achieve sustainable growth. Chaulagain (2015) analysed the financial institutions and provide that financial literacy of consumers of financial institutions provides more chances to get finance from banks.

The financial literature people efficiently meet the needs of wants of banks standard procedure and increase the probability to get finance from the institution. It is not always important that financially literate people act in their own best interest for the purpose of improving their financial well-being and for improving sustainability, in which they make rational decisions. As per Deuflhard et al. (2018), the focus of dual processing theory is on financial functioning. According to this, the human mind is viewed as divided into two systems through which decisions are driven. Financially literate people are good policymakers and they play a key role in enhancing the performance of organizations (Estelami, 2016). Therefore, the following section provides the relational literature on the base on underpinning theory in the current study.

2.1 *Financial Attitude and Bank Sustainability*

Amelia (2018) analysed the productivity and sustainability of the business, the results of research reflect that financial literacy played a significant role in the performance of the corporation, while financial literacy has a negative influence on the outcome of the sustainability of the organization. The financial literacy indicates a positive influence on the performance of the organization as the attitude of stakeholders improves with a higher level of financial literacy. Yip and Bocken (2018) analysed the sustainability models for the success of the banking sector. The authors indicate that innovations are important for banks to achieve sustainable growth and development in order to successfully complete the venture of business and promote the interest of society to gain sustainable growth. The innovation has a positive influence on sustainability. Finney and Finney (2018) analysed the financial literacy role of student loan and attitude of loan provides.

The authors found that financial literacy has a significant impact on the outcome of the financial literacy of the organization and plays a vital role in the determination of the financial literacy of the organization. The financial literacy provides reasonable assurance regarding the character of student loan willingness and provides relevant importance to loan providers regarding the ability to get student loans based on the financial literacy of students. The outcome of the study provides that it has a significant relationship between financial literacy and student loan providers. Buch (2018) described the role of financial literacy and financial stability. The financial literacy has an important role in the determination of financial stability. Although financial literacy does not play an important role in the outcome of financial literacy, instead it provides reasonable assurance regarding the character of the market and helps to understand the character of markets through implementation of standard roles and regulation that helps to positively contribute towards the success of financial institutions and helps to mitigate the risk of investment.

Rasheed and Siddiqui (2019) analysed the attitude of people and financial decision-making (Javed & Husain, 2020). The authors identify that financial literacy has a significant impact on the position of financial literacy and financial literacy do help to understand and eliminate the concept of financial improvement and maximize the results of financial growth and development (Rasheed et al., 2019). The financial literacy helps to improve the position of society and improve the condition of the market through actively managing the affairs of business activities. On the base of the above review, the following hypotheses are proposed:

H_1: Financial attitude has a positive and significant impact on social sustainability.
H_2: Financial attitude has a positive and significant impact on financial sustainability.

2.2 *Financial Behaviour and Bank Sustainability*

Fitria et al. (2019) The relationship between explored the importance of financial literacy, demographics and market information factors that influence the outcome of investment decisions. The investment decision is influenced by the position of financial literacy of organization leaders and can lead to playing an important role in the outcome of success or failure of the investment (Javed et al., 2020). Therefore, the authors indicate higher financial literacy leads to develop a positive impact on the investment outcome. The increased level of financial literacy plays an important role in the determination of financial decisions relevant to investment (Białowolski et al., 2019) analysed the decomposition of financial literacy and develop the model to investigate the level of financial literacy among the respondent and found that financial literacy has a positive relationship with factors used for analysing the level of financial literacy among the respondents and helps to mitigate the risk of investment (Ibadoghlu, 2018) discussed the importance of financial knowledge, inclusion and literacy to define the role of factors on the success factor and help to mitigate the chance of risk aversion through utilizing the skills set that put the negative impact on the growth of the organization (Weber & Feltmate, 2016). The author covers different factors that influence the position of financial literacy, regulation and financial policy that can lead to putting the positive or negative impact on the success of the organization. The paper covers the small and medium enterprises and provides reasonable assurance regarding the character market that can lead to putting the negative impact on the growth of the business (Mersha, 2018) analysed the role of financial literacy in order to assess the position of financial matters that describe the success and failure of an organization (Agarwalla et al., 2015; Brüggen et al., 2017). The financial literacy and presentation of financial reporting to measure the position of attitude, knowledge and behaviour of users while reading the financial information from the sources of the document. The position of financial information varies due to the use of factors that could put a negative influence on the position of the organization. So that following hypothesis is proposed for the current study:

H3: Financial Behaviour has a positive and significant impact on social sustainability.
H4: Financial Behaviour has a positive and significant impact on the financial sustainability.

2.3 Financial Knowledge and Bank Sustainability

Totenhagen et al. (2015) analysed the financial knowledge of youth as consider its key concept to delivery and provide suitable solutions for living. It is important to understand the concept that provides reasonable assurance and success factor that help to determine the positive relationship between the financial knowledge and consideration of positive delivery methods that helps to motivate the investors to achieve sustainable growth (Nyarko-Baasi, 2018) analysed the financial literacy and financial inclusion with respect to the growth of Africa. The paper covers different aspects of financial literacy and financial inclusion and provides reasonable assurance regarding the role of financial literacy and financial inclusion on the growth of Africa. The author found a positive and significant impact on the growth of financial literacy and financial inclusion (Szafranska, 2019) determined the level of financial literacy among the youth and helps to understand the position of financial knowledge vital for the growth of the business. In this article, the writer identifies the position and importance of digital literacy and its influence on the outcome and performance of the institution (Albeerdy & Gharleghi, 2015; Britt et al., 2015) studies the financial knowledge, financial behaviour and financial attitude of youth of China in order to determine the opportunities that the Government can utilize to maximize the benefits for upcoming youth (Purnomo, 2019). The author identifies the importance of financial literacy and its role in the growth of business success through utilizing the opportunity that provides sustainable growth and development to the owner and helps them to achieve long-term benefits from utilizing the opportunity of sustainable growth.

The outcomes uncover a positive relationship between's creative direction, pioneering direction, monetary education and enterprising execution. Thusly, aesthetic direction influences an imaginative company's budgetary and nonfinancial exhibition (Davies, 2015; Drever et al., 2015; Farrell et al., 2016). What's the more, imaginative direction and money-related education give a positive effect on the general execution of an inventive endeavour. In any case, the communication impact of innovative direction and monetary education on the imaginative direction execution relationship is undetectable. The following hypotheses are proposed:

H5: Financial knowledge has a positive and significant impact on social sustainability.
H6: Financial knowledge has a positive and significant impact on the financial sustainability.

2.4 *Mediating Role of Financial Literacy*

Bielova et al. (2018) analysed the mediating role of financial literacy with indicators like social and financial development of the organization. Author agrees that the financial performance is considered as the best instrument to know the financial soundness of the organization (Javed, 2018).The financial literacy plays an important role in the development and growth of society that help to maximize the benefits and growth of the business. Financial literacy does play an important role in the outcome of financial sector growth and social development. The society with a higher level of financial literacy tends to have more diligent and understand the concept of financial sustainability and social sustainability of society. In this exploration, the assignment of checking theories about the presence of a connection between the degree of money-related education and the pointers of monetary and social parts improvement is set (Herdjiono & Damanik, 2016; Sayinzoga et al., 2016).

The article manages the connection between the degree of monetary education and the markers of the improvement of budgetary and social parts as per the information of the EU-28 and nations of the world in general. The outcomes are as budgetary proficiency develops, the borrowers less regularly take cash from a private casual bank and from a family or companions and all the more as often as possible—from a monetary establishment; there is a reverse interrelation between the degree of money-related education among grown-ups and the NPL (nonperforming credits); likewise, for the EU-28 nations, the immediate interrelation between the seriously really denied individuals (% of all-out populace) and the NPL level has been affirmed (Hamza & Arif, 2019) assessed the position of financial literacy as a mediator for investment decisions that help users to make a rational decision. Financial literacy helps to improve the position of investment and achieve sustainability by taking the right decision for the financial decision. However, monetary proficiency has a critical negative effect on venture choices through receptiveness to encounter and a noteworthy positive effect through neuroticism (Tang & Baker, 2016; Van Campenhout, 2015). The investigation improves our comprehension of speculator conduct by considering the intervening job of enormous five character attributes on the connection between monetary education and venture choices. It is suggested that money-related organizations ought to give speculation, directing administrations to eminent financial specialists utilizing the customer profile procedure.

So on the base of the above discussion, the following hypotheses are proposed regarding the mediating role of financial literacy for the current study:

- H_7: Financial literacy significantly mediates between financial attitude and social sustainability.
- H_8: Financial literacy significantly mediates between financial attitude and financial sustainability.
- H_9: Financial literacy significantly mediates between financial behaviour and social sustainability.
- H_{10}: Financial literacy significantly mediates between financial behaviour and financial sustainability.
- H_{11}: Financial literacy significantly mediates between financial knowledge and social sustainability.
- H_{12}: Financial literacy significantly mediate between financial knowledge and financial sustainability.

In Fig. 2 presents the theoretical model of the study for hypotheses testing.

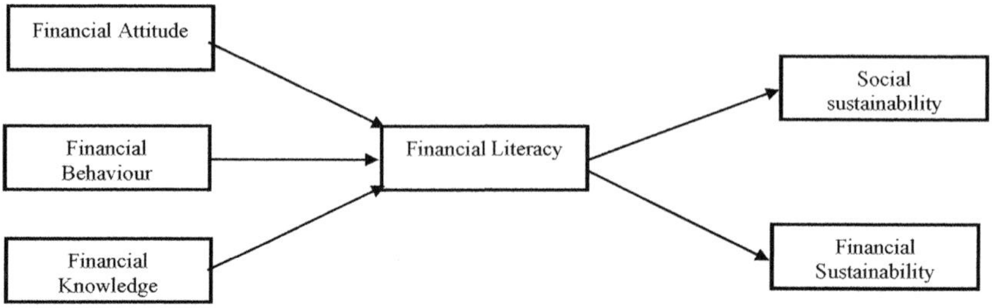

Fig. 2 Research framework (*Source* Prepared by the Authors)

3 Research Methodology

Research methodology describes the adoption of procedures and processes to conduct the research. It indicates a set of procedures that help to complete the procedure of research through the adoption of data collection procedures, techniques, use of tools and measures of the variable that define the character of the market.

3.1 Sample and Population

In order to conduct the research of the sample is consists of from the population of bank managers of leading commercial banks of India. The sample provides reasonable assurance regarding the character of the population as the validity test for data ensures that the sample truly represents the population. The sample indicates the position of data type and data analysis that can lead to putting significant impact on the outcome of the population mean and provide insight into the population. The position population is measured through applying the sampling technique to get insight regarding the level of financial literacy of bank managers and used the outcome to predict financial literacy impact on the social and financial sustainability. Therefore, according to the Kline (2015) in social science, the sample size of more than 300 respondents is enough for generalizability of the results.

3.2 Data Collection

In order to conduct research, we send 380 questionnaires to leading banks managers around India and 61 response was incomplete and are not eligible for data analysis. Hence, data collection of 319 bank managers of leading banks was valid for applying the process of measurement of data. The study was based on the descriptive research design that identifies different aspects of data in order to predict financial literacy level and its impact on sustainability. Convenience sampling method was used for data collection from leading banks. The survey was done using the digital aid of online questionnaires and visit to banks.

3.3 Measures

The study consists of two aspects that include measuring the level of financial literacy and assessing the level of impact on social and financial sustainability. In order to measure the financial literacy, three-domain is used that indicates the level of financial literacy of bank managers. The financial literacy of bank managers measures by utilizing the aid of financial attitude, financial behaviour and financial knowledge. Historically, various authors have measured financial attitude using the six items for current study, this scale is adopted from the study of (Rai et al., 2019). The financial behaviour measure with 5 items scale which is adopted from the study of, and the financial knowledge is also measured on the base of 5 items which is also adopted from the study of, (Rai et al., 2019). To measure the financial literacy of bank managers, a 4 items scale adopted from (Rai et al., 2019) is used. The dependent variables of the study are social and financial sustainability, which is measured on 3 items scale for each and adopted from the study of (Varela et al., 2019).

3.4 Data Analysis Tools

For analysis, we use the tool like AMOS and SPSS to conduct statistical analyses that quantify the financial literacy and help to find the relationship between the dependent and independent variables(Javed & Husain, 2021; Javed et al., 2019). The descriptive analysis helps to identify different aspects of data in order to measure financial literacy through identifying the character of data. The relationship between the variables is measured through financial literacy and bank sustainability.

4 Results and Findings

The classification of data has different demographical profile covert the data into different classes in the shape of gender classification, education and age groups (Table 1).

The classification based on gender indicates male respondent is 52.4% while the female respondent is 47.6%. The graduate is 12.2%, postgraduate is 43.2%, masters are 33.2% and others are 11.3%. The age group 21–30 years indicate 24.8%, 31–40 years indicate 29.6%, and 41–50 years indicate 30.4% and above 50 years indicates 15.4%.

4.1 *Descriptive Statistics & Discriminant Validity*

The descriptive statistics are key to understand the normality of data. The descriptive statistics ensure the data is ideal for the statistical analysis and can utilize for creating statistical inference from the value of data (Table 2).

The descriptive statistics indicate that financial attitude, financial behaviour, financial knowledge, social sustainability, financial sustainability and financial literacy have normal behaviour while discriminant validity indicates that positive correlation between the factors that it is a good indication to get desire outcome from the data analysis. The values of skewness ensure that the data was distributed normally, as the value is in between −1 and +1.

Table 1
Demographical profile

Variable		*Frequency*	*Percent*
Gender	Male	167	52.4
	Female	152	47.6
Education	Graduation	39	12.2
	Post-Graduation	138	43.3
	Masters	106	33.2
	Others	36	11.3
Age	21–30 Y	79	24.8
	31–40 Y	94	29.5
	41–50 Y	97	30.4
	50+ Y	49	15.4

Source Prepared by the Authors

Table 2 Descriptive statistics & discriminant validity

Variables	*Items*	*Mean*	*Skewness*	*FA*	*FB*	*FK*	*SS*	*FS*	*FL*
FA	6	3.5444	−0.829	**0.860**					
FB	5	3.4884	−0.661	0.593	**0.897**				
FK	5	3.5455	−0.763	0.518	0.613	**0.883**			
SS	3	3.4148	−0.214	0.553	0.331	0.388	**0.843**		
FS	3	3.4316	−0.528	0.493	0.350	0.411	0.703	**0.872**	
FL	4	3.5603	−0.834	0.548	0.583	0.472	0.443	0.454	**0.865**

Note FA = Financial Attitude, FB = Financial Behaviour, FK = Financial Knowledge, SS = Social Sustainability, FS = Financial Sustainability, FL = Financial Literacy
Source Prepared by the Authors

4.2 Factor Loading and Convergent Validity

Factor loading the association of constructs items with variables, whereas convergent validity proves that either data is reliable or not. The CR must be greater than 0.70, and AVE must be greater than 0.50 of each construct. In Table 3 shows these results.

Table 3 illustrates the test results of the rotated component matrix. This analysis basically helps in performing the analysis of cross loading factor. Moreover, it prepares the data for further validity tests. The test results acquired in the given table show that all of the values except for one value are greater 0.7. Moreover, none of the variable items is in front of another variable item. Therefore, it can be stated that there is no such issue of the cross-loading factor in the given data.

4.3 Model Fit Indices and KMO

The good fitness of the model is assessed by using the indices. The table provides reasonable assurance regarding the good fitness of model as the value of factors is under the determine level of acceptance that provides a suitable indication of good fitness of model in the determination of the value of model. The KMO value is greater than 0.90 indicates that data suitable for analysis and mode is a good fit based on other indices.

In Table 4, model fit indices have been done in order to check for if the model was effective. The effectiveness of the model has been checked through comparing the current values with the range of threshold. All of the values are within the threshold and it eventually justifies the fitness of

Table 3 Factor loading and convergent validity

	Component loading						*Convergent validity*		
	1	*2*	*3*	*4*	*5*	*6*	*CR*	*AVE*	*MSV*
FA4	0.838						0.944	0.739	0.352
FA3	0.831								
FA5	0.822								
FA6	0.811								
FA2	0.766								
FA1	0.682								
FB4		0.841					0.954	0.804	0.376
FB5		0.830							
FB3		0.822							
FB2		0.819							
FB1		0.778							
FK3			0.877				0.946	0.779	0.376
FK2			0.836						
FK1			0.831						
FK4			0.820						
FK5			0.793						
FL2				0.842			0.922	0.748	0.340
FL3				0.817					
FL4				0.801					
FL1				0.798					
FS2					0.839		0.905	0.761	0.494
FS3					0.831				
FS1					0.805				
SS3						0.829	0.880	0.710	0.494
SS2						0.802			
SS1						0.767			

Note FA = Financial Attitude, FB = Financial Behaviour, FK = Financial Knowledge, SS = Social Sustainability, FS = Financial Sustainability, FL = Financial Literacy
Source Prepared by the Authors

Table 4 Model fit indices and KMO

CFA indicators	*CMIN/DF*	*GFI*	*IFI*	*CFI*	*RMSEA*	*KMO*
Threshold value	≤ 3	≥ 0.80	≥ 0.90	≥ 0.90	≤ 0.08	0.6–1.0
Observed value	2.128	0.869	0.959	0.959	0.060	0.937

Source Prepared by the Authors

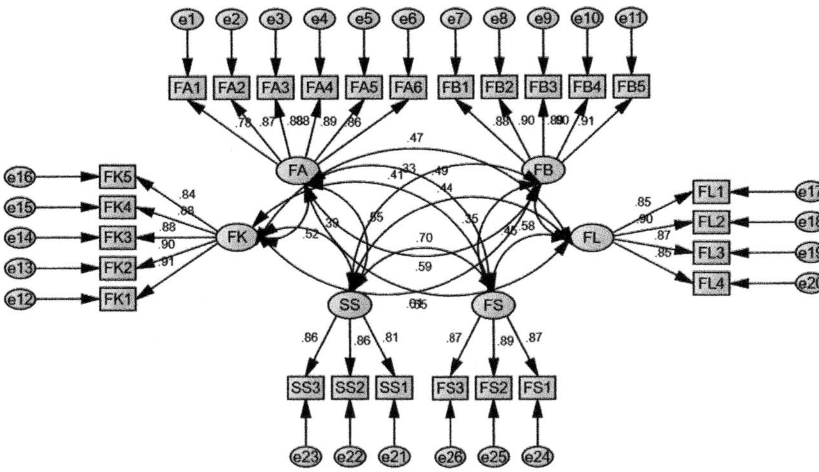

Fig. 3 Confirmatory factor analysis (*Source* Prepared by the Authors)

the model. In Fig. 3, the CFA loading was presented. The CFA analysis provides suitable information and the diagram reflects significant contributions different in order to achieve and satisfy our desire level of model fitness to get the desired outcome from the analysis of different factors that contribute positively towards the determination of the value of the hypothesis. The diagram indicates the contribution of different factors and relationship of different variables to get the desired outcome of the variable.

4.4 *Structural Equation Modelling*

SEM is the statistical technique which provides the multivalve analysis in a single model suggested by many other studies (Sarfaraz, 2017). The outcome of structural equation modelling provides assurance regarding the character of different aspects of structural equation modelling that help to determine the level of significance on the factors to get the desired value of the specific factor. The financial attitude has a positive and significant impact on the determination of social sustainability and indicates a positive and significant impact on the outcome of financial sustainability. Financial behaviour has a negative but insignificant impact on social

Table 5 Structural equation modelling

Hypothesized path	*B-value*	*SE*	*P-value*	*Decision*
FT → SS	0.407	0.061	0.000	Supported
FT → FS	0.293	0.064	0.000	Supported
FB → SS	−0.119	0.063	0.074	Not supported
FB → FB	−0.072	0.066	0.290	Not supported
FK → SS	0.135	0.060	0.024	Supported
FK → FS	0.178	0.062	0.004	Supported
FT → FL → SS	0.054	0.027	0.010	Supported
FT → FL → FS	0.061	0.030	0.018	Supported
FB → FL → SS	0.066	0.029	0.010	Supported
FB → FL → FB	0.074	0.036	0.019	Supported
FK → FL → SS	0.024	0.020	0.158	Not supported
FK → FL → FS	0.027	0.024	0.147	Not supported

Note FA = Financial Attitude, FB = Financial Behaviour, FK = Financial Knowledge, SS = Social Sustainability, FS = Financial Sustainability, FL = Financial Literacy
Source Prepared by the Authors

sustainability and also an insignificant impact on financial sustainability. Hence, why H3 and H4 are rejected.

Moreover, Table 5 shows that financial literacy positively and significantly mediates between financial attitude and social sustainability. Financial literacy also positively and significantly mediates between financial attitude and financial sustainability. Financial literacy positively and significantly mediates between financial behaviour and social sustainability. Same as positively mediates between FB and financial sustainability. Financial literacy positively but insignificantly contributes to financial knowledge and social stability. But the mediating role of financial literacy between financial knowledge and social and financial sustainability is insignificant that's why H11 and H12 are not supported. In Fig. 4 presenting the standardized results of path analysis.

5 Discussion and Conclusion

5.1 Discussion

The financial attitude, financial behaviour and financial knowledge have a positive influence on the financial literacy of bank sustainability. The

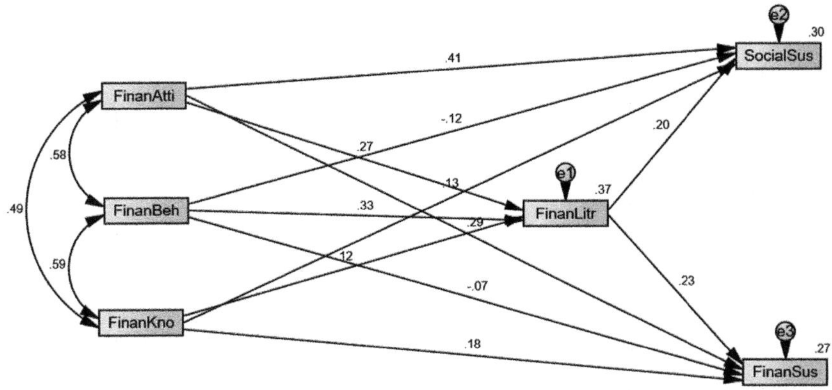

Fig. 4 Structural Equation Modelling (*Source* Prepared by the Authors)

result of first and second hypothesis indicates that (Huston, 2010) financial attitude positively and significantly affects the position of the social sustainability of the bank while financial attitude positively and significantly influences the position of financial sustainability of the financial institution. The third and fourth hypothesis investigates the (Khursheed et al., 2016) financial behaviour of the manager and finds the association with bank sustainability. The results indicate that financial behaviour negatively and insignificantly influences the position of social sustainability and financial sustainability. The result was inconsistent with previous studies due to the lack of variation in determining the financial behaviour of bank employees. The fifth and sixth hypotheses investigate the level of financial literacy in the domain of (Khursheed et al., 2016) financial knowledge and try to build a relationship with the social sustainability of banks. The results reflect that financial knowledge has a positive and significant relationship with the social and financial sustainability of banks. The second part covers the mediating role of financial literacy in order to achieve the social and financial sustainability of banks. In order to identify the mediating role of the financial literacy, hypothesis was developed to identify the position of financial literacy of bank managers. The hypothesis results indicate that financial literacy connects financial attitude and social sustainability of banks. The hypothesis results indicate that financial literacy connects financial attitude and financial sustainability of banks. The hypothesis results indicate that financial literacy connects financial behaviour and social sustainability of banks. The hypothesis results indicate that financial literacy connects financial behaviour and financial sustainability of banks (Ye & Kulathunga, 2019). The hypothesis results indicate that financial literacy connects financial knowledge and social sustainability of banks. The hypothesis results indicate that financial literacy connects financial knowledge and financial sustainability of banks.

5.2 *Research Implications*

The study has contributed in a very significant way in the ways of increasing and positively enhancing the sustainability not only India but also the industries present globally as well because the element of financial literacy can be incorporated in order to build the positive and constructive financial attitude and knowledge so that the financial performance can increase that way. Moreover, the Government can also plan for policies for increasing financial literacy to increase financial performance. Furthermore, the study carries on the specific sector like a financial institution to assess the position of monetary learning of bank employees. It is recommended to banking authorize to develop training for financial literacy enhancement for bank managers to help them positively contribute to the growth of the business. The financial literacy improvement program helps the institution to train their new employees under the experienced managers to increase the financial literacy of bank employees. The results indicate that financial sustainability has a positive association. Hence, training and development programs in the domain of financial literacy help the bank managers to improve the condition of financial literacy of bank employees and contribute positively towards the growth of banks.

5.3 *Conclusion*

In concluding remarks, the purpose of this research is to investigate the impact of financial factors on social and financial sustainability in Indian banks with a mediating role of financial literacy. As through the given research, different factors can be analysed that can make an increment in sustainability performance. The data for this research has been collected from 304 employees of Indian banks through questionnaires. SPSS and AMOS tools have been used for running different tests like CFA has been done to test the reliability and validity of the results, whereas SEM used to test the research hypothesis. In the analysis portion, it can be concluding the financial literacy mediating role in the achieve sustainability of financial institutions. The importance of financial literacy can realize through results of research paper that provides reasonable assurance regarding the degree of influence on the position of financial factors and its impact on the banks' sustainability. Financial attitude, financial behaviour and financial knowledge play an important role in determining the outcome of financial literacy that plays a significant role in sustainability.

5.4 Study Limitations and Future Suggestions

The study has few limitations that put limits on the scope of the study. The study reflects that data from the bank manager that was collected from a specific location in India. Hence, it is hard to generalize the concept of collection for every bank manager who works in the commercial bank of India in different states. The data collection technique was a nonprobability sampling technique hence it can give misleading information when we want to generalize the concept for the whole population of bank managers in India. In order to measure the position of financial literacy of bank managers, it is important to widen the scope of financial concept in the questionnaire. We feel needs to explore the financial concept through questionnaires and investigate the concept of financial literacy of bank managers. In future, the study has scope to explore other sectors, industry and countries for a comparative analysis to explore the position of financial literacy and sustainability of bank managers. The study has the potential to explore different dimensions of financial literacy like physiological aspects of financial decision-making, personal preferences, risk position of the organization, project profitability and environmental sustainability. We recommend to the researcher to replicate the findings with other sectors using probability sampling in order to generalize the sampling for the whole population in order to use its policymaking.

References

Agarwalla, S. K., Barua, S. K., Jacob, J., & Varma, J. R. (2015). Financial literacy among working young in urban India. *World Development, 67*, 101–109.

Alhroob, M., Irbihat, B., Albashabsheh, A., & Javed, S. (2017). Does corporate governance create volatility in performance? *International Journal of Informative & Futuristic Research, 4*(7), 6859–6866. http://www.ijifr.com/pdf save/01-04-2017495IJIFR-V4-E7-075.pd

Albeerdy, M. I., & Gharleghi, B. (2015). Determinants of the financial literacy among college students in Malaysia. *International Journal of Business Administration, 6*(3).

Amelia, Y. (2018). Effect of Financial Literacy for Performance and Sustainability Small and Medium Enterprises in Lampung province. *PROSIDING The 5 th International Conferance on Governance and Accountability (ICGA) 2018.*

Awais, M., Laber, M. F., Rasheed, N., & Khursheed, A. (2016). Impact of financial literacy and investment experience on risk tolerance and investment decisions: Empirical evidence from Pakistan. *International Journal of Economics and Financial Issues, 6*(1).

Białowolski, P. (2019). Economic sentiment as a driver for household financial behavior. *Journal of Behavioral and Experimental Economics, 80*, 59–66.

Batty, M., Collins, J. M., & Odders-White, E. (2015). Experimental evidence on the effects of financial education on elementary school students' knowledge, behavior, and attitudes. *Journal of Consumer Affairs, 49*(1), 69–96.

Bielova, I., Oliinyk, V., Nilova, N., & Nilova, M. (2018). Causal relationship of financial literacy with indicators of the financial and social sectors. *Financial and credit activity: Problems of theory and practice, 4*(27), 457–467.

Britt, S. L., Canale, A., Fernatt, F., Stutz, K., & Tibbetts, R. (2015). Financial stress and financial counseling: Helping college students. *Journal of Financial Counseling and Planning, 26*(2), 172–186.

Brüggen, E. C., Hogreve, J., Holmlund, M., Kabadayi, S., & Löfgren, M. (2017). Financial well-being: A conceptualization and research agenda. *Journal of Business Research, 79*, 228–237.

Buch, C. M. (2018). Competition, stability, and efficiency in financial markets. *In Discussion on a paper by Dean Corbae and Ross Levine prepared for the 2018 Jackson Hole Symposium "Changing Market Structure and Implications for Monetary Policy" Jackson Hole, August* (Vol. 25).

Chaulagain, R. P. (2015). *Financial literacy for increasing sustainable access to finance in Nepal.* Nepal: School of Education, Kathmandu University.

Chu, Z., Wang, Z., Xiao, J. J., & Zhang, W. (2017). Financial literacy, portfolio choice and financial well-being. *Social Indicators Research, 132*(2), 799–820.

Clark, R., Lusardi, A., & Mitchell, O. S. (2017). Financial knowledge and 401 (k) investment performance: A case study. *Journal of Pension Economics & Finance, 16*(3), 324–347.

Davies, P. (2015). Towards a framework for financial literacy in the context of democracy. *Journal of Curriculum Studies, 47*(2), 300–316.

Deuflhard, F., Georgarakos, D., & Inderst, R. (2018). Financial literacy and savings account returns. *Journal of the European Economic Association, 17*(1), 131–164.

Drever, A. I., Odders-White, E., Kalish, C. W., Else-Quest, N. M., Hoagland, E. M., & Nelms, E. N. (2015). Foundations of financial well-being: Insights into the role of executive function, financial socialization, and experience-based learning in childhood and youth. *Journal of Consumer Affairs, 49*(1), 13–38.

Estelami, H. (2016). Cognitive drivers of suboptimal financial decisions: Implications for financial literacy campaigns. *Financial Literacy and the Limits of Financial Decision-Making* (pp. 10–25). Springer.

Farrell, L., Fry, T. R., & Risse, L. (2016). The significance of financial self-efficacy in explaining women's personal finance behaviour. *Journal of Economic Psychology, 54*, 85–99.

Grewatsch, S., & Kleindienst, I. (2017). When does it pay to be good? Moderators and mediators in the corporate sustainability–corporate financial performance relationship: A critical review. *Journal of Business Ethics, 145*(2), 383–416.

Hamza, N., & Arif, I. (2019). Impact of financial literacy on investment decisions: The mediating effect of big-five personality traits model. *Market Forces*, 14.

Herdjiono, I., & Damanik, L. A. (2016). Pengaruh financial attitude, financial knowledge, parental income terhadap financial management behavior. *Jurnal Manajemen Teori dan Terapan | Journal of Theory and Applied Management, 9*(3).

Huston, S. J. (2010). Measuring financial literacy. *Journal of consumer affairs, 44*(2), 296–316.

Ibadoghlu, Gubad, Financial Inclusion, Financial Literacy, and Financial Education in Azerbaijan. (May 12, 2018). *ADBI Working Paper 842*, Available at SSRN: https://ssrn.com/abstract=3183007 or http://dx.doi.org/10.2139/ssrn.3183007.

Jamal, A. A. A., Ramlan, W. K., Karim, M., & Osman, Z. (2015). The effects of social influence and financial literacy on savings behavior: A study on students of higher learning institutions in Kota Kinabalu, Sabah. *International Journal of Business and Social Science, 6*(11), 110–119.

Javed, S. (2018). Does organisation behaviour affect performance of auditing firms. *International Journal of Engineering Technologies and Management Research, 5*, 90–98.

Javed, S., Atallah, B., Aldalaien, E., & Husain, U. (2019). Performance of venture capital firms in UK : Quantitative research approach of 20 UK venture capitals. *Middle-East Journal of Scientific Research, 27*(5), 432–438. https://doi.org/10.5829/idosi.mejsr.2019.432.438

Javed, S., & Husain, O. (2020). An ARDL investigation on the nexus of oil factors and economic growth: A timeseries evidence from Sultanate of Oman. *Cogent Economics & Finance, 8*(1), 17. https://doi.org/10.1080/23322039.2020.1838418

Javed, S., & Husain, U. (2021). Corporate CSR practices and corporate performance: Managerial implications for sustainable development. *Decision*. https://doi.org/10.1007/s40622-021-00274-w

Javed, S., Malik, A., & Alharbi, M. M. H. (2020). The relevance of leadership styles and Islamic work ethics in managerial effectiveness. *PSU Research Review, 4*(3), 189–207. https://doi.org/10.1108/prr-03-2019-0007

Khan, A. A., & Javed, S. (2017). Accounting of post merger financial performance of Punjab National Bank (PNB) and Nedungadi Bank. *International Journal of Mechanical Engineering and Technology, 8*(11), 1043–1062. http://www.iaeme.com/MasterAdmin/Journal_uploads/IJMET/VOLUME_8_ISSUE_11/IJMET_08_11_107.pdf

Malik, A., Khan, N., Faisal, S., Javed, S., & Faridi, M. R. (2020). An investigation on leadership styles for the business productivity and sustainability of small medium enterprises (SME'S). *International Journal of Entrepreneurship, 24*(5), 1–10. https://www.abacademies.org/articles/an-investigation-on-leadership-styles-for-the-business-productivity-and-sustainability-of-small-medium-enterprises-smes-9845.html

Mersha, D., & Ayenew, Z. (2018). Determinants of access to finance of smallholder farmers. *Horn of African Journal of Business and Economics (HAJBE), 1*(1), 129–131.

Nyarko-Baasi, M. (2018). Effects of non-performing loans on the profitability of commercial banks-A case of some selected banks on the Ghana stock exchange. *Global Journal of Management and Business Research.*

Okello Candiya Bongomin, G., Mpeera Ntayi, J., Munene, J. C., & Malinga Akol, C. (2017). Financial intermediation and financial inclusion of poor households: Mediating role of social networks in rural Uganda. *Cogent Economics & Finance, 5*(1), 1362184.

Purnomo, H., & Khalda, S. (2019, November). Influence of Financial Technology on National Financial Institutions. In *IOP Conference Series: Materials Science and Engineering* (Vol. 662, No. 2, p. 022037). IOP Publishing.

Rutskiy, V., Javed, S., Azizam, S. H., Chudopal, N., Zhigalov, K., Kuzmich, R., & Pupkov, A. (2020). *The price determinants of Bitcoin as a new digital form of money*. (R. Silhavy, P. Silhavy, & Z. Prokopova, Eds.). Springer. https://doi.org/10.1007/978-3-030-63322-6

Rai, K., Dua, S., & Yadav, M. (2019). Association of financial attitude, financial behaviour and financial knowledge towards financial literacy: A structural equation modeling approach. *FIIB Business Review, 8*(1), 51–60.

Rasheed, R., & Siddiqui, S. H. (2019). Attitude for inclusive finance: Influence of owner-managers' and firms' characteristics on SMEs financial decision making. *Journal of Economic and Administrative Sciences, 35*(3), 158–171. https://doi.org/10.1108/JEAS-05-2018-0057.

Rasheed, R., Siddiqui, S. H., & Chaudhry, I. S. (2019). Development of SMEs with provision of Islamic finance in emerging economies: A case of Pakistan. *Journal Zia-e-Tahqeeq, 17*, 35–51.

Saeidi, S. P., Sofian, S., Saeidi, P., Saeidi, S. P., & Saaeidi, S. A. (2015). How does corporate social responsibility contribute to firm financial performance? The mediating role of competitive advantage, reputation, and customer satisfaction. *Journal of Business Research, 68*(2), 341–350.

Sarfaraz, J. (2017). Unified theory of acceptance and use of technology (Utaut) model-mobile banking. *Journal of Internet Banking and Commerce, 22*(3), 1–20.

Sayinzoga, A., Bulte, E. H., & Lensink, R. (2016). Financial literacy and financial behaviour: Experimental evidence from rural Rwanda. *The Economic Journal, 126*(594), 1571–1599.

Szafranska, W. (2019). Proceedings before the Minister of Finance concerning Entries in the Land and Mortgage Registers in Favour of the State Treasury Based on International Agreements on the Settlement of Financial Claims. In *Forum Prawnicze* (p. 73).

Tang, N., & Baker, A. (2016). Self-esteem, financial knowledge and financial behavior. *Journal of Economic Psychology, 54*, 164–176.

Totenhagen, C. J., Casper, D. M., Faber, K. M., Bosch, L. A., Wiggs, C. B., & Borden, L. M. (2015). Youth financial literacy: A review of key considerations and promising delivery methods. *Journal of Family and Economic Issues, 36*(2), 167–191.

Van Campenhout, G. (2015). Revaluing the role of parents as financial socialization agents in youth financial literacy programs. *Journal of Consumer Affairs, 49*(1), 186–222.

Varela, L., Araújo, A., Ávila, P., Castro, H., & Putnik, G. (2019). Evaluation of the Relation between Lean Manufacturing, Industry 4.0, and Sustainability. *Sustainability, 11*(5), 1439.

Weber, O., & Feltmate, B. (2016). *Sustainable banking: Managing the social and environmental impact of financial institutions*. University of Toronto Press.

Ye, J., & Kulathunga, K. M. M. C. B. (2019). How does financial literacy promote sustainability in SMEs? A developing country perspective. *Sustainability, 11*(10), 2990.

Yip, A. W., & Bocken, N. M. (2018). Sustainable business model archetypes for the banking industry. *Journal of cleaner production, 174*, 150–169.
Zachary Finney, R., & Finney, T. G. (2018). How does financial literacy impact attitude Ttoward student loan providers? *Services Marketing Quarterly, 39*(3), 193–207.

Promoting Financial Inclusion Through Digital Wallets: An Empirical Study with Street Vendors

M. Rizwana, Padmalini Singh, and P. V. Raveendra

1 Introduction

1.1 Background of the Study

In the present techno-crazed society, digital payments are witnessing a remarkable growth in India "with a compound annual growth rate (CAGR) of 12.7% in the number of non-cash transactions" (*The Economic Times*, 2020). The novel digital era has paved a way for mobile devices and services to flourish as the most prominent tool for financial transactions. Further, the devices and the services have become a basic necessity to foster communication and financial transactions. Due to the high penetration of mobile usage in India, many innovations have resulted in establishing disruptive business models across various industries, and one

M. Rizwana (✉)
Department of Management Studies, Ramaiah Institute of Technology, Bengaluru, India

P. Singh
RV Institute of Management, Bengaluru, India

P. V. Raveendra
Ramaiah Institute of Technology, Bengaluru, India

Ananda S. and D. Singh (eds.), *Financial Inclusion in Emerging Markets*,
https://doi.org/10.1007/978-981-16-2652-4_14

such disruptive innovation is mobile wallet (Bughin, 2013). A mobile wallet is a virtual wallet or a digital wallet which facilitates an individual to pay as well as to obtain payment using an electronic gadget. These virtual wallet services function as cashless payment service, where people need not pay cash or swipe their credit and debit cards while buying any product or services. The mobile wallets have brought in a paradigm shift in traditional financial transaction by providing a scope for financial inclusion among each individual bringing the majority of unbanked population of the country into the financial system. Apparently, the mobile wallets have provided a tremendous opportunity for the unorganized business ventures to make all the transactions more formalized and authenticated. According to ASSOCHAM Report (2016), the total transaction volume of the m-payment in India is expected to grow at a CAGR of 132% during Financial Year 2016–2022 and reach around 460 Billion by the end of 2022. In addition to that, standing next to China and Denmark, India accounts as one of the top markets among global nations in the adoption of mobile wallets (Agarwal, 2018). Though the penetration of mobile wallet is gaining popularity in India, along the road the significance of mobile wallet for financial inclusion is yet to be realized by the unbanked population in India. In addition to this, digital illiteracy coupled with financial illiteracy is creating hurdles in using mobile wallet services. Moreover, considering the businesses in informal sector, particularly the street vendors in India, is under lot of stress due to the transformation of economy towards digital footprints.

1.2 Need for the Study

Among the contributors to the informal economy, the street vendors hold a significant position in catering the needs of human masses that belong to middle and lower strata of the society. Two-third populations in the informal sector constitute 93% of workforce that face array of problems from accessing their legal rights to financial facilities to include them into formalized economy (Prasad, 2018). In par with metropolitan cities such as Delhi, Mumbai, Kolkata, there are around 3 lakhs street vendors in Bengaluru city (*Bangalore Mirror*, 2017). In spite of holding an important segment in exhibiting self-sufficiency as being self-employed, the street vendors are facing lot of problems associated with daily unaccounted financial transactions in the present digital era. Despite numerous government initiatives for hundred per cent financial inclusion, according to the report, 60% population in India does not have operating bank accounts out of which 25 crore population have lack of access to the financial services largely small businesses that includes street vendors are not exposed to the formal financial services (Konwar, 2015). The factors like absence of proper identity proof, poor saving habit, poor financial literacy, lengthy banking procedure and inconsistent income are the major glitches associated with the Financial Inclusion of Street Vendors (Sheik & Sareswathy, 2016). Though street vendors are striving to become digitally inclusive, the extent to which the digital inclusion has brought in financial inclusion among the target audience is yet to be explored that calls for an immediate investigation.

1.3 Statement of the Problem

The problems faced by street vendors range from accessing basic banking facilities due to financial and digital illiteracy. The Indian Government's present agenda to bring in cent percentage financial inclusion has created a major threat to the vendor community. In addition to this, the street vendors are also forced to offer digital wallets payment options which are not in their regular business routine. In order to serve tech-savvy customers, the street vendors are gaining familiarity towards digital transaction to avoid any dip in sales. At this backdrop, the present study is an earnest effort to determine the extent to which mobile wallet services have empowered the street vendors to fall under the umbrella of financial inclusion.

2 Literature Review

These authors have attempted to present the literature work done by the various researchers under the scope of study. Though the number of available literatures in the identified topic of research remains limited, an effort has been made to summarize the important findings that have been reported in Journals and News articles. Pal et al. (2018) attempted to understand the discontent of digital payment among street shop vendors in Mumbai and Bengaluru region. For the purpose of study, a sample of 200 shopkeepers were selected from Mumbai and Bengaluru region. It has been mentioned in the study that the demonetization induced cash shortage has increased the digital payment adoption among the respondents. The study found that the level of adoption of digital payment largely depend up on the factors like type of product sold, nature of transaction and respondents' level of comfort and familiarity with the digital technology. Chopra (2018) investigated the factors that obstruct the acceptance of mobile by street vendors in India. A sample of 551 street vendors were interviewed from Pune, Nasik, Mumbai, Nagpur and Aurangabad. The study found that confidentiality and security of data, protected transaction and reliance are the predominant factors that hamper the approval of M-wallet payment method. The study also found that the apprehensions regarding digital payments are the same regardless of the category of street vendor. (Joshi et al., 2019) have conducted an ethnographic exploration to determine scope of digital money in creating financial inclusion among the marginalized group. In order to accomplish the study objectives, the authors have observed the usage of digital money in the daily practices'. The study found that Paytm has been used by majority of the respondents as everyday digital money. Influence of socio-economic conditions limits the digital transaction to be mainstream in market specially to marginalized section having low level of financial literacy. In most of the cases, due to lack of education and skill sets, the street vendors don't get an opportunity to be a part of remunerative formal job market (Jaishankar & Sujatha, 2016). Sonawane (2017) opined that rapid urbanization has accelerated the migration of rural population to urban areas leading to a parallel growth of informal sector giving rise to employment opportunities as street vendors and small businesses that in not in the purview of banking transaction and formal economy. Everyday challenges of the street vendors include workplace insecurity, confiscation of merchandise and daily earnings, unavailability of formal store setup, inconsistent earnings and so on (Roever & Skinner, 2016). The option of mobile wallets along with cash transactions offered by even the small-scale vendors is influencing the present-day youth to have digital transaction (Prasad, 2018). Influence of socio-economic conditions limits the digital transaction to be mainstream in market specially to marginalized section having low level of financial literacy (Joshi et al., 2019). High adoption rate for digital transaction requires fast data services, a smartphone, Point of Sale (POS) device, discount rate to Merchant, etc. that is capital intensive for marginalized section (D'souza, 2018). Business transactions through digital payments would help businesses to expand business globally with ease of trade between different countries at lowest cost (Singhraul & Garwal, 2018).

Majority of the research paper engages in the discussion regarding the socio-economic status of street vendors and lack of usage of digital wallets by them. The factors inhibiting street vendors to use digital wallets frequently and mobile wallets as a medium for financial inclusions especially for street vendors are yet to be explored.

3 Research Objectives

- To analyse the perspective of street vendors towards e-wallet Payment System.
- To study the factors influencing the street vendors to switch towards e-wallets Payment System.
- To enlist the problems faced by the street vendors in usage of e-wallets Payment System.
- To determine the extent wherein the e-wallets Payment create financial inclusion by expanding the financial capabilities of street vendors.

4 Research Methodology

The research design for this study is descriptive in nature. The study has been conducted with street vendors in urban markets of Bangalore and Mysore region of Karnataka, India. In order to understand the transformation of street vendors from conventional to digital payment system, a survey has been conducted. By using purposive sampling technique a sample of 200 street vendors were interviewed for the study. Data has been collected through interview method to determine the present mode of payment followed for business transaction by street vendors.

To accomplish the objectives of the study fieldwork has been carried out in the Marketplaces of Bangalore and Mysore region. The important market places which were considered for the study are Devaraja Market, Avenue Road, Malleswaram, Jaya Nagar, Gandhi Bazaar where one could observe plenty of street vendors and footfalls of about 5000 people a day and 15,000 on weekends.

In order to provide a meaningful implication for the data collected from the targeted respondents, the authors have selected appropriate tools and techniques of analysis for the study. Percentage analysis has been used to analyse demographic variable like gender, income, factors which motivate and demotivate the usage of digital payment method, repondents' level of inclination towards the usage of mobile wallet and the most preferred mobile wallet. In addition to this, chi-square test has been used to identify the relationship between payment method and access to financial services. The analysis of data has been carried out using the IBM SPSS.

5 Results and Discussion

The researchers attempt to explore how the digital wallets have penetrated among the street vendors and how it has made the street vendors as the bearers of financial inclusion in the selected cities of Karnataka, India can be inferred from the results.

Tables 1 and 2 indicate that majority of the street vendors are male compared to female among the selected respondents and the finding of the first study goes in line with the findings of Kaur (2015) who had opined that street vending business is primarily a male-oriented occupation. Likewise and their average monthly income ranges from Rs. 5000 to Rs. 10,000 which can be corroborated by the findings of (Baliyan & Srivastava, 2016) who found that majority of the male street vendors' average monthly income ranges from Rs. 7000 to Rs. 8000.

Table 3 represents the key determinants that influence the street vendors to use digital payment method is "customer preference" as a prime factor which motivates them to use digital payment options. The

Table 1 Gender of the respondents

Particulars	*Frequency*	*Percentage*
Male	143	72
Female	57	28

Table 2 Monthly earnings of the respondents

Particulars	*Frequency*	*Percentage*
Less than 5000	60	30
Rs. 5001–Rs. 10,000	88	44
>10,000	52	26

Table 3 Opinion regarding the factors which motivates the usage of digital payment method

Particulars	*Strongly agree*	*Agree*	*Neutral*	*Disagree*	*Strongly disagree*
Fast transaction		60 (60%)	20 (20%)	20 (20%)	
Convenience		60 (60%)	20 (20%)	20 (20%)	
Customers preference	70 (70%)	30 (30%)			
Saves time		40 (40%)	40 (40%)	20 (20%)	
Detailed record about all the transaction		25 (25%)		75 (75%)	
Reduced perceived theft risk	25 (25%)	75 (75%)			
Useful for small billings	65 (65%)	35 (35%)			

other factors play a major role include "convenience for small billings" and "reduction of perceived theft risk".

Table 4 presents the inhibitors that limits the street vendors towards the usage of e-payment options which includes "poor knowledge of usage of digital payment methods" and "need for supporting services like active bank account" that aligns with the study of Etim (2014). On considering other problems, "poor infrastructure", "cyber security", "habit of using cash for payment" and "service fees" also limit the use widely among street vendors.

Table 5 indicates that the most predominantly used digital wallets among the selected Paytm is most widely used among street vendors, and they feel that even the small penny can be transferred very comfortably. The finding of the study goes inline with the news published in "*Hindustan Times*" where it has been mentioned that Paytm is widely accepted by small-scale sellers.

Table 6 suggests that major problems faced by street vendors who were using digital payment systems faced "Transaction Failure" as a most frequent interruption. Other problems that occurred frequently are "Duplicate Payment", "Auto Debit" and "Long Transaction Time"

Table 4 Factors which demotivates the usage of digital payment method

Particulars	*Strongly agree*	*Agree*	*Neutral*	*Disagree*	*Strongly disagree*
Poor infrastructure like internet, mobile phone	70 (25%)	100 (50%)		30 (15%)	
Poor knowledge on the usage of digital payment method	200 (100%)				
Cyber Security issues		70 (35%)	30 (15%)	110 (55%)	
Habit of using cash transaction	150 (75%)	50 (25%)			
Transparency		150 (75%)	50 (25%)		
Service fees		70 (35%)	30 (15%)	110 (55%)	
Privacy concern of the customers in using e-wallets	150 (75%)	50 (25%)			
Need for supporting services like active bank account		150 (75%)		50 (25%)	

Table 5 Most preferred mobile wallet

Particulars	*Highly used*	*Moderately used*	*Least used*
Paytm	100 (100%)		
MobiKwik	50 (50%)	50 (50%)	
Airtel Money		30 (30%)	70 (70%)
PayPal		30 (30%)	70 (70%)
Google Pay	81 (81%)	19 (19%)	
Oxigen		10 (10%)	90 (90%)

Table 6 Problems faced with e-wallet

Particulars	*Mostly*	*Frequently*	*Rarely*
Transaction failure	100 (100%)		
Duplicate payment		50 (50%)	50 (50%)
Auto debit		50 (50%)	50 (50%)
Delayed payment			100 (100%)
Long transaction time	25 (25%)	75 (75%)	

and "Delayed Payment" making it difficult for street vendors to use the services at ease.

Table 7 suggests that street vendors strongly feel that they came to know about banking and financial products and services only after using digital wallets that have raised their interest in using digital wallets and

Table 7 Opinion regarding inclination towards usage of digital wallet

Particulars	*Strongly agree*	*Agree*	*Neutral*	*Disagree*	*Strongly disagree*
I have gained interest to know about various options in the usage of digital wallet	70 (25%)	100 (50%)	30 (15%)	-	
I have easy access to various financial products which are available	70 (25%)	100 (50%)	30 (15%)		
Digital transaction helped me to avail various financial services	50 (25%)	150 (75%)			
I have gained access to banking services after using mobile wallets	50 (25%)	150 (75%)			

knowing more about it. In addition to this, the study proved that the usage of digital payment system could reduce the "Financial Capability gap" of small business owners (Deb & Kubzansky, 2012) i.e. street vendors at a significant extent.

Hypothesis H_{01}: The mode of payment method used by street vendors and access to financial services are independent of each other.

From Table 8, it can be interpreted that the chi-square statistic is 58.5307. The p-value is < 0.00001 significant at $p < 0.05$. Hence, null hypothesis (H_{01}) is rejected. It can be concluded that the mode of payment method and access to financial services are dependent of each other. Table 8 suggests that there is enormous opportunity of penetration of digital payment methods among the selected street vendors to access the financial services.

Hypothesis H_{02}: Total monthly earning of the street vendors and usage of e-wallet are independent of each other.

From Table 9, it can be interpreted that the chi-square statistic is 6.0814. The p-value is 0.047803. The result is significant at $p < 0.05$. Hence, the null hypothesis ($\mathbf{H_{02}}$) is rejected. It can be concluded that total monthly earnings and usage of E-wallet are dependent of each other.

Table 8 Cross tab between payment method and access to financial services

	Access to financial services	*No access to financial services*	*Marginal row totals*
Digital	80 (53) [13.75]	20 (47) [15.51]	100
Conventional	26 (53) [13.75]	74 (47) [15.51]	100
Marginal column totals	106	94	200 (Grand total)

Table 9 Cross tab between total monthly earnings and usage of E-wallet

	Using e-wallet			*Not using e-wallet*			*Marginal row totals*
Less than 5000	37	(30)	[1.63]	23	(30)	[1.63]	60
Rs. 5001–Rs. 10,000	43	(44)	[0.02]	45	(44)	[0.02]	88
>10,000	20	(26)	[1.38]	32	(26)	[1.38]	52
Marginal column totals	100			100			

6 Conclusion

By way of conclusion, it can be recommended that the implementation of the government policies to bring cent percentage financial inclusion of the unbanked population requires a bottom-up approach. It is very evident from the present study that the penetration of mobile technology and the cynosure gained by android phones have provided wonderful opportunities for the development of digital payment systems. Further, it has also paved way for so many unbanked individuals who were financially excluded to fall under the purview of banking system. In order to bring digital payment system into mainstream, apart from the government the individual should gain interest to build digital ecosystem by acquiring habit of using digital payment on routine basis.

This study provides an important understanding about the growing interest of street vendors to learn about digital payments. Frequent usage of digital payments has paved a way towards access to banking and financial services. Therefore, financial inclusion of street vendors into formal banking system can be achieved propagating the use of e-wallets by all the street vendors in India over cash payments that are less preferred by the customers these days.

However, the socio-economic background of street vendors suggests that the major problems such as transaction failure and long transaction time need to be addressed by customizing the features of e-wallets for street vendors. Other inferences that can be drawn from the study is that the banking and financial system need to run awareness programmes and train street vendors highlighting the benefits of using digital payment and reconsider service fee that restricts street vendors to utilize the digital payment services.

The study is restricted to two cities of Karnataka State so the results covering the selected street vendors only in two cities of Karnataka may differ in other geographical locations. Escalation in sample size to get accuracy was not possible due to time and money constraints.

Future studies may consider studying street vendors across India to get wider perspective. Two major roadblocks namely low literacy level and lack of training should be studied further to aid the knowledge for designing digital wallets and training programmes.

References

Agarwal, A. (2018). *Mobile wallet adoption*: India story. Retrieved January 15, 2020, from https://medium.com/@callmeastha/mobile-wallet-adoption-india-story-571406dd3a5

ASSOCHAM. (2016). *M-Wallet: Scenario post demonetisation*. ASSOCHAM India.

Baliyan, S., & Srivastava, V. (2016). Socio-economic condition of street venders from the gender prospective. *Journal of Economic & Social Development, 12*(2), 66–75.

Bangalore Mirror. (2017, October 23). 30,000 hawkers on Bengaluru streets: BBMP. https://bangaloremirror.indiatimes.com/bangalore/others/30000-hawkers-on-bengaluru-streets-bbmp/articleshow/61175772.cms

Bughin, M. C. (2013, May 1). *Ten IT-enabled business trends for the decade ahead*. Retrieved from McKinsey & Company | Global management consulting. http://www.mckinsey.com/industries/hightech/our-insights/ten-it-enabled-businesstrends-for-the-decade-ahead

Chopra, K. (2018). M-Wallet technology acceptance by street vendors in India. *Advances in Intelligent Systems and Computing*, 175–182. https://doi.org/10.1007/978-981-13-1610-4_18.

Deb, A., & Kubzansky, M. (2012). *Bridging the gap: The business case for financial capability*. Citi Foundation. https://www.citigroup.com/citi/foundation/pdf/bridging_the_gap.pdf

D'souza, R. (2018). *Two years after demonetisation: Cashless India still a distant dream* | ORF. https://www.orfonline.org/expert-speak/two-years-after-demonetisation-cashless-india-still-a-distant-dream-45682

Etim, A. S. (2014). Mobile banking and mobile money adoption for financial inclusion. *Research in Business and Economics Journal, 9*, 1–13.

Hindustan Times. (2016). Delhi-NCR street vendors get smarter with digital wallets. https://www.hindustantimes.com/delhi/delhi-ncr-street-vendors-get-smarter-with-digital-wallets/story-Uw0wv38FXT4wvrfjfwEY6L.html

Jaishankar, V., & Sujatha, L. (2016). A study on problems faced by the street vendors in tiruchirappalli city. *SSRG International Journal of Economics and Management Studies, 3*(9), 40–43.

Joshi, T., Gupta, S. S., & Rangaswam, N. (2019). Digital wallets 'turning a corner' for financial inclusion: A study of everyday PayTM practices in India. In P. Nielsen Honest & C. Kimaro (Eds.), *Information and communication technologies for development. Strengthening southern-driven cooperation as a catalyst for ICT4D* (pp. 280–293). Springer.

Kaur, B. (2015). Urban informal sector and street vendors. *International Journal of English, Literature & Humanities, 3*(5), 150–164.

Konwar, N. (2015). Financial inclusion of street vendors: With special reference to street vendors of Jorhat Town of Assam. *GIRA—Global Journal for Research Analysis, 4*(12), 195–196.

Niranjan. (2017). A case study of barriers to digital financial inclusion of auto-rickshaw drivers in Viman Nagar, Pune, Maharashtra. *Journal of Political Sciences & Public Affairs, 5*(3). https://doi.org/10.4172/2332-0761.1000272

Pal, J., Chandra, P., Kameswaran, V., Parameshwar, A., Joshi, S., & Johri, A. (2018). *Digital payment and its discontents: Street shops and the Indian government's push for cashless transactions.*

Prasad, B. (2018). Issues and challenges of the weekly market street vendors in Telangana: A special reference to Hyderabad. *Economic Affairs, 16*(1), 46–49.

Roever, S., & Skinner, C. (2016). Street vendors and cities. *Environment and Urbanization, 28*(2), 359–374. https://doi.org/10.1177/0956247816653898

Singhraul, B. P., & Garwal, Y. S. (2018). Cashless economy—Challenges and opportunities in India. *Pacific Business Review International, 10*(9), 54–63.

Sheik, M. A., & Sareswathy, M. (2016). A study on financial inclusion of urban street vendors in Palayamkottai. *International Journal of Research—Granthaalayah, 4*(4), 45–50.

Sonawane, S. T. (2017). Problems and solutions of vendors—A case study. *International Journal of Innovative Research in Science, Engineering and Technology, 6*(1), 940–943.

The Economic Times. (2020). Digital payments growing in India at 12.7% CAGR: KPMG. https://economictimes.indiatimes.com/industry/banking/finance/banking/digital-payments-growing-in-india-at-12-7-cagr-kpmg/articleshow/70890809.cms

Sustainable Economic Growth

Digital Financial Inclusion: Strategic Issues and Imperatives

Pooja Jain, Deepika Upadhyay, and Geetanjali Purswani

1 Introduction

Financial inclusion refers to the process of providing access to different financial products and services at affordable rates to all sections of society. Financial inclusion is globally regarded as a critical measure for the growth and development of any economy. According to 2017 data from the Global Findex Database published by the World Bank, four largest economies with the highest unbanked population are China, India, Pakistan and Indonesia (Demirguc-Kunt et al., 2018). One of the major reasons for the economic backwardness and crippling growth in many countries across the globe including India is the financial exclusion of masses from the formal banking network. Though universal access to banks and banking services started in India soon after the nationalization

P. Jain (✉) · D. Upadhyay · G. Purswani
Department of Commerce, CHRIST University, Bangalore, India
e-mail: pooja.jain@christuniversity.in

D. Upadhyay
e-mail: deepika.upadhyay@christuniversity.in

G. Purswani
e-mail: geetanjali.purswani@christuniversity.in

Ananda S. and D. Singh (eds.), *Financial Inclusion in Emerging Markets*,
https://doi.org/10.1007/978-981-16-2652-4_15

of banks in the year 1969 and then in 1980, but the real push to achieve financial inclusion came only in the year 2005 when the Reserve Bank of India included this in its annual policy statement (Rao, 2018). Financial inclusion in its present form is an outcome of the recommendations given by Rangarajan Committee Report in 2008. According to Demirguc-Kunt et al. (2018), the financial inclusion index of the Indian economy has recovered from 35% in 2011 to 80% in 2017. Indian economy has been taking long strides in achieving financial inclusion. Indeed, there has been a speedy improvement in the statistics wherein the role of Pradhan Mantri Jan Dhan Yojana (PJDY) scheme launched by the Government of India in 2014 has been phenomenal. Later, demonetization of 500 and 1000 currency notes in 2016 also accelerated the process (Maripally & Bridwell, 2017). But as per the latest report published by Demirguc-Kunt et al. (2018) more than half of the bank accounts remain to be un-operational (approximately 48%) that means such accounts were opened without any intention to operate them by the accountholders. Globally this figure is around 25% (Rao, *Opinion*, 2019). Today 69% of the adults across the world have a bank account. But still, it has been estimated that 1.7 billion adults remain unbanked (Demirguc-Kunt et al., 2018). World Bank and G20 nations have been taking deliberate measures to increase financial inclusion in developing and emerging economies to help them fight poverty and other hurdles of economic growth (Ozili, 2018). There are many barriers in the area of financial inclusion. Recent advances have proved that digital technologies provide a viable solution to overcome such barriers and improve access to banking services and financial network.

Fintech solutions can be a viable option to achieve the objectives of financial inclusion through the intervention of technology. The convenience of usage of mobile phones and the accessibility of the internet can lead to quick adaptability of people towards financial products. In the current scenario, the market is embracing digital finance at a very fast pace and things like big data, financial analytics, artificial intelligence, etc. have gradually become common solutions. Many countries like Pakistan, Philippines, China, Mexico, etc. have been adopting digital technologies to ensure financial inclusion. "Digital India Programme" was officially launched in July 2015 by the Government of India to expand and facilitate the digital economy, which also included digital financial inclusion. Digital finance enables the usage of payment gateways which allows instant money transfer with the help of internet or mobile network.

2 Evolution of Digital Financial Inclusion in India

For, digital financial inclusion to be successful, it is necessary that the base is set for the economy to move on. India has evolved over the years in this field and has set the pace right to move forward.

Figure 1 shows the journey of Digital Financial Inclusion in India, according to the BIS paper authored by D'Silva et al. (2019). India has been proactive in ensuring continuous improvement in the field of digital financial inclusion. Infrastructure in India is suitable for tech firms and commercial banks to work hand in hand. Starting in 2010, concrete steps have been taken by the Indian Governments to ensure planned financial inclusion.

The first major step taken in this direction was to provide Unique Digital Identity in the form of Aadhaar in 2010. It has been recognized as one of the most important forms of identity and address proof. It has information like—name, gender, date of birth and permanent and existing address supported by the photograph of the individual with his/her biometric record. All this information is substantial for authentication of the identity of any individual on digital platforms. This platform provided a strong base for other applications to be installed without having their own infrastructure. After this, in 2012, a drive was started by the Banks called e-KYC (Know Your Customers).

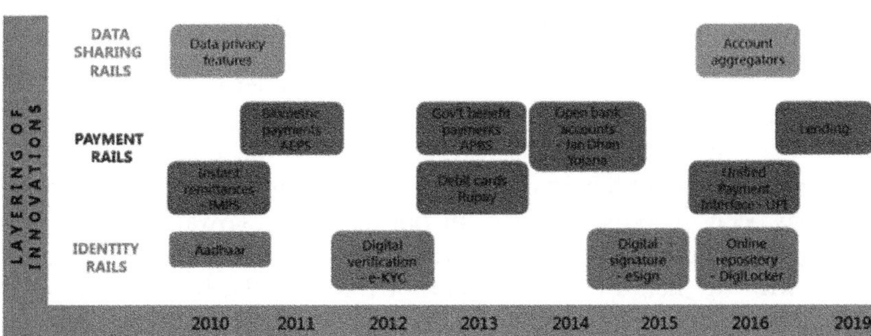

Fig. 1 Evolution of digital financial inclusion in India (*Source* BIS paper [2019], The design of digital financial infrastructure: lessons from India)

In the year 2014, the government launched a nationwide campaign to provide a basic bank account to all citizens under the scheme of Pradhan Mantri Jan Dhan Yojana (PMJDY). The purpose was to provide universal access to banking services to all citizens of the country.

These accounts are zero frills accounts. It does not cost the accountholders any charge to hold these accounts rather, they are used for disbursement of welfare benefits in the form of payment of subsidies by the government. So, the basic motive of opening such accounts was to minimize the leakage in the system so that the intended benefits should reach the deserving population. According to the latest report, the total number of accounts opened under PMJDY has crossed 38crore.

Later, during the year 2015, the Controller of Certifying Authorities (CCA), under the flagship of Ministry of Electronics and Information Technology, launched e-Sign to enable Aadhaar holders to digitally sign an online document. In the same year, RBI provided banking licence to new forms of financial institutions, namely differentiated banks mainly under the category of payment banks and small financial institutions to further expand the horizon of financial inclusion. The increasing number of mobile users and smartphone consumption was acting as a catalyst to the emerging new wave of banking services in the country.

In 2016, the National e-Governance Commission launched the scheme of Digital Locker (DigiLocker) platform to facilitate digital issuance and verification of documents. In the same year, Unified Payment Interface (UPI) was introduced by National Payments Corporation of India (NPCI) under the flagship of RBI to enable virtualization of accounts, a system that works 24/7 without any manual intervention. It can be used for all types of customer to business (C2B), customer to customer (C2C) and business to business (B2B) payments.

Further, with the help of account aggregators, the lending process can become seamless. Other than the above-mentioned initiatives, government has been introducing different policies such as Swabhimaan Yojana (2011), Pradhan Mantri Suraksha Bima Yojana (2015) and Atal Pension Yojana with the help of Reserve bank of India (RBI), Insurance Regulatory and Development Authority (IRDA), Pension Fund Regulatory & Development Authority (PFRDA) towards financial inclusion to provide various banking facilities to all sections of the society using digital interfaces. All these efforts have been instrumental for last-mile delivery of financial services to the end-users.

3 Benefits of Digital Financial Inclusion

Digital financial inclusion has a huge list of advantages. Some of these are as follows:

3.1 Creating Easier Access to Financial Services

Financial institutions all over the world have utilized digital technologies and new business models to increase the accessibility of digital financial services to financially excluded populations. According to World Bank report, digital financial services (DFS), like digital transaction and payment services, served as the gateway to financial inclusion (Ardic et al., 2019). In addition to it, financial institutions are now trying to diversify their products and services. The latest development has been seen in the area of digitizing services such as credit, insurance, savings as well as pension. The advent of Point of Sale (POS) terminals and basic mobile devices have played a vital role in promoting digital savings. These services are far more widespread than analogous channels for traditional savings accounts, such as commercial bank branches. Financial Access Survey (2019) states that in high-income countries banks are closing their branches due to shifting towards mobile and internet banking and on the same line, an increasing trend has been observed in mobile and internet banking in low- and middle-income countries. According to RBI's annual report, 2017–2018, mobile banking services usage increased by 92% in volume and by 13% in value. According to the statistics, the number of point of sale (POS) terminals increased by 21% from 2018 to 2019. In absolute figures, there were 3.08 million POS terminals at end of March 2018. This number increased to 3.72 million by the end of March 2019. In the same period, the number of ATMs reduced from 222,247 to 221,703, which is an indication of acceptance of various other digital financial services by the people and not just being dependent on ATMs. Digital financial services will act as a catalyst to fulfil the vision of RBI to get 600 million new customers' accounts opened by 2020.

3.2 Accessibility, Affordability and Convenience

Digital financial inclusion has the potential to deliver its users, financial services at affordable rates. Recent improvements in technology have played a vital role in providing banking access to millions of people through a secured network. Such user groups also include that section of the population who never used any banking service because of convenience issues. It includes marginal traders and daily wagers who were entirely dependent on cash-based transactions. Therefore, digitized ways of accepting money and making payment helped them to get into the formal banking network. In addition to this, it is easier to do business with Fintech providers.

3.3 Promote Women's Financial Inclusion

Major disparities are seen in the usage of financial instruments and services among males and females. The trend is more prominent in low and low-middle-income countries (IMF Financial Access Survey, 2019). Demirguc-Kunt et al. (2018) report that 65% women as against 72% of men globally are bank account holders. Going by the statistics of India, it can be seen that men had 20% more chances of holding the accounts as compared to women in 2014. There are various reasons for that, for instance, lack of priority among household women for opening an account, their lack of desire to manage their own finances, lack of sufficient documents especially in rural areas for the women prohibiting them from opening the accounts, also sometimes the financial institutions themselves do not support inclusion of women (Murata, & Sioson, 2018; Sioson & Kim, 2019).

The average contribution of women in the GDP globally is 37%. In India, women contribute 17% to the GDP, in China, their contribution is around 41% and 33% in Latin America. Globally, women account for 40% of the labour force whereas this statistic in India is 24% (Woetzel et al., 2015).

A study conducted by Mckinsey & Company in 2018 suggested that India could add up to $770 Bn to its GDP by 2025 if female labour force participation in the country is brought at par with the male section of the population (Woetzel et al., 2018). Here, technology can play a big role by providing new-age financial services to female customers. It can open up wider lending and credit markets such as the promotion of micro-entrepreneurship among women and can integrate women employers in the economic cycle of the country. Fintech companies are also trying to empower women, especially with low literacy, by providing a user-friendly digital interface to reduce their reliance on text. With the use of iconography, voice-based' solutions and customized and design instruments, the requirement of the users can be catered to. Also, initiatives have been taken by the government such as Mahatma Gandhi National Rural Employment Guarantee Act (MNREGA) can bolster the growth of financial inclusion among women. According to this Act, one-third of the beneficiaries of employment for this scheme have to be women. Also, the Act aims at transferring their payment through electronic transfers in their bank accounts. This can ensure more accounts opening in the future for women.

3.4 *Growth of Micro, Small and Medium Enterprises (MSME) Lending*

MSMEs are major drivers of economic growth as they contribute to job creation and innovation. According to the World Bank Report (2018), SME's contribution to national income is up to 40% and they are responsible for creating 70–95% of new jobs. According to Economic survey (2017–2018), though MSME is an integral part of India's economic growth, their share in the total credit generated by Formal Financial lending enterprises is a meagre 17.4% as compared to 82.6%, which goes to big business houses (Borgohain, 2018). The major barriers that obstruct bank lending to SMEs include information asymmetries, high transaction costs, a decline of traditional-relationship lending, and the insufficient financial capabilities of SME owners and entrepreneurs (Nemoto & Korean, 2019). Lack of necessary documentation required for securing a formal loan, not having worthwhile collateral to offer to financial institutions, results in time-consuming and expensive process for MSMEs borrowers and financial institutions. Advancement in technology and favourable government policies have given a boost to Fintech lenders to make the credit lending process simple and speedy. This was possible due to replacement of manual form filing with digital data captures, automated evaluations leveraging on technologies like analytics, machine learning, artificial intelligence and no or little in-person visits (PWC Report, 2019). Digital financial services facilitate Financial Institutions (FIs) to reduce operational costs by minimizing manual intervention, which helps the lenders to pass on the benefits of lower costs to a big segment of customers. Thus, making their digital lending products more attractive. In addition to this, FIs also support the customized credit assessment models which work on behavioural data to detect various typical attributes for charging interest rates that help lending institutions to give loan facilities to more number of customers as per their needs and conditions.

3.5 *To Achieve Sustainable Development Goal*

Financial inclusion indirectly targets eight goals out of seventeen Sustainable Development Goals of the Nations', which it wishes to achieve by 2030. These eight goals include eradicating poverty; ensuring food security and sustainable agriculture practices; curbing hunger, promoting health and well-being; achieving gender equality and economic empowerment of women; enhancing economic growth by providing jobs; increasing innovation and enhancing infrastructure; promoting industrialization, decreasing inequality and mobilization of savings for consumption and investment ("Financial Inclusion and the SDGs," n.d.).

Mckinsey Global report (2016) finds digital finance a very promising option in boosting the annual GDP of developing countries. According to estimates, usage of digital platforms for Finance has the potential to raise the GDP of developing countries by $3.7 trillion around 2025.

Digital payment products, such as use of Unified Payments Interface (UPI) service, debit/credit cards, payment banks, mobile wallets, mobile banking, internet banking, digital payment apps, provide a good opportunity for businesses and government to expand financial inclusion. This can be done, by the digitization of cash payments of wages and transfers, to expand financial inclusion and hence achieve sustainable development goals of the United Nations.

3.6 *Reduction in Corruption*

According to Muralidharan et al. (2014), digitization of government transfers helps the government to cut bribe demands for receiving the payments by beneficiaries by 47%. For instance, digital platforms such as Napanta in India are designed to assist farmers to access real-time information to enable them to make more informed decisions. It helps them to reduce their crop expenditure by 20% and increase the yield by 15% and also sell their products directly to wholesalers. It curtails down the middlemen intervention and ensures more transparency in pricing. It is instrumental in providing better revenues to farmers and also has the potential to reduce hunger and poverty. Similarly, enabling the storing of income in a digital bank account in rural communities boosted domestic savings by 131% within 3 months (UNSGSA, 2018). Over and above this, usage of digital platforms for subsidy and registration purposes has put a dent on the Grey economy and has avoided the tax evasion done earlier in this regard.

4 Digital Financial Inclusion—Challenges in India

While the country is looking forward to increasing the customer base for various online platforms providing financing services, it still has a lot of hurdles to cross in this regard. India being a developing country has its own challenges to overcome. Some of them are as follows:

4.1 High Rural Population

A major portion of the Indian Population lives in rural regions. Rural Population accounts for 65.97% of the total population according to World Bank Collection Development Indicators ("India—Rural population", 2018). Education level in the rural areas is low and their acceptance to technology is also less. And so penetrating in these areas is still very difficult. According to a report by India Brand Equity Foundation, only one-eighth of the Farm household avail credit facilities provided by banks ("India Brand Equity Foundation", n.d.).

4.2 The Low Reach of the Internet

The basic requirement for digital platforms to work is the availability of internet. According to the Keelery (2020), 34.45% of Indians were using the internet in 2017. Without proper access to the internet, providing financial services to prospective users is still a distant reality.

4.3 Low Financial Literacy Levels

According to Standard and Poor (S&P) survey conducted in 2015, 76% of Indian adults do not have a clear understanding of financial products and services ("76% of Indian not financially literate", 2015). They do not understand the benefits provided by various financial products like Insurance, mutual funds, wealth maximization through Compounding, etc. There is a dire need for the financial institutions to propagate their work and educate the masses about the benefits of Financial Inclusion. A big part of the Indian Population believes in keeping their savings in the form of cash. Gold is considered as the second-best option of saving by them. Gold also holds a sentimental value among Indians. A huge inclination has been seen in investment in gold by the people irrespective of its ever rising prices. People do not trust Financial Institution with their money and would not want to avail the facilities as long as possible.

4.4 *Lack of Regulatory Framework*

Changes in technology are very frequent. And the usage of technology for conducting the fraud is rampant. To curb this misuse of technology, the regulatory system also needs to change frequently. Biggest challenge in the digital world is safety and security of data and funds of the people. Therefore, in the absence of apt norms and security measure in place, people cannot be expected to shift from their age old ways of dealing with their finances.

4.5 *Gender Gap*

Literacy rate, access to various opportunities and facilities are high for the males as compared to females in India. This can also act as a hindrance in the path of digital financial inclusion. As in 2017, the gap between the holders of account between males and females stood at 6%. Around 60% of unbanked adults in India is represented by women according to the Global Findex Report 2017.

These and many other issues can act as a bottleneck in the area of digital financial inclusion. But this also can be taken as an opportunity to develop a sound financial ecosystem in future.

5 Road Ahead

A robust and efficient digital infrastructure is a prerequisite of universal access to financial services. To penetrate the financial inclusion to remote rural areas, a strong digital financial infrastructure needs to be provided to co-operative banks, payment banks, Panchayats, common service centres, etc. (National Strategy for Financial Inclusion 2019–2024). People in the country will be attracted towards financial inclusion only if they are offered a variety of financial products such as insurance products, mutual funds, pension products, etc. through seamless delivery. Adoption of Fintech by financial institutions can make financial services accessible by all at a lower cost.

One of the biggest hindrances in the way of financial inclusion is the lack of financial literacy among the masses. Financial literacy and education can be imparted through training programmes in small target groups, advertisements and short films can be projected for a better understanding of the products and processes involved. Financial literacy needs to be made a compulsory part of school and college education.

On the other hand, digitization of information comes with its own challenges. Cloning, phishing, malware, hacking, etc. can put customers' Right to privacy at stake. Therefore, strong customer protection architecture and robust Regtech are imperative to gain the confidence of people and ensure the safety of their information. Inclusive growth is inevitable for any economy, therefore concentrated and coordinated efforts of all stakeholders such as government, financial services providers, other regulators, and training institutes is a demand of time to enable the people to use financial services in a sustained manner.

While India has taken a lot of efforts to penetrate financial inclusion to the grass-roots level but still a lot of further work is needed to ensure that underserved and unserved population should not only get adequate access to the financial services but also use these services for their inclusive growth.

References

76% Indians not financially literate. (2015, December 15). https://www.financialexpress.com/economy/76-indians-not-financially-literate-says-sp-survey/179025/#:~:text=As%20much%20as%2076%20per,Ratings%20Services%20survey%20said%20today

Ardic, O., Gradstein, H., Istuk, I., & Michaels, L. (2019). *Financial inclusion beyond payments: Policy considerations for digital savings.* World Bank Group Working Papers (136101).

Borgohain, A. (2018, January 29). Economic survey: Large businesses corner 82.6% of credit, MSMEs get a paltry 17.4%. *Economics Times.* https://economictimes.indiatimes.com/small-biz/sme-sector/economic-survey-large-businesses-corner-82-6-of-credit-msmes-get-a-paltry-17-4-/articleshow/62693254.cms?from=mdr

Demirguc-Kunt, A., Klapper, L., Singer, D., Ansar, S., & Hess, J. (2018). *The Global Findex Database 2017: Measuring financial inclusion and the fintech revolution*. The World Bank.

D'Silva, D., Filková, Z., Packer, F., & Tiwari, S. (2019). *The design of digital financial infrastructure: Lessons from India*. BIS Paper (106).

Financial Inclusion and the SDGs. (n.d.). https://www.uncdf.org/financial-inclusion-and-the-sdgs

Global Findex. (2017). Measuring Financial Inclusion. (2018). Retrieved from World Bank. https://globalfindex.worldbank.org/sites/globalfindex/files/2018-04/2017%20Findex%20full%20report_0.pdf

India Brand Equity Foundation. (n.d.). https://www.ibef.org/download/Banking-July-2020.pdf

India—Rural population (2018). https://www.indexmundi.com/facts/india/rural-population

IMF Financial Access Survey. (2019). https://www.imf.org/en/News/Articles/2019/09/27/pr19359-imf-releases-the2019-financial-access-survey-results

Keelery Sandhya. (2020, October 20). *Internet penetration in India 2000–2017*. https://www.statista.com/statistics/255135/internet-penetration-in-india/

Maripally, A., & Bridwell, L. (2017, July). The future of financial inclusion and its impact on poverty reduction in India. In *Competition forum* (Vol. 15, No. 2, pp. 329–334). American Society for Competitiveness.

Muralidharan, K., Niehaus, P., & Sukhtankar, S. (2014). *Payments infrastructure and the performance of public programs: Evidence from biometric smartcards in india*. National Bureau of Economic Research.

Murata, A. and Sioson, E. P. (2018). *Financial literacy programs for remittances. Migration and Remittances for Development in Asia*. ADB-World Bank Co-Publication.

Nemoto, N., & Korean, M. (2019). Digital innovation can improve financial access for SMEs. *SME Policy Faced With Development of Financial Technology G20 Japan, 1*, 1–11.

Ozili, P. K. (2018). Impact of digital finance on financial inclusion and stability. *Borsa Istanbul Review, 18*(4), 329–340.

PWC Report. (2019). *A wider circle digital lending and the changing landscape of financial inclusion*. https://www.pwc.in/assets/pdfs/consulting/financial-services/fintech/publications/a-wider-circle-digital-lending-and-the-changing-landscape-of-financial-inclusion.pdf

Rao, K. S. (2018, July 11). *Money & Finance*. Retrieved from Ideas for India. https://www.ideasforindia.in/topics/money-finance/financial-inclusion-in-india-progress-and-prospects.html

Rao, K. S. (2019, January 23). *Opinion*. Retrieved from The Hindu Business Line. https://www.thehindubusinessline.com/opinion/financial-inclusion-is-fast-losing-steam/article26071996.ece

RBI Annual Report 2017–18. https://www.rbi.org.in/Scripts/AnnualReportPublications.aspx?year=2018

Sioson, E.P., & Kim, C. J. (2019). *Closing the gender gap in financial inclusion through fintech*. ADBI Policy Brief. https://www.adb.org/sites/default/files/publication/498956/adbi-pb2019-3.pdf

UNSGSA. (2018). *Igniting SDG progress through digital financial inclusion*. United Nations Secretary-General's Special Advocate for Inclusive Financial Development.

Woetzel, J., Madgavkar, A., Gupta, R., Manyika, J., Ellingrud, K., Gupta, S., & Krishnan, M. (2015). *The power of parity: Advancing women's equality in India*. McKinsey Global Institute.

Woetzel, J., Madgavkar, A., & Sneader, K. (2018). *The power of parity: Advancing women's equality in Asia pacific*. The McKinsey Global Institute Report, Shanghai.

World Bank. (2018). *Small and Medium Enterprises (SMEs) finance. Improving SMEs' access to finance and finding innovative solutions to unlock sources of capital*. https://www.worldbank.org/en/topic/smefinance

Inclusive Finance and Income Inequality: An Evidence from Saudi Arabia

Fatma Mabrouk and Noreha Halid

1 Introduction

Income inequality remains a hardy challenge in Saudi Arabia and experiences rapid expansion changes in previous decades. Financial inclusion is often considered as a serious component that marks inclusive growth in order to develop a tailored product for low-income segments. Inclusive finance can enable consumers and firms to make longer-term consumption and sustainable investment schemes, contribute to productive activities and face with unanticipated short and long-term shocks. Saudi Arabia targets multiple goals through the Vision 2030 implantation at national and international levels. The main objective is to achieve an economic, political and societal inclusive development by reducing poverty and inequality. The Financial Sector Development Program is one of the 12 governing programs launched by the Council of Economic and Development Affairs to attain the objectives of Vision 2030 (National Planning Commission, 2013) and aims for five principles financial objectives: diversity, stability, digital transformation, depth of the financial sector and

F. Mabrouk (✉) · N. Halid
Department of Economics, College of Business Administration, Princess Nourah Bint Abdulrahman University, Riyadh, Saudi Arabia
e-mail: FMMabrouk@pnu.edu.sa

Ananda S. and D. Singh (eds.), *Financial Inclusion in Emerging Markets*,
https://doi.org/10.1007/978-981-16-2652-4_16

inclusiveness. The Financial Sector Development Program seeks the development of the national economy by diversifying its sources of income and boosting savings, finance and investment (Vision 2030). Unbanked people cannot save, thus contribute to weakening the saving mobilization internal ratio and the national saving income-generating activities. Financial inclusion aims, in priority and particular, to bank the poorest, enables them to finance their activities, save, satisfy their needs and protect themselves against the risks of everyday life.

This research seeks to explore the relationship between inclusive finance and income inequality in Saudi Arabia using new microdata published by the World Bank (2017). It aims to contribute at the present economic literature and analysis by:

- Developing financial inclusion study using recent cross-country microdata.
- Evolving studies on developing Saudi Arabia's economy and financial sector.
- Designing and implementing recommendations that can help policymakers how to expand access to financial services, driving to the decline of poverty incidence and income equality.

The expected results of the study are presented in the following propositions:

H_1: Financial inclusion is defined as the mechanism that ensures the ease of access, availability and usage of formal financial activities in the economy (Sarma, 2008).
H_2: There is a significant connection between financial inclusion and income inequality in Saudi Arabia during 2017 the year study period 2017.
H_3: Financial inclusion can be considered as a veritable channel to alleviate poverty and develop the Saudi economy (King Khalid Foundation, 2018).

The remainder of this paper is structured as follows: Section 2, we review existing studies on inclusive finance and income inequality. Section 3, we present the research methodology based on the econometric framework with precision to the data and models employed.

Section 4 examines and discusses results. To finish, Sect. 5 takes out the conclusion and policies implications.

2 Literature Review

Contrary to the exhaustive studies analyzing the link between financial inclusion and growth (Erlando et al., 2020; Kamalu et al., 2019; Sethi & Sethy, 2019), studies connected to the financial inclusion and inequality issues are not various. Most of the existing researches are testing the macroeconomic impact of financial inclusion or financial development to the growth, poverty or inequality, scare investigations point up the microanalysis aspect.

Park and Mercado (2018) test the connection between financial inclusion, poverty and income inequality for many countries including 37 from developing Asia, in their study, they established a financial inclusion index using various macroeconomic and country-specific contributors affecting the degree of financial inclusion. Their results show that various dimensions of financial inclusion, as availability and usage are significantly reducing poverty and lowering income inequality. In fact, findings suggest that per capita income, rule of law and demographic factors impact financial inclusion, and contribute to poverty reduction and lower income inequality. In the same vein, Honohan (2008) checks the significance of financial inclusiveness in reducing income equality for more than 160 countries. The results show that higher financial inclusiveness level significantly reduces income. More precisely, Gini coefficient as a measure of financial access is contrary linked to income inequality, and explained that access to a formal account does more for those somewhat higher up the ladder than the $2 a day poor. The author reemphasizes the importance of wider financial development, with its favorable impact both on economic growth and on the degree to which growth is pro-poor.

Another study done by Turegano and Herrero (2018) supposes that a nation with a developed level of financial inclusion probably has a more equal revenue distribution after relevant factors regulation, mainly economic development and fiscal policy. In the same line of thought, another more developed analysis is reported by Jin (2017), who investigates in different regions the relationship between the inclusiveness finance level and poverty alleviation in a group of 86 Asian, Africa and Latin America nations during the period 2004–2013 by applying generalized method of moments. As a matter of fact, results show that the impact of inclusive finance on poverty reduction estimated by the Gini coefficient seems to be different through regions as a possible negative correlation or inverted U-shaped association. The study shows that inclusive finance expands the income gap initially, but at certain level of financial development, it can play an important role to restraint the income gap and ultimately reduce poverty.

Recent research presented by Van Velthoven et al. (2019) concludes that finance used to contribute to economic growth, although probably in a non-linear way, its overall effects on well-being should therefore be positive, the authors estimate a fixed-effects panel model for a large sample of countries between 1975 and 2005 and test the hypothesis of the finance contribution compared to others factors for a greater redistribution of income than inequality. The authors line up their study on the effects of finance on inequality to other recent studies and deduce that inclusive finance is indirectly positively related to poverty.

Analyses based on time series data (Hathroubi, 2019; Onaolapo, 2015) contribute also on how financial inclusion can be a veritable channel to alleviate poverty and develop the economy by examining the effects of financial inclusion on economic growth. For example, Onaolapo (2015) tests the Nigerian case during a period of 30 years. The overall results of the regression estimations show that inclusive financial highly influences poverty reduction. However, the effect on national economic growth and financial intermediation through enhanced Bank Networks is marginal. Recently, Hathroubi (2019) tried to confirm the assumption that financial inclusion has an impact on reducing inequality and poverty in the Saudi Economy. His paper constructed a new and original widespread index to measure the impact of financial inclusion on Saudi Arabia growth and human development through a set of socio-macroeconomic indicators. By applying a GMM methodology, the author finds that financial inclusion is highly and positively correlated to human development index, and to employment, but is insignificantly negatively correlated to per capita real GDP and highly negatively correlated to the share of rural population and women in adult population.

3 Research Methodology

Beyond the drivers of income inequality mapped out in the existing literature and using The Global Financial Inclusion Database (Global Findex)

Table 1 Source of data

Survey	*Description*	*Frequency*	*Country coverage*	*Publicly available*
Global F-index	Cross-country, nationally representative survey of households 'finances	Triennial rounds, annual rounds for selected questions	Global	Yes

Source World Bank

published by World Bank-2017, this study tries to explain the relationship between income quintile and financial inclusion in Saudi Arabia. The quintile estimations explain more the effect of the explanatory variables on the explained variable. It produces different effects along the quintiles distribution of the income variable. Indicators of financial inclusion measure how people borrow, save, make secure payments and deal with risks. They are collected for all adults by key demographic characteristics (gender, age, education and employment status) and covering 1009 individuals (Table 1).

The income variable is defined as a dependent variable. In this instance, this dependent variable is cardinal measure and considered as a score and simple linear regression model Ordinary Least Squares is suitable to estimate the impact of financial inclusion on income:

$$\mathrm{Zi} = \alpha + \beta\, W_i + \varepsilon_i \qquad (1)$$

where, Zi is a cardinal measure of income and Wi is a vector of independent variables.

Under the ordinarily assumption, ordered Logit or Probit models assuming a continuous and latent measure of the dependent variable which is given by:

$$\mathrm{Zi}^* = \alpha + \beta\, W_i + \varepsilon_i \qquad (2)$$

where, i = 1…0.5
i=1; Poorest 20%
i=2; Second 20%
i=3; Middle 20%
i=4; Fourth 20%
i=5; Richest 20%

Table 2 Income distribution of the respondent

Income	*All Sample*	*Men*	*Women*
1 = Poorest 20%	17.54%	17.80%	17.08%
2 = Second 20%	18.24%	17.65%	19.28%
3 = Middle 20%	18.24%	16.72%	20.94%
4 = Fourth 20%	21.61%	22.60%	19.83%
5 = Richest 20%	24.38%	25.23%	22.87%

Source Author's calculations based on The World Bank Data (2017)

The specification of the ordered probit /logit model implies that in order to estimate any parameter that could be interpreted, marginal effects must be considered. We estimate several income regressions by taking account of diverse independent factors: (1) Demographic and socioeconomic factors (2) Financial inclusion (Access, Usage and Quality). In this study, we adopt the definition of Sarma (2008) and World Bank (2014) which presents financial inclusion as the ease of access, availability and usage of the formal financial system by all members of the economy. Model (1) includes only demographic and socioeconomic characteristics; model (2) adds financial inclusion (Access) while models (3) and (4) take into account the usage as an important pillar of the financial inclusion. Finally, model (5) estimates the impact of these three set of potential independent variables inducing the quality pillar.

About 17% (equivalent to 177), 18% (equivalent to 184), 21.6% (equivalent to 218) and 24% (equivalent to 246) of the respondent report receiving low, second and middle, fourth and high income distribution, respectively (Table 2).

Tables 3 and 4 present the descriptive statistics and correlation matrix. Descriptive statistics are presented in percentage for all the sample and by sex. Correlation matrix reveals a very high significant connection between most of the variables at the level of 5%. No issue of multicollinearity problem detected, all the variables will be included in our model regression.

4 Results

Table 5 represents ordered probit regression of income quintile and financial inclusion. Five models are estimated. Model (1) includes only demographic and personal characteristics. Models (2), (3), (4) and (5)

Table 3 Descriptive statistics

Variables	*All Sample*	*Men*	*Women*
Age			
15 to 25	26.60%	19.70%	38.80%
26 to 35	43.10%	45.80%	38.30%
36 to 44	15.80%	17.80%	12.10%
≥ 45	14.60%	16.70%	10.70%
Education			
Primary education or less	7.60%	7.40%	8.00%
Secondary education	55.20%	55.10%	55.40%
Tertiary education	37.20%	37.50%	36.60%
Employment status			
In workforce	77.60%	90.25%	55.10%
Out of workforce	22.40%	27.88%	72.12%
Access			
Has an account	74.53%	82.35%	17.65%
Doesn't has an account	25.47%	17.65%	39.39%
Saving			
Saved in the past year	49.75%	51.55%	46.56%
Doesn't saved in the past year	50.25%	48.45%	53.44%
Borrowing			
Borrowed in the past year	58.28%	63.62%	48.76%
Doesn't borrowed in the past year	41.72%	36.38%	51.24%
Has loan from a financial institution for home, apartment, or land	17.24%	23.68%	5.79%
Doesn't has loan from a financial institution for home, apartment, or land	82.76%	76.32%	94.21%
Borrowed in past 12 months: for medical purposes	11.10%	11.46%	10.47%
Doesn't borrowed in past 12 months: for medical purposes	88.90%	88.54%	89.53%
Borrowed in past 12 months: for farm/business purposes	7.43%	9.29%	4.13%
Doesn't borrowed in past 12 months: for farm/business purposes	92.57%	90.71%	95.87%
Availability			
Used mobile phone or internet to access FI account	31.22%	38.54%	18.18%
Doesn't used mobile phone or internet to access FI account	68.78%	61.46%	81.82%
Made bill payments online using the Internet	37.26%	46.13%	21.49%

Source Author's calculations based on The World Bank Data (2017)

Table 4 Correlation matrix

	1	*2*	*3*	*4*	*5*	*6*	*7*	*8*	*9*	*10*	*11*	*12*	*13*	*14*	*15*
1-Income	1.00	−0.03	−0.02	−0.01	0.139**	−0.260**	−0.01	0.198**	0.172**	−0.02	−0.190**	−0.152**	−0.100**	0.073*	−0.03
2-Female		1.00	−0.171**	−0.151**	0.00	0.01	−0.405**	−0.240**	−0.05	−0.145**	0.211**	0.245**	0.227**	0.02	0.094**
3-Age			1.00	0.981**	0.227**	−0.120**	0.105**	0.166**	−0.102**	−0.05	−0.04	−0.01	−0.118**	0.02	0.070*
4-Age^2				1.00	0.204**	−0.087**	0.063*	0.120**	−0.085**	−0.067*	0.00	0.02	−0.085**	0.04	0.073*
5-Completed secondary education					1.00	−0.854**	0.05	0.110**	0.04	0.05	−0.172**	−0.134**	−0.02	0.03	0.00
6-Completed tertiary education or more						1.00	−0.123**	−0.177**	−0.133**	−0.06	0.261**	0.226**	0.05	−0.04	0.01
7-Employed							1.00	0.292**	0.092**	0.216**	−0.193**	−0.208**	−0.195**	−0.107**	−0.089**
8-Has an account								1.00	0.127**	0.211**	−0.394**	−0.262**	−0.237**	−0.076*	−0.096**
9-Saved in the past year									1.00	0.102**	−0.185**	−0.188**	−0.02	−0.02	−0.179**
10-Borrowed in the past year										1.00	−0.223**	−0.241**	−0.232**	−0.299**	−0.240**
11-Used mobile phone or internet to access FI account											1.00	0.609**	0.208**	0.03	0.078*
12-Made bill payments online using the Internet												1.00	0.218**	0.03	0.094**
13-Has loan for home, apartment, or land													1.00	0.073*	0.141**
14-Borrowed for medical purposes														1.00	0.140**
15-Borrowed for farm/business purposes															1.00

**The correlation is significant at the 1% level (2-tailed)
*The correlation is significant at the %% level (2-tailed)

Table 5 Income quintile and financial inclusion: ordered probit regressions

	Model 1	*Model 2*	*Model 3*	*Model 4*	*Model 5*
Basic model elements					
Demographic and personal characteristics					
Female	−0.1325*	−0.0743	−0.0803	−0.0366	−0.0544
	(0.0786)	(0.0797)	(0.0798)	(0.0802)	(0.0812)
Age	−0.0602***	−0.0797***	−0.0720***	−0.0749***	−0.0744***
	(0.0176)	(0.0181)	(0.0183)	(0.0186)	(0.0183)
Age^2	0.0007***	0.0009***	0.0008***	0.0009***	0.0009***
	(0.0002)	(0.0002)	(0.0002)	(0.0002)	(0.0002)
Completed secondary education	−0.7301*** (0.1382)	−0.6809*** (0.1421)	−0.6245*** (0.1437)	−0.6198*** (0.1459)	−0.6039*** (0.1441)
Completed tertiary education or more	−1.3097*** (0.1444)	−1.2257*** (0.1480)	−1.1536*** (0.1504)	−1.1420 (0.1523)	−1.1084*** (0.1522)
Employed	−0.1512*	−0.2478***	−0.2400**	−0.2596***	−0.2412**
	(0.0904)	(0.0926)	(0.0938)	(0.0936)	(0.0941)
Financial inclusion					
Access					
Has an account		0.5033*** (0.5937)	0.5049*** (0.0887)	0.4564*** (0.0888)	0.4664*** (0.0928)
Usage					
Saved in the past year			0.2170*** (0.0693)	0.2098*** (0.0703)	0.1987*** (0.0700)
Borrowed in the past year			−0.1467** (0.0711)	- -	−0.1707** (0.0722)
Has loan for home, apartment, or land				−0.2386*** (0.0908)	
Borrowed for medical purposes				0.2211** (0.1115)	
Borrowed for farm/business purposes				−0.0301 (0.1373)	

(continued)

Table 5 (continued)

	Model 1	*Model 2*	*Model 3*	*Model 4*	*Model 5*
Availability-Quality					
Used mobile phone or internet to access FI account					−0.0939 (0.0973)
Made bill payments online using the Internet					−0.0824 (0.0891)
Nb. Obs	1009	1009	1009	1009	1009
Log pseudo-likelihood	−1557.70	−1540.06	−1533.49	−1530.33	−1531.55
Wald χ^2	114.61	146.53	159.11	164.25	164.38
(p. value)	(0.0000)	(0.0000)	(0.0000)	(0.0000)	(0.0000)
Pseudo R^2	0.0358	0.0467	0.0508	0.0528	0.0520

Notes Robust standard-errors are reported into brackets.
Levels of statistical significance: ***p < 0.001, **p < 0.05, *p < 0.1
Source Author's calculations based on The World Bank Data (2017)

include financial inclusion variables. Three indicators are considered and estimated consecutively to check the stability of the model: access, usage and quality. Models (3) and (4) distinguish between different types of usage as the brow for home-apartment, or land and the brow for medical, farm/business purposes. The objective is to stress different possible purposes for investment that can contribute in poverty alleviation. Model (5) includes demographic, personal characteristics and all dimensions of financial inclusion. Results are stable as all variables are significant except female and quality of financial inclusion for the whole estimations. 60% of Saudi women are not banked and they are ranked second after the stateless (King Khalid Foundation, 2018). In spite of its relative lack of value, the Pseudo R^2 points up an increasing degree of variables explanation from model 1 to model 5. The marginal effects linked to each variable and each value of the income level are displayed in Table 6.

Results show that Saudi financial inclusion is valid through mechanism that ensures the ease of access and usage for different proposes, but not

Table 6 Marginal effects for income quintile regressions[1]—Models 1 to 5

Model 1

	Poorest	Second	Middle	Fourth	Richest
Basic model elements					
Demographic and personal characteristics					
Female	**0.0322**	**0.0167**	0.0035	**−0.0124**	**−0.0401**
Age	**0.0146**	**0.0076**	**0.0016**	**−0.0056**	**−0.0182**
Age^2	**−0.0001**	**−0.0001**	**−0.0001**	**0.0001**	**0.0002**
Completed secondary education	**0.1778**	**0.0923**	**0.0194**	**−0.0683**	**−0.2212**
Completed tertiary education or more	**1.3189**	**0.1656**	**0.0349**	**−0.1226**	**−0.3968**
Employed	**0.0353**	0.0196	0.0051	**−0.0129**	−0.0472
Model 2					
	Poorest	**Second**	**Middle**	**Fourth**	**Richest**
Basic model elements					
Demographic and personal characteristics					
Female	0.0177	0.0096	0.0020	−0.0072	−0.0222
Age	**0.0190**	**0.0103**	**0.0022**	−0.0077	−0.0238
Age^2	**−0.0002**	**−0.0001**	**−0.0001**	**0.0001**	**0.0002**
Completed secondary education	**0.1624**	**0.0885**	**0.0188**	**−0.0662**	**−0.2037**
Completed tertiary education or more	**0.2925**	**0.1594**	**0.0340**	**−0.1191**	**−0.3668**
Employed	**0.0550**	**0.0334**	**0.0099**	**−0.0206**	**−0.0778**
Financial inclusion					
Access					
Has an account	**−0.1348**	**−0.0567**	−0.0018	**0.0576**	**0.1358**
Model 3					
	Poorest	**Second**	**Middle**	**Fourth**	**Richest**
Basic model elements					
Demographic and personal characteristics					
Female	0.0190	0.0105	0.0022	−0.0079	−0.0239
Age	**0.0170**	**0.0094**	**0.0020**	**−0.0071**	**−0.0214**
Age^2	**−0.0002**	**−0.0001**	**−0.0001**	**0.0001**	**0.0002**
Completed secondary education	**0.1478**	**0.0820**	**0.0176**	**−0.0615**	**−0.1860**
Completed tertiary education or more	**0.2730**	**0.1516**	**0.0326**	**−0.0113**	**−0.3437**
Employed	**0.0530**	**0.0327**	**0.0097**	**−0.0204**	**−0.0749**
Financial inclusion					

(continued)

Table 6 (continued)

Model 1					
Access					
Has an account	**−0.1343**	**−0.0576**	−0.0020	**0.0584**	**0.1355**
Usage					
Saved in the past year	**−0.0513**	**−0.0284**	**−0.0061**	**0.0212**	**0.0646**
Borrowed in the past year	**0.0343**	**0.0194**	**0.0044**	**−0.0140**	**−0.0440**
Model 4					
	Poorest	**Second**	**Middle**	**Fourth**	**Richest**
Basic model elements					
Demographic and personal characteristics					
Female	0.0086	0.0048	0.0010	−0.0036	−0.0108
Age	**0.0176**	**0.0099**	**0.0021**	**-0.0074**	**−0.0222**
Age^2	**−0.0002**	**−0.0001**	**−0.0001**	**0.0001**	**0.0002**
Completed secondary education	**0.1459**	**0.0819**	**0.0177**	**−0.0615**	**−0.1841**
Completed tertiary education or more	**0.2689**	**0.1510**	**0.0327**	**−0.1133**	**−0.3394**
Employed	**0.0566**	**0.0356**	**0.0108**	**−0.0220**	**−0.0811**
Financial inclusion					
Access					
Has an account	**−0.1196**	**−0.0534**	−0.0029	**0.0526**	**0.1234**
Usage					
Saved in the past year	**−0.0494**	**−0.0276**	**−0.0060**	**0.0207**	**0.0623**
Has loan for home, apartment, or land	**0.0561**	**0.0315**	**0.0068**	**−0.0236**	**−0.0709**
Borrowed for medical purposes	**−0.0520**	**−0.0292**	**−0.0063**	**0.0219**	**0.0657**
Borrowed for farm/business purposes	0.0070	0.0039	0.0008	−0.0029	−0.0089
Model 5					
	Poorest	**Second**	**Middle**	**Fourth**	**Richest**
Basic model elements					

(continued)

through the availability. There is a significant relationship between financial inclusion and income inequality in Saudi Arabia during the year study period. In fact, age, education and employment are strongly significant in any case. Unfortunately, female variable is not significant and this can be explained as Duvendack and Mader (2020) discussed in their study that the effects on women's empowerment seem to be generally positive,

Table 6 (continued)

Model 1

Demographic and personal characteristics					
Female	0.0128	0.0071	0.0015	−0.0053	−0.0161
Age	**0.0175**	**0.0098**	**0.0020**	**−0.0073**	**−0.0221**
Age^2	**−0.0002**	**−0.0001**	**−0.0001**	**0.0001**	**0.0002**
Completed secondary education	**0.1425**	**0.0798**	**0.0170**	**−0.0596**	**−0.1797**
Completed tertiary education or more	**0.2616**	**0.1465**	**0.0312**	**−0.1095**	**−0.3298**
Employed	**0.0530**	**0.0330**	**0.0097**	**−0.0206**	**−0.0752**
Financial inclusion					
Access					
Has an account	**−0.1227**	**−0.0543**	−0.0026	**0.0537**	**0.1260**
Usage					
Saved in the past year	**−0.0469**	**−0.0261**	**−0.0055**	**0.0195**	**0.0591**
Borrowed in the past year	**0.0397**	**0.0227**	**0.0052**	**−0.0163**	**−0.0513**
Availability-Quality					
Used mobile phone or internet to access FI account	0.0221	0.0124	0.0026	−0.0092	−0.0279
Made bill payments online using the Internet	0.0194	0.0108	0.0023	−0.0081	−0.0245

Notes (1) Marginal effects account for the change in the conditional probability of income quintile (Poorest/ Second/ Middle/ Fourth/ Richest) for an infinitesimal or discrete change (respectively) in each continuous or dichotomous independent variable; Bold characters denote the fact that the coefficient associated to the variable is statistically significant (at least at 10%)
Source Author's calculations based on The World Bank Data (2017)

but it depends on feature programs that are often related to the financial service availability, cultural, traditional and geographical circumstances.

Education and employment reduce the probability to be in the fourth and richest quintile. Access reduces the probability to be in lowest and second quintile. This result can be explained by the great efforts made by the Saudi Government in terms of education and employment and how this can impact the poverty. Continuous huge hard work even during the COVID-19 for online education and work. The impact of saving usage reduces the probability to be in the tree first quintiles. The effect of borrowing increases when we distinguish between borrowing for home, apartment or land, borrowing for medical purposes, borrowing for business purposes is not significant.

Our findings are conforming Al-Hanawi et al. (2020) results which suppose that financially involved persons are probably more likely in both borrowing for medical purposes and coming up with emergency resources, related to those who are financially left out. The same applies that persons in low-income groups are more likely to be financially excluded and have a reduced chance of coming up with emergency resources and borrowing for health determinations.

In conclusion, we can confirm that financial inclusion can play the role of catalyst for enhancing equality. Access and usage pillars of inclusive finance are significantly reducing the probability to be in the lowest and second income quintile. However, the availability-quality pillar is not significant. The overall deduction is that financial inclusion can be a veritable channel to alleviate poverty and enhance equality income in the Saudi economy.

5 Conclusion

This study is motivated by the necessity to consider simultaneously the difficulties of access and use and the need for clear and quick regulation to develop a financially inclusively society. Using the Global Financial Inclusion Database (Global F-index) published by the World Bank and Probit models, we tried to explain the impact of financial inclusion on Saudi income.

Inclusive finance plays an important role in the economy and for Saudi Arabia, it can be considered as a strategy to reduce poverty gap by contributing to raising the income of individuals and stimulating the economy by merging the informal and formal sector projects, through micro-corporations, home enterprises and entrepreneurship. This allows the government to increase its tax revenues and contribute to the integration of the poor. The study results confirm that financial inclusion can be a veritable channel to alleviate poverty and develop the Saudi economy.

Finally, we address four basic policy recommendations to intensification this effect.

- Facilitate the use of innovative and advanced technologies in the banking sector by increasing the Fintech implementation to support potential growth and poverty reduction through financial inclusion and efficiency. Actually in Saudi Arabia, many universities are including in their study plan the Fintech axe.

- Strengthen financial infrastructure and promoting sustainable and inclusive financial development by diversifying financial products.
- Encourage savings and stimulate it toward productive investment, by applying an interesting interest rate that motivates people to save.
- Foster women's access to the banking system, indeed, greater women's financial inclusion necessitates a more gender-inclusive financial scheme that reports the exact demand and supply obstacles that women face. An inclusive adjusting relevant environment is desirable.

Acknowledgements This research was funded by the Deanship of Scientific Research at Princess Nourah bint Abdulrahman University through the Fast-track Research Funding Program.

References

Al-Hanawi, M. K., Chirwa, G. C., Kamninga, T. M., & Manja, L. P. (2020). Effects of financial inclusion on access to emergency funds for healthcare in the Kingdom of Saudi Arabia. *Journal of Multidisciplinary Healthcare, 13*, 1157–1167. https://doi.org/10.2147/JMDH.S277357

Beatriz, A., & Marc, L. (Eds.). (2011). *The handbook of microfinance*. World scientific, p. 704. https://doi.org/10.1142/7645

Conroy, J. (2005). APEC and financial exclusion: Missed opportunities for collective action? *Asia Pacific Development Journal, 12*(1), 53–80. https://www.unescap.org/sites/default/files/apdj12-1-full.pdf

Duvendack, M., & Mader, P. (2020). Impact of financial inclusion in low-and middle income countries: A systematic review of reviews. *Journal of Economic Surveys, 34*(3), 594–629. https://doi.org/10.1111/joes.12367

Erlando, A., Riyanto, F. D., & Masakazu, S. (2020). Financial inclusion, economic growth, and poverty alleviation: Evidence from eastern Indonesia. *Heliyon, 6*(10), e05235, 1–13. https://doi.org/10.1016/j.heliyon.2020.e05235.

Haque, M. I. (2020). The growth of private sector and financial development in Saudi Arabia. *Economies, 8*(2), 39. https://doi.org/10.3390/economies8020039

Hathroubi, S. (2019). Inclusive finance, growth and socio-economic development in Saudi Arabia: A threshold co-integration approach. *Journal of Economic Development, 44*(2), 77–111. http://jed.or.kr/full-text/44-2/4.pdf

Honohan, P. (2008). Cross-country variation in household access to financial services. *Journal of Banking & Finance, 33*(11), 2493–2500. http://www.sciencedirect.com/science/article/pii/S0378-4266(08)00097-6
Jin, D. (2017). The inclusive finance have effects on alleviating poverty. *Open Journal of Social Sciences, 5*(3), 233–242. https://www.scirp.org/pdf/JSS_2017033112022135.pdf
Kamalu, K., Wan Ibrahim, W. H. B., Ahmad, A. U., & Mustapha, U. A. (2019). Causal link between financial developments, financial inclusion and economic growth Nigeria. *International Journal of Scientific and Technology Research, 8*(12), 2757–2763. https://www.researchgate.net/profile/Kabiru_Kamalu/publication/340273746_MY_IJSTR_PAPER/links/5e81d110299bf1a91b8a55ba/MY-IJSTR-PAPER.pdf
King Khalid Foundation. (2018). *Financial inclusion in Saudi Arabia: Reaching the financially excluded*. Policy Design and Advocacy Program, p. 12. https://kkf.org.sa/media/ipuh5olx/2-financial-inclusion-in-saudi-arabia-2018.pdf
National Planning Commission (2013). *National development plan vision 2030*. Ministry of Economy and Planning. https://www.mep.gov.sa/en/development-plans
Onaolapo, A. R. (2015). Effects of financial inclusion on the economic growth of Nigeria (1982–2012). *International Journal of Business and Management Review, 3*(8), 11–28. http://www.eajournals.org/wp-content/uploads/Effects-of-Financial-Inclusion-on-the-Economic-Growth-of-Nigeria-1982-2012.pdf
Park, C. Y., & Mercado, R. (2018). Financial inclusion, poverty, and income inequality. *The Singapore Economic Review, 63*(1), 185–206. https://doi.org/10.1142/S0217590818410059
Pinos, F. (2015). *Inclusion financière et populations précarisées: effets des business models des services financiers en France*. Doctoral dissertation, p. 401. https://tel.archives-ouvertes.fr/tel-01252570
Sarma, M. (2008). *Index of financial inclusion* (Working Paper Number 215). Indian Council for Research on International Economic Relations, p. 26. http://icrier.org/pdf/Working_Paper_215.pdf
Sethi, D., & Sethy, S. K. (2019). Financial inclusion matters for economic growth in India. *International Journal of Social Economics, 46*(1), 132–151. https://www.emerald.com/insight/content/doi/10.1108/IJSE-10-2017-0444/full/html
Turegano, D. M., & Herrero, A. G. (2018). Financial inclusion, rather than size, is the key to tackling income inequality. *The Singapore Economic Review, 63*(1), 167–184. https://doi.org/10.1142/S0217590818410047
Van Velthoven, A., De Haan, J., & Sturm, J. E. (2019). Finance, income inequality and income redistribution. *Applied Economics Letters, 26*(14), 1202–1209. https://doi.org/10.1080/13504851.2018.1542483

Vision 2030. *Financial sector development program charter delivery plan 2020.* https://vision2030.gov.sa/en/programs/FSDP

World Bank Group. (2012). *Financial inclusion strategies: Reference framework.* World Bank Publications. World Bank, Washington, DC 20433, USA, p. 60. http://documents1.worldbank.org/curated/en/801151468152092070/pdf/787610WP0P144500use0only0900A9RD899.pdf

World Bank Group. (2014). *Global financial development report 2014: Financial inclusion.* World Bank Publications. World Bank, Washington, DC 20433, USA, p. 224. http://hdl.handle.net/10986/16238

Index

Ananda S. and D. Singh (eds.), *Financial Inclusion in Emerging Markets*,
https://doi.org/10.1007/978-981-16-2652-4

Printed by Printforce, the Netherlands